D0810634

ACTING ON THE WORD

BOOKS BY BERNARD HÄRING

The Law of Christ
Shalom: Peace
This Time of Salvation
Christian Maturity
Toward a Christian Moral Theology
A Sacramental Spirituality
Christian Renewal in a Changing World
The Christian Existentialist
What Does Christ Want?

BERNARD HÄRING

ACTING ON
THE WORD

"Blessed are they who hear the word
of God, and act on it."

FARRAR, STRAUS AND GIROUX

NEW YORK

INTRODUCTION

Since religious life is a charism and therefore a service, its meaning should be understood as fully as possible by those who have committed themselves to this way of life. It should also be understood by all those to whom it is intended to be a service, a message, a witness. A charism, a special gift of God, is a vocation in view of the common good of the whole People of God, indeed of all men. The following of Christ through the practice of the evangelical counsels will bear witness to the greater good and will perform a better service if all religious come to the full realization that their message and service must be relevant for the men of this era. Religious will maximize the present opportunities only to the extent that they distinguish the eternal realities from their changing expression.

The present work is directly addressed to those who have received this charism, who are eager to deepen their appreciation of it and to live it in a way likely to convey its message to their fellow men. This is what I urge on all young men and women who are considering the choice of such a vocation. I would happily be an interpreter of the evangelical counsels to every reader, whether religious or not, because this message deepens our understanding of the Church in her manifold functions and our understanding of the full Christian life as such. It is not given to all to follow the evangelical counsels literally, but all are invited to live on the same plane in their own vocation. The meaning of the evangelical counsels is, at the present moment, an important theme of the ecumenical dialogue and (though to a lesser extent) of the dialogue between Christians and modern men in general.

Many of the chapters in this book have come out of the conferences which I was honored to give at annual meetings of major superiors of religious men and women in the United States and Germany. Other chapters were judged pertinent to a well-rounded presentation of contemporary religious life and are thus presented for further enlightenment.

I am most grateful to Sister Gabrielle L. Jean of the Grey Nuns of the Cross, Chairman of the Psychology Department, Rhode Island College, Providence, who helped me most effectively in collecting the material and editing it. I want also to express my gratitude to Sister Joan Bland of Notre Dame de Namur, Professor at Trinity College, Washington, D.C., who helped us greatly in the final editing, and to the group of Mercy Sisters who contributed valuable criticism and offered many helpful suggestions to the author.

In an Appendix the reader will find the text of a proposed Interim Rule with which I would be very much in agreement. The draft was prepared by members of the Interim Rule Committee of the Maryland Province of the Sisters of Notre Dame of Namur, to be submitted to the General Chapter of their congregation. I want to express my gratitude to the Sisters for permitting me to print it.

B.H.

Union Theological Seminary
New York City
January, 1968

CONTENTS

ONE | THE RELIGIOUS IN THE
POST-CONCILIAR CHURCH 3

Witness to the Fullness of the Times | Humility | Unity in Variety | The Spirit as Life-giver | A Pioneering Group | Witnesses to the Church of the Poor | Collegiality in Religious Life | Preach the Gospel | Spirit of Initiative | Holiness in Charity | Silence and Charity | The Rule and Authority

TWO | IN THE LIGHT OF THE GOSPEL 20

Joyous Witness | Spiritual Renewal | Witness to Holiness | Bountiful Gifts | Law and Spirit | Spirit of the Poor | Consecrated Virginity | Enlightened Obedience

THREE | RELIGIOUS WITNESS IN THE WORLD 36

Dynamic Social World | Mary: Image of the Church and of Womanhood | Mary Magdalen and the Modern Religious | Ecclesial Gardening | Treasuring Up His Words in Our Hearts | The Hour of Favor | The Balance Sheet | The Risk of a New Approach

FOUR | CONTINUITY OF LIFE 55

Normal Times | "Normal Times" for St. Paul | Witness to Fidelity | Mary Ward and Charles Borromeo | God's Fidelity to Abraham | God's Fidelity to the Primitive Church | Fidelity in Creation | Preserving the Image | Fidelity, Not Minutiae | Virtues for Times of

Change and Renewal | 1) Readiness to Change 2) Continuity 3) Spirit of Prayer 4) Patience 5) Dialogue 6) Greater Charity | *Christian Maturity*

FIVE | PROGRESS IN MATURITY 79

Conscience Formation | *What Is Conscience?* | *Conscience and Faith* | *Law and Value* | *The Rule and the Law* | *Divine Law and Human Responsibility* | *Openness to Values* | *The Law of Grace* | *The Bridegroom's Voice* | *The Letter and the Spirit* | *Love and the Law* | *The Place of Obedience* | *Maturity and Personal Fulfillment*

SIX | FREEDOM IN OBEDIENCE 102

Moral Freedom | *Conciliar View of Obedience* | *Christ: Our Exemplar* | *Obedience: Service of Freedom* | *Spirit of Love* | *Enlightened Obedience and Initiative* | *Open Dialogue* | *Obedience and Authority in Love* | *Synthesis of Love* | *Conscience and Obedience* | *The Realm of Obedience*

SEVEN | RENEWAL THROUGH PRAYER 121

What Is Prayer? | *Dialogue with God* | *Gospel Message* | *"My Eyes Are Always Looking to the Lord"* | *Hearken to the Call* | *Initiating Dialogue* | *"Lord, Teach Us How to Pray"* | *Prayer in the New Law* | *Prayer and Celibacy*

EIGHT | UNDIVIDED LOVE AND SERVICE 136

Elements Human and Divine | *A Spiritual Unction* | *Primacy of Love* | *Fidelity to Celibacy* | *Spirit of Poverty and Humility* | *Covenant Between Christ and the Church* | *Eschatological Reality* | *Ascesis and Chastity*

NINE | MEANINGFUL ASCETICISM 151

Conciliar Directives | *Archaisms* | *The Gospel Message Today* | *The "Old Man"* | *Loving Service* | *Collegiality* | *Unity in Community* | *Ascetical Realism* | *Source and Goal* | *Ascesis in Obedience* | *Openness to the World and Poverty*

TEN | HUMILITY OF THE POOR 163

Spirit of the Poor | Essence of the Beatitude | The Following of Christ | Perfect Charity Through Poverty | Common Life | Church of the Poor | Corporate Witness to Poverty | Poverty and Effectual Apostolate | Solidarity in Corporate Witness | Personal Responsibility in Poverty | Rules and Superiors | Renunciation of Inheritance | Human Dependence | Common Law of Labor | Asceticism in Poverty

ELEVEN | THE EUCHARISTIC EXPERIENCE
OF COMMUNITY 189

Humble Service | Humble Avowal | Community of Faith | Humble Self-surrender | Openness to Joy | Community of Hope | Power of Solidarity | Community of Love | Cost of Discipleship | In the Holy Spirit | Prayerful Support | Community Prayer

TWELVE | CONTEMPORARY ISSUES 203

I. RENEWAL IN PRAYER

Prayer House | Forms of "Houses of Prayer" | Objections to the House of Prayer

II. MOTIVATION TO RESPONSIBILITY

Religious Leitmotiv | Individual Values | Specific Motives | Worldliness | Personal Responsibility | Humility

III. PRIMACY OF CONSCIENCE

Historical Approaches | Formation in Faith and Love | Formation Through Imperatives | Commercial Approach | Dialogue Approach

IV. PRIORITIES IN THE APOSTOLATE

Weighty Decisions | New Ventures

V. FEMININE SPIRITUALITY

Gifts of Women | Women and Beauty | Women in Theology

THIRTEEN | THE CHALLENGE OF THE FUTURE   229

Church of the Future | Novel Features | Religious of the Future | Cooperation and Dialogue | Conscience, Not Conformity | Witness to the Gospel

APPENDIX   241

PROPOSED INTERIM RULE

PROPOSED INTERIM CONSTITUTIONS

INDEX   263

The following system of abbreviations is used in referring to the documents of Vatican Council II:

LG — *Lumen Gentium*
Dogmatic Constitution on the Church.

GS — *Gaudium et Spes*
Pastoral Constitution on the Church in the Modern World.

PC — *Perfectae Caritatis*
Decree on the Appropriate Renewal of the Religious Life.

ES — *Ecclesiae Sanctae*
Norms for the Implementation of the Decree *Perfectae Caritatis.*

We praise you, Lord of the Church and Redeemer of the world, for being privileged to live in this great and difficult age. We thank you for the earthquake that has jolted us out of our drowsiness; you have driven away our self-complacency and tolerance of mediocrity. We thank you for the growing pains and tensions, for the new and never before dreamed-of opportunities of giving witness to you, the living God and Brother of all men.

Lord, make us firm and joyful in faith, hope, love of God and of neighbor. Grant that we may read correctly the signs of this time of salvation and grow in maturity and openness. Give us the fortitude and wisdom to bear the risks of the full Christian life. When we make mistakes—and, being human, we shall—help us to correct them with peace of mind and a sense of humor. Help us to outdo each other in mutual respect and charity and to bear each other in patience and good cheer.

Lord, teach us how to pray and to transform life into prayer, into a colloquy with you. Teach us that holy worldliness which brings life and religion together and praises you, our Creator and Redeemer. Renew our hearts and minds, our passions and affections, that we may be able to fulfill our role in the renewal of the Church and society.

ACTING ON THE WORD

ONE | THE RELIGIOUS IN THE POST-CONCILIAR CHURCH

By the charity to which they lead, the evangelical counsels join their followers to the Church and her mystery in a special way. Since this is so, the spiritual life of these followers should be devoted to the welfare of the whole Church. (LG, 44)

The Church introduces herself in the Constitution on the Church as a body giving testimony to the charity of Christ. The Church is a witness to Christ's love both as a mystery of the union of Christ with his Father in the Holy Spirit, and as a juridical structure involved with the distribution of roles among its members. The dogmatic Constitution presents charity *first* as a visible sign or mystery and then as a structure from which flows, with greatest efficacy, charity as experience and commandment. Differing from human laws and precepts, charity is the internal union with Christ; it is the whole Church as a community of love inviting us, and urging us to give the response of love. When the Church is referred to as the germ and beginning of the kingdom of God through charity, humility, and self-sacrifice (LG, 5), the reference applies to the whole Church.

The Constitution on the Church is of great importance for the future of religious congregations. It is interesting to note that in the plan of this key conciliar document, the chapter on religious (6) follows immediately those dealing with the laity (4) and

3

the universal call to holiness (5). Religious are Christians in the pursuit of perfect charity in a special way through the continuous practice of the evangelical counsels of chastity, poverty, and obedience. The Constitution states explicitly that their future in the Church will depend directly on their affinity with the Pilgrim Church.

Witness to the Fullness of the Times

In the sixth chapter of the Constitution on the Church, a religious community is described as a joyful family whose primary goal is progress in charity. True charity is based on faith and on the sacraments of faith. Through a life based on the evangelical counsels, religious become outstanding witnesses of the heavenly kingdom and thus help all the members of the Mystical Body respond generously to the great Christian vocation. Religious proclaim to all Christians that they die to sin and are consecrated to God through baptism. They bear witness to all the faithful that they have no everlasting city here below; however, the text is careful not to make Christian life *merely* a preparation for heaven. Our life even *now* is a life in Christ. Therefore the Constitution continues by saying that religious manifest to all believers the presence of the heavenly good possessed here below (LG, 44). Already on their earthly pilgrimage they live in the intimate friendship of God; in a sense they experience the joy of heaven since they believe. The power of the kingdom of God, the love of God, is so mighty that it fills their lives.

The same chapter of the Constitution on the Church explains that the religious vocation must be viewed in relation to the Church. There are not two kinds of vocation: one for personal sanctification and another in the service of one's fellow man; rather, sanctity must be seen as a total consecration to Christ in the service of the Church. "The spiritual life of these followers should be devoted to the welfare of the whole Church" (LG, 44). Through a life of prayer and dedication, religious are consecrated to charity, to the praise of God's love, and to serve as witnesses to God's mystery and commandment of love. Religious are primarily witnesses. They are called to live in an outstanding way the common vocation of all Christians, and to such an extent that they instruct others in the fullness of Christian life. Their spirituality must, first of all, be that of genuine Christians; only subsequently can they develop a distinctive spirituality for their religious group. Religious are first and foremost living members of the Church.

Faced with the mystery of Christ, the Church attains true self-understanding. She emerges as a mystery and a sacrament, that is, as a visible and efficacious sign of union with God and a sign of unity binding the whole human race together. The life of religious men and women consecrated to celibacy for the kingdom of God must be viewed in the same perspective. The whole of religious life is an efficacious sign of their union with God and with all the redeemed. Those who consecrate themselves by vows offer themselves as Christ himself did for the redemption of mankind. It is not for selfish reasons but as living members of the Church that they wish to fulfill the role which Christ himself has prepared for them in the Mystical Body. By their lives, they seek to manifest in a special and distinctive way that the highest reality for them is union with God, and thus service to fellow men.

The Church is the mother of all the living because she is the beloved and loving bride of Christ. The more she loves him, the more will she manifest herself as mother of all the living. Her apostolate and service will be a function of her growth in union with Christ; so it is with religious who, united with his redeeming love, carry out the work of redemption in hundreds of different ways. Furthermore, if the whole Church is the mystery of salvation, a sacrament, consecrated religious must manifest to all members of the Church and even to those outside the Church that the source of their union with mankind and their humble service to men is their union with Christ.

Humility

The Church is called "the germ and the beginning of the kingdom of God." The implication is that the Church is not allowed to seek her own will, her own glory, but that in all things she humbly seeks the will of the beloved Spouse. Christ did not come to seek his own will, his own glory; he did not come to be served but to serve.

Religious are expected to reflect the same attitude of service, both in their humble way of obedience and in the superior's humble exercise of authority. The one great concern must be adherence to the loving will of God. This in no way precludes the possibility of speaking to superiors and explaining difficulties relating to any assignment; however, in the end, obedience must always be a witness of supernatural faith. The goal of obedience as well as that of authority is growth in humble obedience to the law of grace, recognition of the present opportunity as an invitation to respond to the grace of the Holy Spirit in genuine initiative.

Poverty must be envisioned in the same light. The Church is called upon to be the Church of the poor, and she will be a credible witness to the kingdom of God if, instead of amassing stately fortunes and mansions, she seeks to serve those bereft of earthly riches. Religious communities owe it to themselves to pray much, and together, to think of ways by which poverty can permeate their style of life. Their poverty must become visible in the sense that, as religious, they do not seek exemptions and privileges for themselves but wish only to serve. In their humble service they may use the earthly goods and modern means available, always being careful, however, to express the spirit of poverty: humility, service, and detachment. Earthly possessions should never be sought for self-enhancement, for personal advantage, or for power; they are intended to promote a better service to neighbor.

Unity in Variety

The Church, the Mystical Body of Christ, is characterized by a great variety of functions in its members (Eph 4; I Cor 12). As a body, it should never expect uniformity or conformity but rather unity in great diversity. There is ample evidence of variety in religious congregations and orders: variety in tasks, services, ministries, and within communities; this diversity, when fully appreciated, strengthens solidarity. Greater freedom and variety should prevail among the provinces. Let the American sisters be good American sisters, living members of the American community, and let the German, Dutch, or Italian sisters be good members of the Church in their area. With variety, unity will be more easily preserved than by a scrupulous and compulsive endeavor to enforce conformity to a set custom, language, or even routine.

Furthermore, every member has a special gift of God. One of the principal points of the Constitution on the Church is to make much of this great variety of individual gifts. This holds for communities as well as for individual persons; God is infinitely rich. "All these gifts are the work of one and the same Spirit, distributing them separately to each individual at will" (I Cor 12:11). So every religious must regard the gifts of all with a view to serving the Mystical Body, and his own gifts as intended for service to his own community and to the whole Church. For superiors, this means care to avoid arbitrary appointments and, more specifically, care not to appoint people to tasks for which they are not fitted. Assignments must be made after prayerful, considerate study, and particularly in a manner respectful of the giver of gifts, God. Attention must be given to such questions as: What does God expect of these sisters or brothers in view of their personal gifts? What does he intend for them? Where can they best develop the qualities they have received from God? In this way only can superiors be true to God and manifest to others the true nature of the Church. All must give the best service possible to the Church and this requires a deep religious formation. Therefore as many religious men and women as possible should receive a sound theological formation that will enrich their communities and give them the inspiration so direly needed in our time.

The Spirit as Life-giver

The Constitution on the Church treats of the Messianic people of God in terms which clearly indicate that for Christians the "law" cannot mean conformity to external criteria; rather, the guide is the Holy Spirit moving their heart. The great commandment is that of love; the dignity and freedom of Christians emanate from their filial relationship to God and from the dwelling of the Holy Spirit in them as in a temple. The liberty of the sons and daughters of God, then, means docility to the promptings of the Holy Spirit. Consequently, there must be watchfulness, vigilance for the signs of the times by which the Holy Spirit and charity rule our lives.

Christians must be determined not to resist the grace of God. When confronted with a special invitation from God, they can never excuse themselves by saying that there is no written law, for the very laws of Christians are the gifts of God, the love of God. Love is *the* commandment. No law obliges us to enter a religious community; it is an invitation of the grace of God. If religious congregations wish to have vocations, they need only give their sisters, brothers, and Fathers a proper formation in the freedom of the sons and daughters of God, namely, a thoughtful docility to the gifts of God. The guiding principle cannot be: "Must I do this?" Rather it should be: "What can I render to the Lord for all he has done for me? How can I please the Lord? How can I respond to his love? How can I follow through on his plans for me?"

God's invitations are to be accepted freely, for he seeks our cooperation in freedom. It is imperative that our growth in freedom be according to grace and not merely freedom according

to the law. The Council Fathers agreed that the goal of obedience consists in a readiness to respond to the internal guide, the
Holy Spirit. "Religious obedience will lead to greater maturity
in consequence of that enlarged freedom that belongs to the
sons and daughters of God" (PC, 14).

It is not sufficient for one to enter a religious community freely
because of the urgent appeal of Christ. It is also necessary that
one's life be a free and joyous service to the whole Church, that,
in great spontaneity, one always try to do more than what is
externally or legally imposed There must be respect for meaningful and valid laws, but if a Rule is cluttered with trivia, spontaneity will be stifled, with a consequent loss of freedom for
God's sons and daughters. The first Rule for all religious must
be the Gospel, and it must be translated into their lives in terms
of the great commandment of love: love of God and of others as
he loved us. Religious must be witnesses to a spontaneous kind
of obedience that prompts them to do more than what is com-
manded by external regulations.

A Pioneering Group

The second chapter of the dogmatic Constitution on the Church
also represents the Church as a body of forward-looking pilgrims.
Were she to identify herself with a past era, she would condemn
herself to death; she must look forward. It would be unrealistic,
in the wake of the recent Vatican Council, to expect legislation
to be passed that will immobilize the Church for another two
hundred years. We must be prepared to move, to progress, but
to move nearer to the Lord and to what he has in mind for the
future. Religious are especially called to be witnesses to the true
nature of the Church; they cannot be like the wife of Lot who,
at a critical moment when people were being saved from Sodom
and Gomorrah, looked back in spite of the warning of God, only
to become a pillar of salt.

It seems that some religious today resemble Lot's wife; may

she never become the patroness of religious congregations. If the whole Church is to look forward, religious orders must do so more than others. One cannot justify clinging to the past by saying: "Our holy founder laid down this rule . . ."; the founder's relics are not your most important possession, but his life, his spirit. Founders were children of their age and society; however, they felt deeply and displayed great sensitivity to the real needs of their time. In the same way we must realize the needs of our era. In an age of rapid change, we must not be bound by too many traditions. Pope Pius XII, in a letter sent to the major superiors of Portugal shortly before his death, repeated the warning of Our Lord: "Why do you transgress the law of the Lord because of your traditions?"

We must test our relics, the relics of our traditions, in the light of the Constitution on the Church, in the light of the present thinking of the Church, in the light of the Great Commandment: How can we, *here and now*, manifest our love for God and neighbor and fulfill our mission? To set our sights on the future, to be forward-looking means more than mere external adaptation; it means a continuous conversion of the individual and of the community. No Christian belonging to the Pilgrim Church can be allowed to be self-righteous and complacent. Every Christian must grow continuously, while those who are special witnesses to the true nature of the Church—religious orders and congregations—must take greater pains to achieve a deeper conversion, a greater purification. For this reason there must be in our daily living and in our prayer life, as well as in the reform of our structures, a greater effort to sustain one another in our striving for sanctity and in our never-ending attempts to respond more fully to present opportunities, to the present needs of the Church and the world.

Witnesses to the Church of the Poor

The Church encompasses with love all those afflicted with human infirmity and recognizes in the poor the image of its poor and suffering Founder (LG, 8). This is one aspect of the *agape* of God, movement from on high to the humble. While such love characterizes the whole Church, religious orders and congregations are particularly urged to scrutinize their consciences on this point. In America, the good sisters, brothers, and religious priests, by a modest life of poverty in past generations, have built up the tremendous colleges that now serve the country's youth. These institutions of higher learning also are a reflection of the generosity of the American people. Therefore, why could these colleges and universities not become the property of the people of God, of their alumni or of the families who send their children there to be educated? Could not the administration and/or ownership be entrusted to capable laymen who would take over supervision of the estates and property and share in the responsibilities? Would not religious then enjoy greater freedom to advance toward the Lord and bear a more effective witness, unencumbered by the problems of estate management? In view of their role in the People of God, we must look to the charisms of the laity and assign them greater responsibility in the Church. There are many dedicated laymen who could take over these temporal and financial concerns; many are eminently qualified to act as good administrators.

There is no doubt that too much emphasis is being placed on administration in the lives of our superiors; they are overburdened with administrative tasks. If there is to be initiative and spontaneity, if religious are to be leaders in the spiritual life, then superiors must be charismatic leaders who inspire religious life as such; they must not waste most of their time in fund-raising, building activities, and the like. Administration must never be the primary concern of religious superiors.

Religious are witnesses to a spirit of responsibility in poverty. Can they be said to be witnessing to this spirit of poverty if, for example, sisters are required to ask for their daily necessities, e.g., stamps, soap, shoelaces? Are they not wasting the superior's (and their own) precious time? There are more essential things to claim their attention, an essential one being spiritual guidance; well-prepared superiors are sorely needed today. Local and major superiors should have at least the same spiritual preparation as priests if they are to fulfill their role in communities as charismatic spiritual leaders.

Collegiality in Religious Life

According to the concept of "collegiality" in the Constitution on the Church the bishops and the pope stand in a definite relationship to each other (LG, Ch. 3); while the bishops are under and dependent on the pope, they are still members of the same college headed by the pope and share responsibility with him. Furthermore, in elaborating on the structure of collegiality the point is made that bishops are not meant by Christ to shoulder the entire saving mission of the Church themselves. . . . "It is their noble duty to recognize the services and charismatic gifts of the faithful" (LG, 30). Chapter four goes a step further in saying that bishops must not only allow the laity to express their concern for matters related to the Church, but at times, in view of their competence, laymen are obliged to speak freely to pastors regarding things that affect the spiritual good of the Church. In the light of this fundamental conciliar document, it appears that the state of charity, freedom, and frankness is fitting for the sons of God and brothers of Christ.

The concept of collegiality, then, has a special significance for the religious life. Every religious has the right to explain his wishes if, by his good ideas, he can contribute to the good of the congregation. Above all, superiors should listen to those religious who show in all things a spirit of humility as well as signs of discernment and spontaneity. Some have good ideas but cannot carry them out because they do not set a good example; however, the good idea should be heard and used if it can contribute in any way to the welfare of the group. All should be encouraged to bear their share of responsibility, to contribute within the realm of their competence to the attainment of the group goals. Collegiality is an expression of love and it implies a relationship of friendship. There is a mutual solidarity, not only between those in higher and lower positions, but between brothers and sisters—all are responsible for the common good. Some adjustment of roles must be made to do justice to this aspect of collegiality. The dogmatic Constitution (LG, 29) speaks of deacons who, by the grace of their state, should represent Christ and become the servants of all. Should it not also be the role of superiors to be the personification of humility, mercy, goodness, but remembering always that goodness is not weakness?

Preach the Gospel

The Constitution on the Church informs bishops and priests that their chief task is to preach the Gospel, the message of joy (LG, 25, 28) The superior's task is somewhat similar in that his mission is to be carried out in a spirit of joy. The superior's chief responsibility is to preach the Gospel in his own way, by his example, by his conversation and correspondence. He must bring the good news, not in small postscripts, but by giving priority to the message of joy, of goodness. This point is of paramount importance when considering how we, as religious, can be witnesses to the essential mission of the Church.

In a way, the role and style of life of the religious differ from those of the laity (LG, Ch. 4), but from the viewpoint of divine revelation (LG, Ch. 6) religious belong to the laity and not to the hierarchy. However, what is true of the laity holds in an outstanding and even more significant way for religious. The laity must collaborate at different levels, always with mutual respect being shown between bishop, pastor, and laity, and among lay collaborators. The same rule applies to religious orders: they

must be prominent witnesses of mutual respect, especially in relation to the gifts bestowed by God on every one. Religious should
have a spirituality specific to themselves because of their celibacy
for the kingdom of God, their obedience, and their service in
poverty. However, it should be clear that the basic Christian life
is the same: one in the joy of the Lord under the great "Rule of
the Gospel."

We cannot witness in an outstanding way to Christianity unless
we know what is the common inheritance of Christians, what the
spirituality of baptism is. Therefore, the essential formation of religious consists in becoming eminently good Christians, formed by
the Gospel in the dual commandment of love of God and neighbor. The laity are said to have a priestly function, a prophetic
office: they are witnesses to the kingdom of God in their joyous
and humble service, in their relation to the Christian community.
The witness of religious orders must attest to these same attributes. Dedicated religious, whose whole life is conceived as a
glorification of God, know that they glorify God above all by
charity, unity, and solidarity, and thus direct everything to the
praise of God.

Need any more be said to emphasize the great importance of
the spirit of prayer and especially of the liturgy? The liturgy
proclaims the Gospel and makes the whole of life praise God.
The prophetic office of religious consists in their witnessing in
this present age to the power of the kingdom of God, to the love
of God which bears fruit in fraternal love. This love of God must
be so strong in them that they do not feel frustrated in their religious community; this will be true only if life as such is strong
in them—the life of charity, goodness and humility.

Spirit of Initiative

The Constitution on the Church speaks about the importance of
the spirit of initiative (LG, 37). Religious superiors should not
despise but encourage good initiative. Theirs is the obligation to

strive for discernment of the Spirit; they must view initiative as coming from a right spirit, but with openness toward the signs of the times. A timely instance in this country is initiative in relation to the problem of racial integration. We cannot bring the Eucharistic Bread and the Gospel to the Negro if we are not concerned with justice, with his daily position in the community of faith and in civil life; we will not be believed. We must show our concern that Negroes be accepted as persons, as full-fledged members of American society.

America has, by Divine Providence, a decisive role to play for the solidarity of nations, for peace on earth. Should America remain unable to solve its racial problem, its whole task as peacemaker of the world will be significantly crippled if not jeopardized. Therefore religious communities should also be greatly concerned and ready to promote courageous initiative on this social issue. At times, it may not be advisable for a superior to send out sisters or brothers for civil rights demonstrations, but one could at least indicate approval and delight for an initiative manifested at the right moment, guided by Christian prudence and fortitude. The superior may hesitate to allow representatives of the congregation to become involved in a civil rights march but should look favorably on volunteers from the ranks who wish to line up with laymen on the issue of brotherhood for the glory of God, Our Lord. We are all blessed when we are called to suffer something for the sake of justice, goodness, kindness; but, above all, religious must be witnesses to the universal vocation of sanctity through their all-embracing spirit of love.

Holiness in Charity

All Christians are called to holiness; this vocation is clearly prescribed for all in the dogmatic Constitution (LG, Ch. 5). Religious orders have no monopoly on sanctity, but they become eminent servants and witnesses if they are outstanding in charity, since sanctity consists in genuine love. God sanctifies us by his overriding love and we accept sanctification as coming from God if we love one another. Therefore, the conscience of the religious must be formed not merely in the light of the Decalogue; this cannot be enough for Christians. Can a Christian boast about not having committed adultery? The law of the Christian is proclaimed in the Sermon on the Mount, in the directive that Christians are to be good, even as their heavenly Father is all-good. They are to be all-compassionate even as their heavenly Father is all-compassionate: "Love one another as I have loved you."

The whole formation in the novitiate must be centered about this great ideal of charity. In times characterized by lack of any meaningful fulcrum for life, by dispersion and dissipation of energies, the religious witness must be that of a life of synthesis, seeing all things in the light of the love of Christ Jesus. Our whole life is to express the fact that he loves us, that we love him, and that in him we love our neighbor.

There should be less asceticism in orders apart from that of charity, but more asceticism inherent in charity showing that love functions as the center of all sacrifice. Some forms of asceticism practiced by religious communities do not involve great sacrifice or real selflessness, but they may make sense as symbols calling for a life of service and self-denial. However, if the symbols are outdated, totally unrelated to actual daily living, they become escapes from the realities of life, from real charity. Life demands asceticism; love itself imposes asceticism, the kind found in a good Rule and beyond the Rule. The novice master or mistress must know how to explain the Rule as an application of the great Holy Rule, namely, the great commandment of love of God and neighbor. If a Rule cannot be explained in this light, indicating that it serves charity, application must be made to the provincial for an explanation; if the provincial cannot explain it, the point should be referred to higher authorities for clarification. If it still cannot be explained, we must be humble and confess: "I do not see how this serves charity," and this specific Rule should no

longer be imposed or stressed. It is meaningless if it has no bearing on charity. Some Rules have, indeed, lost their value; but there
are others that could be brought to life again if viewed in the
perspective of the great commandment of love and service.

Silence and Charity

Silence contributes much to charity; it is not irrelevant. There
should be silence at least in some parts of the house· around the
chapel, for example, and at some hours, at least in the evening.
But silence strictly for the sake of silence, in the form of "evening silence after eight or nine o'clock" in such a way that no one
dares say a kind word to another (in spite of the fact that they
may listen to loud voices on television)—such silence lacks mean-
ingfulness. Personally, I think that there always should be ex-
ceptions on one evening or another; the Rule of silence must be
flexible.

Generally, silence performs a tremendous service of love because it provides a foundation and a source of thought, a necessary atmosphere if we are to be men and women of prayer.
Silence is needed for listening to God, as a preparation for the
dialogue with God and neighbor. This becomes an impossibility
in the midst of noise and confusion. The times and places of
silence, however, depend on the particular institute. It is evident
that it must reasonably serve charity. If you see your confrère
or sister frustrated or in deep sorrow, charity prompts you to say
a few kind words of understanding. You should be allowed to
speak to each other under such circumstances; this can be done
in an atmosphere of silence without disturbing the peace and
quiet of others. Charity takes precedence over silence and is to
be served by it.

The Rule and Authority

General Chapters and each superior of an order should examine
the Rules very carefully, asking: "Do these Rules today foster

and promote a service of salvational charity?" In a talk during July, 1965, Pope Paul VI pointed out that the whole function of authority is to serve charity and salvation. The Rule, a positive reality, must express and promote this spirit of service.

Formation must find its great unity, its great synthesis, in this salvational charity. The Sermon on the Mount gives us many clear hints about discerning charity. The evangelical counsels must be accepted as directives of Christian fulfillment. What can celibacy for the kingdom of God mean other than union with God in an outstanding way and freedom for the service of others? We are not convincing if we take a vow of celibacy or virginity and then act heartlessly toward each other, or without warmth or special kindness in our interpersonal relationships. No one will believe in us as witnesses to God's love. The Rule must foster and not stifle this warmth demanded by the exigencies of a truly human Christian friendship.

St. Alphonsus was a great friend of religious; he himself founded a religious congregation of men and an order of contemplative women. There were some however who entered the monasteries without real vocations; the many Rules overburdened them. He once wrote a letter to a superior who refused to grant any dispensations: "By acting in this way, you make every law a great infraction and great sin against charity. There is an indubitable need for dispensations."

Obedience must be increasingly manifest as a loving obedience; in turn, loving obedience will only be possible if there is a humble and loving exercise of authority. The superior's obligation to see this point is great in that he is expected to be a charismatic spiritual leader. If anyone is capable of being a good superior, let him be a superior; do not bog him down with mere administrative tasks. It is far more important to have good superiors who exercise authority lovingly, respectfully, and in a way likely to inspire enthusiasm and bring joy into the community.

Such is the meaning of the evangelical counsels. The world today needs persons who act from conscience and act joyfully, with enthusiasm and fortitude. This is the witness to be given by our obedience, service, and humility.

TWO | IN THE LIGHT OF
THE GOSPEL

Since the fundamental norm of the religious life is a follow-ing of Christ as proposed by the gospel, such is to be re-garded by all communities as their supreme law. (PC, 2)

In a recent conversation, a Protestant minister, extolling our late Pope John, attributed his great influence to three descriptive words: "this humble, kind, and holy" man. Humility is indeed the first of the beatitudes and, with kindness, it permeates all the evangelical counsels. The *aggiornamento* introduced by Pope John and supported by his successor, Pope Paul VI, is thoroughly inspired by the spirit of the evangelical counsels. Our openness to what is going on in today's world and our involvement in today's world must be motivated by the eschatological reality of the heavenly kingdom already present yet leading us to a fulfillment beyond this world.

I am sometimes concerned to see that even some religious are inclined to accept Harvey Cox's *The Secular City* as the fifth gospel. Harvey Cox says many good things which have to be said, but I feel that he is partial in the expression of his views. His thinking evolves along the following lines: We do not know whether something exists beyond this world . . . surely there is nothing in the heights and nothing in the depths. Therefore, we must develop a political language: the open future—that's God! Cox is not yet sure whether he will commit himself to atheism, according to the *Secular City Debate;* he believes that in the open future there is something that sounds like God; it may be that in our hope we will find God. Of course, there is something in the open future, but in another sense. God has given us the pledge of the open future not only in this world but beyond this world. The Second Vatican Council in its Constitution on the Church in the Modern World accurately and emphatically says that the reason for our commitment to the world of our own day is the hope of a world to come, a life beyond this world.

In this context of eschatological hope, St. Paul appeals to all Christians on the level of the evangelical counsels: "The time we live in will not last long. While it lasts, married men should be as if they had no wives; mourners should be as if they had nothing to grieve them, the joyful as if they did not rejoice; buyers must not count on keeping what they buy, nor those who use the world's wealth on using it to the full. For the whole frame of this world is passing away" (I Cor 7:29-31). This is said to all in a context where Paul is speaking of the witness of those who profess themselves celibate for the sake of the kingdom of God.

Joyous Witness

Religious should be joyous and exemplary witnesses of a deeply Christian life. The Pauline text describes Christian life in the spirit of the evangelical counsels. Of course married men must live fully as married men; spouses are called to love one another wholeheartedly; but in their love they must be concerned, above all, with being free for God and the kingdom of his love on earth. Only thus will they truly love each other. Mourners must realize that they are called to bear the cross, but they can do so only if they perceive the heavenly kingdom as already present yet destined to be finally fulfilled. Those who rejoice are invited to rejoice in the Lord; unavoidably however they will engage in questionable pleasures, superficial leisure activities, a halfhearted seeking after self-actualization, unless they rejoice in all good things as well as in something which is beyond this present world. "Buyers must not count on keeping what they buy." Those who use the world's goods should use them with the knowledge that they can possess and utilize them for their true fulfillment only to the extent of their unselfish love and spirit of self-denial.

In his epistle, St. Paul appeals to us and encourages us to use all of God's gifts well without clinging to the ephemeral. Our awareness of the truth that this world is transient will move us to make the best use of opportunities of wealth and skills in the development of our potential of love. The evangelical counsels, as a witness to the world and as a service to the whole of mankind, are the essence of religious living. The evangelical counsels do not separate us from the rest of mankind; they link us wholly with the Christian world and are the best way to serve the secular city.

Spiritual Renewal

The Decree on the Appropriate Renewal of the Religious Life says that since religious life intends above all else to lead those who have embraced it to the imitation of Christ (PC, 2), to union with God through the profession of the evangelical counsels, it becomes evident that even the most desirable changes in view of contemporary needs will fail unless a renewal of spirit gives them life. Indeed, only an interior renewal can successfully promote and sustain exterior works. The interior renewal required as a condition for our external adjustment to present needs is anchored in the spirit of the beatitudes, the Sermon on the Mount, the evangelical counsels. Therefore, this whole era of change in the Church impels us to meditate deeply on the meaning of the evangelical counsels. A serious examination of our innermost thoughts and desires and structures is mandatory; we must ask ourselves whether they witness to the reality of the counsels and beatitudes. Our answer to this question will reveal the direction and gauge the intensity of our renewal effort.

The goal of the evangelical counsels is the following of Christ in the pursuit of perfect charity (PC, 1). The essential point is the "following of Christ" on that road where one never reaches the point of satiation. We can always love more; we can always discover, in a more joyous, more grateful way, how God loves us and how he enables us to love each other more. Thus we follow Christ. The Decree says that the "following of Christ" lies in the pursuit of perfect love through the exercise of the evangelical counsels; these are the blazing emblems of the heavenly kingdom (PC, 1).

What is the heavenly kingdom? It is that realm where God guides us by his own love, by his gifts, to the gracious manifestation of his own love. In the kingdom, love is eminently visible. This love is visible now but present only in a limited way. At the Parousia of the Lord, in the final manifestation, all who consented to be guided by the love of God will be called together in him. His love is a rallying call! This is the lesson we must learn at the present time. It should be clear to us that the evangelical counsels open us totally to God's love; this openness to God's love is tested by our readiness to accept each other in a great variety of temperaments, characters, and, above all, in the open-mindedness of liberals and conservatives to opposing points of view.

Love is always linked to Christ. There is no understanding of what love is if we do not look fixedly toward Christ and, through him, to our neighbor. He has shown us the Father; he has manifested to us the full extent of God's love (Jn 13:1). Christ himself is a witness; having been rich in heavenly beatitude, he became poor. This alone is what gives meaning to our becoming poor. Christ did not become poor to drag us into misery; he became poor in order to enrich all men, to endow us with the heavenly richness of love. Christ became obedient in order to manifest that the heavenly Father guides him and guides us by his love, and he brings us together in the one kingdom of love. Christ also revealed to the world that one can be a perfect man without marriage, without confining one's love to a few persons. He has paved the way for Christian marriage by his own witness to the fullness of manhood in virginity, in a life of celibacy. In an all-embracing love he has chosen his Church as spouse. Genuine Christian virginity, celibacy for the sake of the kingdom of God, can never be a cover for selfishness; nor can it be a frustration, because it is not a search for self-fulfillment. It is an enrichment in Christ's love and therefore a growth toward an ever greater potentiality for love of neighbor.

Witness to Holiness

That the evangelical counsels testify to the holiness of the Church is a point strongly emphasized in the Constitution on the Church (LG, 39). The holiness of the Church is manifested unceasingly through those fruits of the grace of the Holy Spirit produced in the faithful. It is expressed in multiple ways by those individuals who, in their walks of life, strive for the perfection of charity and thereby help others to grow in love. In a particularly effective way this holiness is radiated by the practice of the counsels customarily called the evangelical counsels.

The conciliar decrees explain the theology of the evangelical counsels. They cannot be viewed as proceeding from man's own initiative. There should be a great emphasis on initiative but not on the kind which has man as its center or which begins with man. The kind I am referring to is initiative considered to be the fruit of the Holy Spirit. It comprehends the initiative of the Holy Spirit and man's generous response in total dependence on the Spirit's grace. "Since the Spirit is our life, so let the Spirit also direct our course" (Gal 5:25). Such an approach does not focus on the purely natural law but bespeaks a total confrontation with Christ; it looks to the gifts he has bestowed upon us.

The great gift that Christ has poured forth in our hearts is the Holy Spirit. In this perspective we must look at all gifts of God, the Creator and Redeemer, including the full scope of individual gifts given for the service of others. It is the Spirit who gathers all into oneness through the variety of his gifts, and everyone who accepts the gifts of the Holy Spirit produces the fruits of the Holy Spirit. One's only desire should be to know: how can I contribute to the growth, to the building up of the Church? How can I serve the world today? While the multiple ways of unredeemed individuals tend to separate, the Spirit brings together all those who follow the pattern of the redeeming love of Christ as so many limbs, so many members, of the One Body.

In the dogmatic Constitution, we learn that the Holy Spirit prompts us to practice these counsels (LG, 39). When a Christian lives on that spiritual level, his whole way of life helps others strive toward holiness. The presence of a person truly living according to the spirit of the counsels attracts men to the God who inspired this life of love. It speaks loudly of the mercy of God, of his continuing presence, his love and kinship with men. Religious life, then, must be lived in such a way that all Christians can learn the essentials of a life according to the Gospel. Therefore, we should not overemphasize accidental things, for these would conceal the essentials of the counsels and our witness. This, I believe, was why some communities partially failed; they believed in so many little things and to such an extent that they forgot the essentials. They gave the Spirit little chance to direct their lives; therefore, they were not a model of holiness for the whole world. The life of religious men and women must be, above all else, a life witnessing to "the law of the Spirit who gives us life in Christ Jesus" (Rom 8:2). This implies a witness to the freedom of the sons and daughters of God who are set free from the quest for self-fulfillment, freed from a slavish, external conformity to laws. Religious are Christians who are set free to plumb the depths of the law of God, namely, to build up a community of love, to be totally free for him and for the needs of their neighbor, to be grateful for all the love they are receiving from God through their neighbor.

Bountiful Gifts

The evangelical counsels are not limited to poverty, celibacy, and obedience. There are many counsels, since every grace of God, every gift of God, becomes a "counsel." Confronted by such a gift, can a friend of Christ ever say, "Your gifts do not bind me, Lord; you have forgotten to make it a law"? This is the thinking of the slavish man. In the New Testament God chiefly "legislates" by his gifts; it is of the very nature of the New Covenant that man should accept the gifts of God as his own innermost law, as his rule of life. Full Christian life is gratitude, i.e., a grateful acknowledgment of the gifts of God through our contribution of services needed here and now.

The same rule of life applies to superiors. They must never stifle the Holy Spirit; God distributes his gifts as he wills. It should also deter individual members from insisting on a selfish use of their gifts in the narrow perspective of personal fulfillment. The grace of the Holy Spirit is operative only where there is humility. Therefore, humility is one of the fundamental criteria for the discernment of spirits.

The law of the Spirit makes us humble, grateful, and constantly prompts us to search for the best way in which we can serve. We are not allowed to be so nearsighted as to serve only our immediate environment; we must extend ourselves to serve mankind in the all-embracing perspective of a Church on pilgrimage toward the heavenly kingdom, a Church engaged in a process of community-building, in charity and in humility. Since it is a form of life under the influence of the Holy Spirit, the practice of the counsels rightly understood will lead to Christian maturity. The latter implies growth in an ever-increasing knowledge of God's gifts and their relation to the building up of the Christian community, their relation to the witness of Christian freedom, the fruit of unselfishness. The initiative of the sons and daughters of God is based on docility to the Holy Spirit and manifests itself in respect for one's neighbor, one's community, and all of mankind.

If we busy ourselves with constant attention to meticulous laws, we will all too often stifle the Spirit and shroud the witness of the evangelical counsels. We of course need structures; we need laws to help man on his way toward an ever greater maturity. However, the protection afforded by these laws should not be that of a smothering parent who protects the child to such an extent that he is driven either to rebel against her authority or else settle for infantilism for the rest of his life.

Law and Spirit

All man-made laws should lead toward the law of the Spirit, toward a better understanding of the gifts of God and how they can serve the unity of the whole community with proper regard for initiative and charity. The evangelical counsels call for initiative in docility—initiative as a loving response to God's own initiative. The decree on religious life says, "Those who profess the evangelical counsels love and seek before all else that God who took the initiative in loving them. Such dedication gives rise and urgency to the love of one's neighbor for the world's salvation and the upbuilding of the Church" (PC, 6).

It is because of God's initiative, which seeks always to build up a community of love, that this great sign of salvation, the Church, thrives on unity in variety and variety in unity. The Church is a sign of charity. The evangelical counsels make us free for God and, being free for God, we are then truly freed for our neighbor. Therefore, the evangelical counsels cannot be lived by those who do not believe in the prime importance of prayer; this is the crucial question for the religious of our time.

Formerly there was a trend in the Church that imposed on parents the duty to desire as many children as possible; however, they were not to love one another too much. Love was accorded only a secondary place; it was not to interfere with the primary duty of procreation. The Council corrected this faulty thinking; using the Bible as a source and relying on a deepened self-understanding of what the Church is, the Council's message for parents now is that they can never love one another too much. If their mutual love is true and strong, they will want to have children to share in their mutual love and they will be willing and able to educate them well. The Church as a whole will be the mother of all the living, an attractive and great sign of love in the world, only insofar as she is a loving spouse of Christ.

As religious, our witness should be in the same direction. We should be deeply convinced that if we do not have enough time for meditation on the Gospel, if we refuse to take time to look on the countenance of Christ, to be with him, then we will never really be set free for the true service of our neighbor. We will always be erroneously motivated and the work in which we engage will be slanted or biased. In contrast to Harvey Cox's new gospel, the evangelical counsels set us free for the world to come—the heavenly kingdom which begins here but goes beyond this world; they make us free for a personal God who has shown us his countenance in Christ who is with us. Personalism in the community begins with prayer, in being with Christ; only then can we learn to be truly with our neighbor.

The evangelical counsels, then, promote great love for the neighbor. Those who live in the Spirit will have the greatest spiritual fecundity. The Constitution on the Church declares: "By the charity to which the evangelical counsels lead, they join Christ's followers to the Church and her mystery in a special way" (LG, 44). The mystery of the Church is, above all, her being loved by Christ; he has chosen her and she is totally linked to him. In all things she can proclaim, "Thee, Christ alone, do I know." Only by knowing Christ can the Church truly know the world and discover the needs of the world. So it is with the evangelical counsels. The source of our power is humble prayer; such was the power of Pope John: his prayer, his love of God, his meditation on the Gospel, his listening to the word of God con-

tained in Scripture. It becomes easier, in this way, to accept all
events as a calling from God, a word, a message from him.

It will prove helpful to consider the three individual evangelical counsels in the broader perspective that every gift of God
becomes a "counsel," a law of the Spirit for the recipients of the
gift, because given in view of the Church.

Spirit of the Poor

Poverty must be seen in the perspective of the first beatitude,
"How blessed are those who have the spirit of the poor" (Mt
5:2). This is humility. In view of the richness of the heavenly
kingdom, we empty ourselves of selfishness, we give up an egotistic search for self-fulfillment. This we can do only in deep
faith, a faith that is a joyous, humble, grateful reception of the
gifts of God, of his beatifying love. It is a joyous surrender to
Christ, to the Message and to the Messenger. In him we are rich
and being rich in him, we can put to death selfish desires. It is a
constant gratitude, a persistent awareness that we have not
chosen the Lord but that he has chosen us; a docile humility that
never considers man's initiative apart from God's gifts, from
God's intention to bring us together. Poverty enables us to renounce many earthly things, yet without the risk of feeling frustrated because we are filled with his love, with his joy. We rejoice
in being servants, in bringing kindness, goodness, and peace to
others.

In view of conditions in the world of today, the spirit of
poverty must be lived in a sense of responsibility. There is too
much conformity among contemporaries. We find a definite lack
of personalism; people are guided only by social pressures and
prejudices, with no insight into the dynamics of their behavior.
Because of this, it is more important today than at any other time
for the individual to assume responsibility. In practical terms,
this means that a religious will not ask the superior for permission before answering the question: "Do I please the Lord by this

request? Am I asking for this permission in a spirit of service, of humility and unselfishness?" If one is not sure and insists on asking the superior, he should at least inform his superior that his motivation is questionable, that he is not sure whether he can justify the permission being sought. This represents a humble admission that he needs help in making the right decision. At times the superior may say: "I have not the insights or criteria to make a wise decision in this case. May I suggest that you go first and pray for ten minutes before the tabernacle. If you can face the Lord and know for sure that your request pleases him, then go ahead. . . . You have my permission." Greater maturity means face-to-face encounters with Christ who has become poor for us in order to enrich us. We must become aware of the fact that we have to be witnesses, witnesses of a mature, responsible use of our own wills, our own skills and earthly goods.

Consecrated Virginity

It is in the same light that the evangelical counsel of celibacy for the kingdom of God must be considered. Above all this demands openness for God's blissful love. Celibacy cannot be lived without the experience of a kind and gentle love. Allow me once again to present the problem within the present times, within the framework of the modern world. We are living in an age geared to business and management. People live under the threat of being manipulated, totally administered and managed. They are guaranteed everything save assurance of their dignity, of personal love. In this world there has developed a personalism which insists that in marriage the spouses be accepted as persons and not as objects to be exploited sexually. This personalism also means the desire to see the children as persons and to have them educated fully to maturity. Therefore it is more important today than in former times for celibacy to be lived with a warm heart for each other.

In religious life there seems to be a pressing need today for smaller communities. If a community comprises three hundred people in one house, it must be structured according to the principle of subsidiarity. The Redemptorist Rule says that a normal house should not have more than nineteen or twenty members: about twelve priests together with a number of brothers. Larger houses will have to be restructured. We must always be the friend of all, but is this possible in large and impersonal communities if they are so lacking in structure as to leave no room for friendship within smaller units? We need more personal communities. Our communities must be restructured but in a way that will not destroy the great communities. Neither must we destroy the unity of a large congregation, but it must be structured differently, possibly with a margin of flexibility.

The Decree on the Appropriate Renewal of the Religious Life says, "Above all, everyone should remember, and especially superiors, that chastity is safeguarded in a community of true fraternal love of Christ and all its members" (PC, 12). The chief witness of celibacy is that of a warm heart, a genuine friendship, a brotherly kindness for all who need us, the kind of spontaneity and generosity that excludes maternalism and paternalism. Our communities should foster this kind of love. A contemporary Protestant theologian, Theodor Bovet, says that it is a good thing to renounce marriage, but it is not a good thing to renounce living in the warmth of human friendship and community. Only if we are this one, personal community paying loving attention to each other, respecting one another, can we truly be committed and bear witness. Celibacy, then, will not be a frustrating experience. The problem of celibacy for many young priests arises from the fact that the pastor does not give his curates sufficient attention and due respect, has no kind words for them or shows no interest in them. An impersonal situation of this kind causes them to seek consolation elsewhere. The Council says very clearly that for the clergy celibacy can be lived as a witness if there is fraternal love, brotherhood, and community life among secular and religious priests. It is this full, integrated approach to love that makes it possible for the celibate to be consecrated to God and at the same time become a mature person. The wholeness of the person is very important.

Enlightened Obedience

Obedience in religious life must also be seen in the perspective of a witness to Christian sanctity in our own day; there is so much wretched conformity to be counteracted! To meet the needs of the present times especially, for greater love of God and of neighbor, religious obedience must foster mature personalities, not external conformism. Obedience must be based on insight and must not suppress the person by meaningless laws, laws that are truly museum exhibits. There must be some kind of structure; this is obvious. Life must go on in an orderly fashion, but we do not need useless laws, laws educating seminarians to be eternal seminarians and novices to be eternal novices. The novitiate must be realistic in its approach to the mature life of a professed sister or brother destined to live a full religious life in the missions or in the colleges of today.

There must be an integration of authority and obedience in the perspective of Christ's humility. He is the Lord and Master. He revealed the origin of authority in his Church by washing the feet of his disciples. The superior must bear witness to humility; his mission is not to be served but to serve. Obedience and authority can only be understood within the framework of love. Authority must be a source of love; it must be an inspiration to live the spirit of the Gospel in joy and peace. Authority must always be exercised with a view toward the building up of a community of love based on the truth of the Gospel.

When faced with the problems posed by the pace of changes today and the proper handling of discussions and disputes, superiors would do well to look to the example of Pope John and Pope Paul and try to keep the same goal in mind. They should note that the good shepherd takes three steps forward and occasionally one step backward in order to maintain unity, to bring all together. Some of our religious (and not only in America) are so impatient that they dissipate their precious energies in all directions. One group runs ahead of the other; unlike John who outran Peter on Easter morning and then waited for him, the others keep forging ahead. If the Johns are on the run in such a way that the superior cannot even explain to them: "We are on the move, but let us pause to get our bearings, to find out if we are moving in the right direction," it will not be possible to bear witness. We cannot be credible if we do not talk to each other, convince each other, and listen to each other. It is sometimes advisable to wait for slower colleagues. The Church will move much more quickly in this era of change if we are kind and lovingly patient with each other. The role of the superior becomes one of coordination, but not in the sense of cold management. The superior must be a coordinator of hearts and ideas; for this, he (she) must have a loving heart and a discerning mind. Let the one who understands finances best be the treasurer, but do not choose superiors from the ranks merely of expert managers. The prime requisites for a superior are a loving heart and a spirit of brotherhood.

Obedience and authority are not something apart from the order of love; they are totally linked to the understanding and building up of a community of love, a community capable of witnessing to love, that can operate in unity and creativity but that, above all, tries to build its family ties upon fellowship in Christ. Religious obedience is possible only under the influence of the Holy Spirit. Superiors, for their part, must be *spiritual* men and women; this means that they must be fully docile to the Holy Spirit whose pleasure is often served by teaching them through those "under authority."

The superior must also maintain an open-door policy. He must have time to listen to people; however, even this will not be done with benefit unless he listens to the Holy Spirit and meditates on the Gospel. The good superior will show docility toward the members of the community, fully realizing that he has no monopoly on insights. He must learn docility to the Holy Spirit by being docile to the other brothers or sisters. It is not only brothers and sisters who must admit that at times they do not listen to the superior. The superior must sometimes admit that he did not listen to the brothers when they were right, or when they were eager and able to contribute. If a superior is humble, if he can listen to others, then he will finally be able to say the last word.

Today, more than ever, the goal of obedience must be maturity. The decree on religious life states: "Realizing that the religious are giving service for the upbuilding of Christ's Body according to God's design, let them bring to the whole execution of commands and to the discharge of assignments the resources of their minds and wills and their gifts of nature and grace" (PC, 14). Religious obedience is to be an enlightened obedience but also a humble obedience. Thus people will know that religious orders are not only made up of orderly people but also of mature, responsible people in the discipleship of Christ where there is the greatest respect for each person. Therefore, superiors must not merely tell others what they are to do. Superiors should ask others gently whether they would like to do a certain thing. The mature person will always want to do and like to do the right thing. Superiors must be earnestly considerate for the good of the entire community and for all persons within the community. The relationship between superiors and sisters (or brothers) within the community must be one of true love; this means more than loving a superior because of his (her) role or office. Superiors have a right to be loved as persons because of their good qualities and their human frailties. Why do we so readily overlook this? We should never look at the faults and imperfections of another person without a deeper awareness of our own personal faults and imperfections, mistakes and defects. Only then can we accept each other truthfully as we are. Only then will we be able to help each other become more fully what Christ wants us to be.

Obedience, says the Constitution on the Church, "does not detract from the genuine development of the human person. Rather, by its very nature it is most beneficial to that development" (LG, 46). In the present post-conciliar era, this attitude must be the norm for the exercise of authority, both with regard to obedience and the reform of religious rules. Rules and precepts which do not help to build up a genuinely Christian community of mature persons and which fail to promote an apostolic activity as a witness to unity must be courageously altered. Likewise, superiors assume responsibility for applying the rules, but this should not be done mechanically. Instead, rules should be interpreted according to the criteria of fraternal and sisterly love, always in openness toward the "signs of the times," and hence, in a spiritual sense. Similarly, superiors should gently endorse and promote those customs which express or encourage genuine love and reflect an alertness to the needs of the Church today.

The theology of marriage declares that the sacramental grace of marriage bears its most precious fruits if the spouses, by their mutual love, bring each other and their children to an enthusiastic knowledge of "How good God must be!" It is evident that in religious life, religious obedience and authority are meaningful but distinct services of love. In this regard, an altogether different charism is expected of superiors, namely, that of manifesting the love with which God loves his own sons and daughters. If they do this, religious will continue enthusiastically to recognize God's love and their love for each other. Nevertheless, we must also acknowledge that the love of the superior has its limitations, just as married couples acknowledge limitations in each other while continually trying to enrich each other. If we insist that the superior remain in an icebox of impersonalism, we cannot expect a warm heart in return. In pre-conciliar days, the emphasis was placed mostly on what superiors expected of their subjects and only rarely was any consideration given to the reverse set of expectations; it is necessary to consider both. We must enrich each other humbly.

THREE | RELIGIOUS WITNESS IN THE WORLD

... The counsels are especially able to pattern the Christian man after that manner of virginal and humble life which Christ the Lord elected for himself, and which his Virgin Mother also chose. (LG, 46)

The Constitution on the Church states that the laity can and ought to be "witnesses to the resurrection and to the life of the Lord Jesus as a sign that God lives" (LG, 38). What is the *raison d'être* of religious in the Church if the same role of witnessing to the risen Lord is not expected of them, in a more outstanding way? They especially must give testimony to the resurrection and the life of the Lord Jesus as a symbol of the living God in the present age. Their relevance will depend on their understanding of this role in both the Church and in the world, because the Church is in the world and the world is in the Church.

In the present context, the world may be defined as the whole of mankind inclusive of the created universe; it encompasses the physical, geographical, social, and psychological environments of contemporary man. The Church and the world are related to each other on very many levels. The relevance of the Church for this last third of the twentieth century will be convincing only if its members are witnesses to the Gospel in love and in service. As a group, religious orders and congregations are expected to be pioneers in the Church, trailblazers, locomotives rather than the caboose at the end of a long freight train.

The new Pentecost ushered into the Church by the recent Vatican Council is forcing her out of her centuries-old immobilism, especially the kind reflected in the stereotyped formalism of the liturgy. There was not complete immobility, of course, but enough to cause many good Catholics and even religious superiors to think that the best Catholic, the best religious was the most unchanging, the most immobile one. Since Vatican Council II, Catholics and non-Catholics are being confronted by a redefined Church. Pope John saw clearly the need for the Church to be renewed and to show her real countenance to the world as a church on pilgrimage, a living Church.

In this new epoch in Church history everything centers around the great mystery of the death and resurrection of the Lord, as declared in the Constitution on the Sacred Liturgy. The whole emphasis in renewal is to bring about an awareness that we have died to sin with Christ and are risen with him; that the Church is the Church of the *risen* Lord. Therefore, the Church as a whole is called to give witness to him, to the mystery of his unselfish love, to the victory of his selfless life. His is a victory of *life*, not the victory of the grave. In the Gospel of St. John, it is shown that women were the first to receive the message of the resurrection of the Lord, and they were sent to the Apostles, even to Peter and John, to bring them the great message of joy: the Lord is risen! In the Church of the future the importance of religious orders is bound to increase. In a sense, we are only at the beginning of Church history and the development of religious orders and congregations.

Dynamic Social World

We are living in the most dynamic age in the history of mankind, in an era characterized by new events, new inventions, and far-reaching programs, e.g., in space exploration. This new world has seen the emergence of an image of man different from the one that dominated Greco-Roman or humanistic culture. The new image of man is strongly colored by the modern sciences, especially psychology, sociology, the biological and physical sciences, and mathematics. The life-space of man is inescapably enmeshed in the mass communications media. For the first time in the world's history there is the possibility of all cultures and religions drawing together. Ours is a pluralistic society in which each one can choose his own system of values; ours is a time when religious liberty and tolerance are being promoted while at the same time atheism is being politically organized and attempts are being made to impose an alien ideology on the masses by violence. Add to the ever-growing web of social forces the rise of new forms of personalism, a new awareness of the value and dignity of the human person, and we can get some idea of the innumerable complex forces impinging on contemporary man.

There is a great danger of losing equilibrium, the happy balance between the practical sciences progressing at a geometric rate and developments in man's theological and philosophical formation, *i.e.*, an understanding of man's nature and his relationship to God and to the world. The fantastic evolution of science is accepted as a sign of the liberation of man's intellectual power to control his own destiny. The resulting pseudo-security with regard to man's mastery of the physical universe is counterbalanced by a tremendous feeling of insecurity with regard to moral judgment. The witness of religious can be particularly helpful in offsetting the prevalent malaise.

An attempt will be made to show how the different developments solemnly proposed by the Council affect religious, especially religious women. One of the essential contributions of the Constitution on the Church in the Modern World is that it deals with the new role and image of womanhood in the world. The emerging feminine image is totally different from that of two hundred years ago, or the role and possibilities open to women at the time of St. Paul. At the present time, we must combine fidelity to tradition, divine tradition, with the opportunities and needs of the moment. With great courage we must distinguish between a divine revelation that is abiding and human traditions capable of being legitimately changed or abolished. We must look to Christ, the living God, who gives life and is at the same time the absolutely faithful One. He is the founder of the Church and is ever faithful to her; the Church strives to mirror the image of Christ's fidelity, that of the living Word of God.

Mary: Image of the Church and of Womanhood

Religious have much to gain by meditating on the Church, the image of Christ, the faithful and true witness. In Mary, the Church not only has her perfect prototype but also the image of womanhood. Indeed, God created woman with her characteristic virtues and capabilities, but he made her this way in view of Mary and the Church. One of the noblest attributes of woman is her tenacity to life. This is something totally different from a mere arbitrary shaping of the external results of history, something completely different from immobile clinging to the mere letter of the law. Every woman has an inborn intimacy, one might say complicity, with tradition, but tradition understood as continuity of life. Such is the power of her humility that she is more able than man to bring together essence and existence in holiness.

The Constitution on Divine Revelation presents Holy Scripture as the expression of the living tradition of the Church. Scripture was written by inspired disciples of Christ who understood him, and therefore dared to translate his very words into a language capable of being understood and reconciled with new experiences and new views. It is from Holy Scripture, the book of a living tradition, that we come to know Mary.

In Mary, Virgin and Mother, all that is best in womanhood reaches its fulfillment. Hers was the highest privilege conceivable for a mere creature; she is the great deaconess of salvation. As the humble handmaid of the Lord, she sang for us the perfect song in praise of the Redeemer; she is proposed, therefore, as the

mirror of the Church. She is presented as a prototype of the
Church in her faithful expectation of the richness to come and
in her constant watching for the advent of the heavenly Bridegroom with the fullness of grace. Her humility allows her life to
be completely permeated by the Word of God whom she conceived not only in her womb but also in her heart.

St. Luke mentions the woman who praises Christ's mother for
having borne a great son. Jesus replies, "Blessed are those who
hear the word of God and keep it," acting upon it. Luke also
mentions twice in the same chapter the words, "Mary treasured
up all these things in her heart" (2:19, 51). She pondered on
them; he did not say that she memorized them. She did not commit the *Magnificat* to memory after having uttered it nor did
she repeat it exactly later on to Luke. She did not memorize the
words of the Lord, but she treasured them up in her heart and
acted upon them. Thus she entered into the tradition of the
Church. She had come upon their meaning and could tell John
or Luke, later on, what happened.

What lesson concerning the history of salvation do we learn
from Mary? She is obedient to the Word of God, but she is a
prototype of enlightened obedience since she asks how all these
things shall be accomplished. She is not a slave who does not
wish to know what the master is doing; she asked, "How shall
these things be?"

Her faithful treasuring up of events in her heart becomes, in
an ineffable way, a constant opening to the call of the moment.
The angel said to her, "No word of God shall lack power." Her
answer, "Behold the handmaid of the Lord," opens her virginal
womb to the eternal Word of the Father. At the same time, she
proves her fidelity to the changing call of the moment. Mary rose
immediately and went with haste through the hill country into
the city of Juda to attend her cousin Elizabeth. If she had been
a nun at the beginning of the nineteenth century, there would
have been no provision in the Rule to cover this situation. Once
she had told her superior, there could have been no question of

her going to the hill country without a companion. Thank God that she was free to do it!

The Blessed Virgin had faith; at all times she treasured up words and happenings in her heart. Mary's faithfulness to the Word and devoted response to the special service demanded of her came from the same source, from a profound humility and a living faith. Mary is the prototype of the Church. Our Lord has entrusted his Word to the Church, his bride, and has bestowed the Holy Spirit on her. The Word is the seed that bears fruit a hundredfold. This Word was not entrusted to the Church primarily for inclusion in a book that would contain everything once and for all. It was committed to her care by the living Word of God, through the Holy Spirit. Therefore, the inspired writer allowed himself to speak about the events he was recording for different cultures in different ways, so that all could understand the message and its significance for them. With the same purpose of meaningful communication, the Holy Spirit at Pentecost caused the apostles to speak in all languages so that all could hear the same message.

Devotion to the Blessed Virgin, then, becomes more than an emotional affair. It is a commitment to her openness, to her deep faith, and to her way of treasuring up the Word of the Lord. A few pages about the Blessed Virgin reveal this openness and readiness to respond in service. The angel did not tell her to go to the hill country but only told her that her cousin Elizabeth was also blessed. In Cana, at the wedding feast, nobody told her about the wine shortage, but she saw that the newlyweds were in a rather precarious situation. It was she who was vigilant, open-minded, openhearted, and faithful to the changing call of the present moment.

Mary Magdalen and the Modern Religious

We must now look at another Mary; it may be that we are closer to this other Mary than we are to the Blessed Virgin. We refer to Mary Magdalen, not the great sinner or woman of perfected faith, but the one who painfully had to grow in faith. St. John gives us a tremendous portrait of Mary Magdalen, one so very different from that presented in the Synoptics (Jn 20:1-18). The Synoptics summarily dismiss Mary Magdalen by saying that she came to the tomb, saw the Lord, and brought the message to the disciples. It all seemed very easy for her. St. John, however, develops an aspect of Mary's story which the Synoptics did not deny but simply failed to mention. That aspect of Mary Magdalen has relevance for our own lives, namely, her slow growth in faith. We see this Mary as the good woman who had the unique privilege of bringing the message of the great mystery of Christ's resurrection to the apostles, but she was not quick to understand. Mark (16:5-9) and John (20:11-18) specifically indicate that the pious women received quite a shock. They were coming to visit the grave of the Lord. Very early on that Sunday morning they came to the tomb carrying the spices they had prepared. Finding that the stone had been rolled away, they went inside the tomb but the body was not to be found. While they stood there, utterly at a loss, two men in dazzling white garments suddenly appeared at their side; they were dumbfounded.

The situation of some religious men and women today is similar. The point was dramatically made five years ago at a conference in Chicago when the question was addressed to me from the floor: "After the Council, do you not think that the rules and laws of the Church will again be formulated once and for all?" Stated differently, the question meant: "After the Council, will we be able to capture the Lord and bring him back to his tomb?"

We have to adjust ourselves to the fact that the world is moving ahead; we live in a dynamic world. The emphasis of the Constitution on the Church is the same as that of the Constitution on the Sacred Liturgy. Christians are living in a time of great favor, a time when the victory of Christ's love has appeared fully in his resurrection. Christians of every age must be forward-looking, because they live between his first and his second coming. We are living in the twentieth century, in a mobile and dynamic age, in a highly progressive society. How can we forget the most essential aspect of our faith and give the impression that we find ourselves in a situation analogous to the three days the Lord rested in the tomb? He wishes us to become witnesses to his life.

Let us study closely how patient he was with Mary Magdalen, the privileged messenger of his resurrection to the apostles. Luke says clearly: "She was utterly at a loss." She saw that the stone had been moved away from the entrance and she ran to Simon Peter and to the disciple whom Jesus loved. "They have taken the Lord out of his tomb," she cried, "and we do not know where they have laid him." Then we have that wonderful passage where John outruns Peter. He has to wait until the older, heavier Peter comes up. It is the intention of the holy writer to indicate that there are slow and fast runners. An interesting thought in this connection is that even in the best religious congregations some outrun others even though all are truly running toward the risen Lord. Should they not also have the same charity as John? He peered in and saw the linen wrappings lying there, but he did not enter. Sometimes we realize what should be done, but for a while—not for all eternity but for a short time—we must wait for the older confrères or sisters to catch up with us; they are running hard but they are getting out of breath.

The disciples, however, went home. Had they seen the risen Lord? No, but they believed although their faith had not yet attained its fullness. Mary, however, stood at the tomb outside, weeping and crying. As she wept, she peered into the tomb and saw two angels in white sitting there, one at the head and one at the feet, where the body of Jesus had lain (Jn 20:10-12). They asked her why she was weeping; she told them that they had taken her Lord and she did not know where they had put him. She then turned around and saw Jesus standing there; but she did not recognize him. Jesus said to her, "Why are you weeping? Who is it you are looking for?" Thinking that he was the gardener, she said, "If it is you, sir, who have removed him, tell me where you have put him and I will take him away." Jesus appears in the image of the gardener (who takes care of growing life) but Mary is still seeking him among the dead.

Jesus called, "Mary!" She turned to him and said, "Rabboni! My Master!" Jesus said to her, "Do not cling to me this way for I have not yet ascended to the Father, but go to my brothers and tell them that I ascend to my Father and your Father, to my God and your God" (Jn 20:17-18). Mary Magdalen went to the disciples with the joyful news. "I have seen the Lord," she said, and she gave them his message.

We have a tremendous development here but not an easy one to understand. Mary Magdalen went through a crisis. The crisis came out of the depths of her heart because she loved the Lord and believed in his love; but she had not grasped the mystery of the risen Lord, the living Lord. Is this not often the case with us? We love him, but we cling to old stereotyped forms. We do not distinguish between the tomb of centuries, i.e., the sepulcher of outdated traditions and that which is divine tradition: the torrent of life, divine life. The Church is the Church of the Risen Lord. Her chief message to all times, and especially to our dynamic age, is: "What are you looking for? What do you expect to find?" Are you waiting only for little things, a little rule, a little security instead of the continuation of salvation history in which the living Lord goes along with us, preparing in us his final coming?

Ecclesial Gardening

The Second Vatican Council presents the Church under the image of the Virgin ever watchful for the coming of the Lord. Mary Magdalen is the model of the Church on pilgrimage. The Blessed Virgin is the model toward which she has to strive. As for religious, theirs is the outstanding vocation to be witnesses to the true nature of the Church, the virginal bride of Christ. The virgin, then, must give high value to prayer, to the liturgy, to being with Christ.

The Church looks to see what her Divine Bridegroom is preparing for her in the life that is now going on. As a Gardener, he is cultivating life. In presenting himself to Mary Magdalen as a gardener, Christ indicates that the first step to a realization that he is the living Lord is to take care of life. The Church has also been entrusted with the care of life, growing life. Therefore those who witness to the real nature of the Church must have the same orientation. The role of gardeners of life does not coincide with that of custodians and guardians of the tomb, keepers of the stereotyped formalism of past eras. We must always be mindful that the living word of God takes precedence over all long-established traditions. There is a tendency even today to imprison the word of God, to preserve it in a shrine—not to say a grave—of set forms and archaic laws. We do this with a completely good conscience, one that is all too secure; our motives may even spring from the love of Our Lord who has given us his Word. There is love in our attitude but a love that has not yet been purified, a love not yet afire with the Spirit of Pentecost, a love not yet filled with trust and grounded on faith in the risen Lord.

In our own way we believe in the mystery of the resurrection, but we were told about the Lord in a fashion that smacked too much of the world; we encountered him in the imperfect beginnings of our faith. Now we are called to believe unreservedly, with a faith permeating all aspects of our life, that Christ is risen; we can then become messengers of the resurrection. John's Gospel has a wonderful twentieth chapter; it presents a woman who lived quite some time before understanding the full import of Christ's resurrection. It is this same woman who was sent to the apostles and disciples bearing the message of the risen Christ.

It may be that at special moments in the life of the Church, woman, and, in an eminent way, sisters, have a special mandate to bring the message to priests and the faithful: Christ is risen! Their mission is not that of capturing him and bringing his body back to the tomb; they must live and show in their lives that the Lord is risen, that he has sent the Holy Spirit. All reli-

gious must make a serious endeavor to break away from some
of their more obsolete traditions. We must seek the experiences
that will help us to be credible when we bring the message joyfully to the disciples: Christ is risen indeed!

Treasuring Up His Words in Our Hearts

The ideal of nearness to the life of God and to the world of today
springs from the Gospel. In the farewell discourse that summarizes his teachings, Our Lord says: "If you dwell in me, and if
my words dwell in you, then ask what you will and you shall
have it" (Jn 15:7).

The words of the Lord must *dwell* in us. We see Mary, the
mother of the Lord, in the mystery of the Incarnation. She received the living Word of God; but she first heeded the message,
the words that prepared her life for this event. Notice her reaction to the intimation: "Your cousin Elizabeth is also in good
hope." The angel did not say, "You must go to her." Just one little
cue and she, who was ever watchful, hastened over the hills to
sing in the house of her cousin Elizabeth the *Magnificat,* the song
of joy. She was vigilant and she praised God in humble service.

When the woman from the crowd cried, "Blessed the mother
that bore you," Our Lord replied, "Indeed, blessed are those who
hear the word of God and act upon it." Mary is, above all,
blessed, not only because of her blood relationship as the mother
of Christ but because she is the prototype of the Church in her
total dedication to Christ and her neighbor (LG, Ch. 8). First,
she is watchful for the word of the Lord; she treasures all these
happenings, all these words. The different translations of the
term "word" assume great meaning here; it stands for both *word*
and *happening.* When something happens, God speaks to us
through that event.

Today more than ever we must try to view all things in the
light of the Bible; this should be the fundamental book for our
novices. The holy Rule and all other regulations must be seen

in the light of the Gospel; so must present happenings—the events of the Second Vatican Council and all that happens in the world —all must be viewed as messages coming from God. We must treasure up all these happenings, these words in our hearts and meditate on them, close to the Lord. We too are called on to imitate the vigilant virgin who is open-minded and watchful for the coming of the Lord in all events, in the whole of salvation history. We must try to understand the meaning of the present age both in its great events and in the modest happenings that characterize our daily lives.

The Hour of Favor

In Holy Scripture the key word to New Testament morality is *kairos,* "the hour of favor." Christ himself often speaks of "his hour." He sees the present moment in the light of the great "hour of favor," the hour which his Father has prepared for him, namely, the hour of the Paschal Mystery, of his death and resurrection. At Cana when Mary's vigilance for the needs of others prompted her to say, "They have no wine," the Lord replied, "My hour has not yet come." However, he performed a miracle that foreshadowed the great hour of his own wedding in his own blood. Every moment of decision must be seen in the light of the decisive hour of the Paschal Mystery. In all events the Lord makes present his hour, always the hour which his Father has prepared for him.

In our lives, in our Institutes, we must also endeavor to see everything in the light of the great hour, that of the Paschal Mystery of the death and resurrection of the Lord. The power of the resurrection reaches us through these events; and if the power of his resurrection reaches us, he is preparing us for his Second Coming. In decisions at the present time, the present moment, this great aftermath of the Second Vatican Council, we are being put to the test. If you say that you believe in the risen Lord and in his final manifestation, the Parousia, the Second Coming, but you still decide to avoid risks—you decide to remain immobile —you are testifying to the world that you do not believe in the risen Lord, that you are not watchful virgins. You refuse to accept the working of the Holy Spirit and of Christ Jesus through the Holy Spirit, as he prepares us for his coming. We have to be watchful, but we will grasp the real meaning of the present hour only if we treasure up in our hearts the words of the Lord, the teachings of the Church, and the happenings we experience with a living faith. By joyfully singing, praying, celebrating the Paschal Mystery every day, we come a little closer to the image of the Church and the Blessed Virgin because all events enable this mystery to reach us here and now. Such is the meaning of witnessing "to the resurrection and the life of the Lord Jesus" and being a sign that God lives.

St. Paul appeals to Christians to "use the present opportunities to the full, for these are evil days" (Eph 5:16). How can one reconcile the two things: "a special opportunity" and "because days are evil"? There is no doubt that for those who do *not* use to the best advantage present opportunities, the days are bad. The message of St. Paul is faithful to the preaching of the Lord: we are living in a time of favor, a time of grace. However, there are many sleepy people and others about who, like Lot's wife, keep looking backward, always crying and weeping for the "good old times." These somnolent and passively resistant individuals keep saying by their acts: "The world would be so restful if everything were settled once and for all; but everything is on the move. Look at all these changes. The Council has disturbed us!"

We can see that a great vision has been presented to us in the Bible. Christ relates every moment of his life to the great hour, the hour of his wedding to the Church, the hour of the Paschal Mystery. Death and resurrection are always presented as a unified thing. We then see how Christ relates the life of the Church to his second coming by his continuous exhortation in the Gospel to be watchful because we do not know when the bridegroom is coming. We do not know when the *kairos*, the moment of favor, is coming.

God prepares his coming for us in present opportunities, the present favorable time, the great possibilities being offered to us. We will not be ready to greet his second coming if we are not watchful. Christ represented his Church, holy Church, according to the image of the Virgin because she was always vigilant for the coming Lord. Those who are in an outstanding way signs of the Church, the virginal brides of Christ—religious—must be relevant for the world, but they will be so only to the extent of their watchfulness, never according to a mechanical external obedience.

Why do some of you seem to belong so much to the past? A look at seventy or one hundred congregations reveals that they constitute a perfect museum of all the customs, costumes, and clothing of past centuries. Outlandishness does not make for a relevant witness in the modern world; it merely signifies a predilection for antiques. We are pertinent to the mission of the Church by watchfulness and we are outstandingly relevant if we present the right countenance of the Church, the corrected image of the Church, by our vigilance and loving service, not only by a new garb.

In his second epistle to the Corinthians, St. Paul indicates what the word *kairos* means: "Behold the time of favor has arrived; behold the time of salvation has come" (II Cor 6:2). Of equal relevance is the admonition: "Do not receive the present grace of God in vain" (II Cor 6:1). *Kairos* is the crowning event, the external opportunity, or better, the internal call of the Holy Spirit to those who are docile and genuinely spiritual men and women. They understand what God has prepared for them at the present moment. Our time, the time of Vatican Council II, is a time of salvation. This is the great hour prepared for us by God.

In one of those long sermons in which Our Lord tried to convert lawyers from their attitude of external formalism and mechanism, he said, "Why do you transgress the law of God because of your well-established traditions?" (Mt 15:3-4). We must feel the same way today. If we observe only the external letter, outward tradition, we are mummies and therefore witnesses against the faith that Christ has risen. Two thousand years later we are still at the stage of Mary Magdalen's wavering faith, in the hour the Lord was preparing for her.

Nothing could be worse than to insist merely on the letter of the law, forgetting about the tremendous appeal of the present hour prepared by God, especially if we also forget the appeal of the heart. Many accept life in conformity to external pressures and seem totally oblivious of issues related to social justice. Their greatest preoccupation is to maintain their dignity and self-styled security, and this they do by blocking the apostolate. They make the witness of the religious inefficacious and in many cases there is even a real disobedience to the essential laws of God because of external obedience to man-made laws.

Many moralists were trained in schools of theology that gave chief attention to the positive law. Positive law has meaning only for the community that is watchful for the signs of the time. Therefore the problem is one of determining how to follow the signs of the time while remaining within the law of God. If members of a community can deal effectively with new situations in our rapidly evolving times, these things undoubtedly are according to God's plan and show that the law cannot be rigid. One example that touched me profoundly will serve to illustrate the point.

The Sacred Congregation for Religious issued a decree requiring seminary professors to teach in Latin. This was before the time of Pope John though he, later on, in the unfortunate constitution *Veterum sapientiae*, stated that only those who were capable of teaching in Latin were obligated to do so, and those who were not were to be replaced as soon as possible. This was explained by a Roman canonist to mean normally "as soon as you die." As a result of the earlier law, a Father General informed his provincials that the law had to be observed literally and without exception. The provincial then notified the professor of dogma of his obligation to teach in Latin. Until then, the professor of dogma had celebrated Mass every Sunday for two little towns. He could no longer minister there because he had to learn Latin. So two thousand persons went without Mass. Besides, every week the same professor taught heresy because, knowing so little Latin, he was deceiving his students by his poor use of the language. They either laughed throughout the class or else slept. He was not helping to train priests for the future. Great personal harm ensued; the professor lost his optimistic outlook and developed stomach ulcers. Anger and frustration marked the atmosphere of a house where nonsense in the name of God and the Church was causing so many laws of God to be violated.

The Balance Sheet

We are well aware that there is a certain loss of vocations today. It seems that a very thorough study should be made of the different reasons for this phenomenon. Some losses are actually gains. It may be that in the case of some religious, they have perhaps for the last several years been in a state of "internal emigration" and when they finally left the community, the congregation was liberated not only of troublemakers but of people who had no faith, and who did not believe in the living Lord. There are others, however, who leave because of activism. Religious very much dedicated to their work sometimes lose the spirit of prayer; it soon follows that they no longer find any reason for remaining in the congregation. They are better able to serve their activism by leaving. There are also legalists who constantly cry, "Observance, observance," because they no longer believe in the *living* Christ Jesus and persecute those who wish to pursue a more effective apostolate in our time. These spiritless men and women are a constant source of frustration and often are a cause of the loss of the best vocations. There are cases of sisters and brothers who leave out of impatience because their superiors act like the classical guardians of the tomb of Our Lord—perhaps out of love for him, but all the while lacking faith in the living Lord. If these religious had more of the love and faith of John, they would recognize in their overcautious superior another Peter who is well on the road to the risen Lord but must be helped by the patience of John.

I have been trying to persuade many religious men and women to remain in their communities even though their congregations are evidently far too conservative, too tradition-bound. I urge them to try to work within the congregation to improve things: "Stand together; show a proper spirit, obedience, humility, patience, and courage." Their stock answer is: "Father, we will have this superior for another ten years, and in ten years we will all be crazy." This is what frustration does; but is there any reason for them all to be crazy? They could retain their sanity and mental balance by standing together in humility, by promoting good ideas and right courses of action, by giving more credit to their superiors, by showing that they really do believe in the Risen Lord. The fact remains, however, that there are sometimes good people who are weak and disturbed by a spirit of discouragement, and during discouragement all kinds of temptations can flourish.

The losses occur, then, for very many reasons. We should rejoice only when religious leave who do not wish to lead a life of faith in the Risen Lord. Some are immobile and lacking in spirit; they cannot tolerate changes of any kind. Losing these people amounts to a gain for the congregation. However, before losing them, the community should do everything possible to awaken them, to jolt them out of their torpor, to help them. Patience and kindness have a soothing effect, but as a last resort, if they do not wish to live on the level of witnesses of the living Lord, it is better for them to depart.

Woe to the communities, however, that lose those who wish to be witnesses of the living Lord but who, provoked by wrong-headed conservatism, run to a wrong-headed progressivism.

These are the two extremes. We soon became aware at the opening of the Council that the greatest danger was not that from extreme traditionalism so much as from a misleading progressivism in reaction against this traditionalism. We must be on guard to discern what real progress means: renewal in the Spirit and in greater depth. Extreme progressivism of the wrong kind is almost always provoked by extreme advocates of archaic traditionalism. If we wish to conserve the best of what we have, we can do this only by continuity of life. A gardener cultivates life, helps life to grow, to continue. We are witnesses to the living Lord in our courage toward new ways. A good initiative must always manifest the *spirit* of continuity, but not the lifeless clinging to old forms and formulas. God is always a living God. He speaks in every age, according to the signs of the times. We must dare to take the initiative, to promote the necessary changes.

The Risk of a New Approach

I confess and humbly acknowledge that my books do some harm to persons who pick and choose words here and there, lifting them out of context. They do not study the work as a whole. In the foreword of my books, I warn that statements should always be viewed in the full context. Nevertheless, we must take risks; we must alert people but still take the risk involved in a lively initiative, the risk of growth in depth by bringing the message of Christ to the world today. If we do not, we are making a decision for suicide, and suicide is a greater risk than the constant risk of growing life.

The reason for the existence of a religious congregation is to serve as pioneers of a new epoch or at least to act as the most alert sectors of a Church on pilgrimage. The congregation must always be in the vanguard, looking forward to the coming of the Lord, always watchful. If I were a Counselor of Devils—which thank God I am not—I would advise all demons to tempt those in authority (major superiors and others) to retain all the old formulas and to complain as loudly as possible about the "rest-lessness" of open-minded religious. I would not tempt them to schism, but to trail, for security's sake, far, far behind the rest of the Church. It would be the most effective way of destroying these communities.

What reason can justify membership in a religious congregation if the group has no other goal than to lag behind the rest of the Church? Our religious vocation summons us to be pioneers in the Church, to effect a real renewal, all the while treasuring up the words of the Lord in our hearts, being vigilant for present opportunities, pioneers in relevance to the times, bringing the message of the Gospel to bear so that the times can be sanctified.

The inestimable vocation of the religious is to be allowed to know the signs of the time, to be watchful, to do what is here and now required by the hour of favor, the time of opportunity. We must face the world as it is; we have new tasks to perform. There are new dangers, and there must be new emphases to protect values particularly endangered today. In all these things religious have a special task assigned them, namely, to be, in an outstanding way, witnesses to the Christian life in general, witnesses "to the resurrection and the life of the Lord Jesus and a sign that God lives" (LG, 38).

FOUR | CONTINUITY OF LIFE

The appropriate renewal of religious life involves two simultaneous processes: (1) a continuous return to the sources of all Christian life and to the original inspiration behind a given community and (2) an adjustment of the community to the changed conditions of the times. (PC, 2)

------❧------

It is a humbling experience for American priests to have to admit that they are being outdone by religious women in the process of adaptation, but the point is valid. The praise is all the more deserved since the sisters themselves admit that they need further improvement. This insight together with the readiness to move in the desired direction are indeed praiseworthy attributes for any group.

Normal Times

In spite of the progressive spirit of most religious, however, there are still a few who are inclined to groan like the good monsignor I encountered a few weeks ago. He asked me rather impatiently: "Father, do you think we will ever have 'normal times' again?" I asked what he meant by "normal times." He meant "times when everything would be settled once and for all and we would have no further changes." Such "normal times," of course, are encountered only by those reposing in cemeteries.

The Acts of the Apostles depict "normal times" as the springtime of the Church, times of growth and new horizons, times of personal differences and tensions, even tensions between God and man. We need only recall the fact that God himself intervened in the case of the headstrong though basically well-disposed Peter. God revealed to him a vision of "unclean animals" (signifying the Gentiles) and bade him eat. Peter refused at first, saying: "I never ate unclean things." However, he understood the implication of the invitation to eat, since at that time, the young Church demanded that converts from paganism first be cleansed according to Hebrew rituals before being admitted into the Christian community. Peter then yielded to the Spirit. After having preached the Gospel to the household of Cornelius and after witnessing the descent of the Holy Spirit upon the still unbaptized Gentiles, he dared to obey God's command and baptized them all. This act of Peter incurred the censure of the people of the "Holy Office" of that day, headed by St. James. This group openly accused him in the public assembly saying: "How could you baptize these pagans before they had been circumcised?" Peter humbly apologized maintaining, "It is not I that dared since I never intended to act in this manner; yet how could I do otherwise when the Holy Spirit had already descended on them?" The incident clearly testifies to the humility of the first pope.

"Normal Times" for St. Paul

At that time the largest Christian community was undoubtedly that of Antioch. Paul and Barnabas had agreed to dispense most of their converts from following the old holy rule of the Israelites, namely, circumcision. Because of this, Peter was informed by James (or rather, by those surrounding him) that it was high time to investigate Paul's activities at Antioch where a new "situation ethics" was making havoc of all the established "holy rules." Peter thus felt compelled to go to Antioch where he met Paul of whom he was personally very fond. Peter neither intended to join Paul in his activities nor to justify his actions. Yet, since the first council of Jerusalem had decided in his own favor in the case of Christians of Gentile origin, he could offer no objections. Peter himself had eaten meat with the Gentiles.

However, due to mounting pressures from the people of the "Holy Office" who followed him to Antioch, Peter kept aloof from the company of the uncircumcised who ate "unclean" food. The situation caused tension in the new Christian community; they lost confidence in both Peter and Paul. Therefore, in the presence of the whole assembly, Paul asked Peter how he could justify his present conduct since he himself, in the case of Cornelius, had baptized the Gentiles without imposing on them the Jewish law of circumcision. Paul resisted Peter "to his face," as he declares in his letter to the Galatians (2:11). The tension thereafter subsided although it involved an act of humility on the part of Peter and much grumbling from the people surrounding James and constituting the then "Holy Office."

Tensions increased further for St. Paul. He was accused, shackled, and sent to Rome where some were intent on preaching the Gospel in a contentious manner in order, as Paul himself testified, to embarrass him and cause him to be condemned to death. Even before Paul's imprisonment, a most embarrassing incident occurred which has been recorded, for our edification, in Holy Scripture compiled under the inspiration of the Holy Spirit. After having personally brought a generous donation from his Christian community in Antioch to the needy brethren in Jerusalem, St. Paul was met by the recipients of his bounty saying: "We are sorry, Paul, but you are accused of teaching contrary to our 'holy rule.' Therefore you must perform some work of justification. Since some of our people, faithful to the holy rule, are at this moment offering acts of reparation in the Temple, we suggest that you join them and pay the required ransom offering. Our conjecture is that since you brought these huge sums of money from your people, you must also carry substantial amounts in your pockets wherewith you can pay the required offering." Paul did have some money with him, but little did they realize that it was the money which he himself had earned by working day and night when not preaching the Gospel.

The incident instructs us not only with regard to tensions in the early Church but also on how to cope with them. After an exhausting journey, Paul, a man with innumerable sufferings who had been repeatedly stoned, scourged, and imprisoned, immediately proceeded to the Temple to perform the penitential rite instead of taking a well-deserved rest. He executed the orders of this self-righteous group surrounding James. Paul's appearance in the Temple caused considerable consternation and resulted in his imprisonment. It is not unlikely that Paul had some inkling of the ignoble desire to allow him to be delivered into the hands of the hostile Jewish authorities; however, during his lifetime Paul never once insinuated or expressed such a suspicion. Even if the people surrounding James never directly intended Paul's incarceration, the fact remains that they made no attempt to have him released. The situation was grave indeed.

We should never despair of any situation. The Church made progress because of great pioneers like Paul; he did not retreat like some angry priests today who say: "Good-by, I've had enough of the whole system." Men like Paul went on in patience, denying the egotistical self, enduring great sufferings for the sake of unity and renewal. This is the lesson we must learn in our present "normal times."

The Church is growing; it is growing out of a narrowness very similar to that of the James clique who wished to keep the Church under Jewish law, under Jewish regulations and customs —in short, who wanted a Church of Jewish culture. The Church grew out of the ages of Constantine and Charlemagne, eras when the successors of the humble apostles not only became "princes" of the Church but princes of the Holy Roman Empire, ruling according to the high-handed spirit of those days, not according to the spirit of the new age of the Gospel.

Witness to Fidelity

Never before in the history of mankind have we witnessed such dynamic and rapid changes as characterize most societies today throughout the world. The Church of the Word Incarnate is involved in this history and as a consequence it cannot be spared the pains relating to the birth of a new age. Because this epoch is fraught with many risks, we cannot be foolish and run all kinds of unnecessary risks; on the other hand, unless we face justifiable risks, we will be building the Church outside the secular city, a Church out of touch with present needs. We will be condemning it to a graveyard unless we accept the risks of revitalization in this post-conciliar period.

Not in spite of the need for change and renewal but rather because of this need, we must witness to fidelity. Throughout the ages and until the second coming of Our Lord, Christian life will have to bear the marks of the Covenant, and this Covenant between God and the Church rests on God's compassionate and long-lasting fidelity. Christ, the faithful One, expects all Christians but especially the religious of our time of renewal to be outstanding witnesses to the New Covenant in unfailing fidelity and continuity of life. Understood properly, continuity of life has nothing to do with continued lifeless formalism. Let me explain by a few examples how these two concepts can be confused.

Mary Ward and Charles Borromeo

One Sunday in 1947 I happened to be in a parish where a Mother Provincial was visiting two of her sisters. While discussing the difficulty of recruiting lay sisters, Mother Provincial expressed the opinion that young girls were no longer very humble; no one was showing any interest in becoming a lay sister. I ventured to suggest that possibly humility was lacking elsewhere; had not Pope Pius XII urged the abolishment of different classes between religious in the same community? Mother Provincial replied that she was cognizant of the pope's desire, "but our General Chapter decided to remain faithful to our foundress."

The irony of the situation was that their foundress, Mary Ward, was one of the bravest, most courageous women of the whole sixteenth century. She founded her congregation of English ladies in an age of persecution. She was a child of her time. She belonged to the high nobility and graciously allowed one of her handmaids to enter the same congregation with her. It was a mark of great humility in those days to consent to have only one of her dozen attendants. Other ladies belonging to the high nobility who had remained faithful to the Catholic Church were also allowed to take one servant with them. Although there were two classes in the community, these handmaidens considered it a great privilege to share religious life with their ladies even though they belonged to a lower social class. They were not educated women but humble attendants. However, in the twentieth century, when daughters of farmers and middle-class employers and businessmen decided "to remain faithful to the foundress," the action was contrary to the spirit of Mary Ward. Her modern successors had succumbed to the temptation of "guarding the sepulcher" instead of looking to the risen Lord.

Once I had pointed out the historical background of Mary Ward's congregation, I asked Mother Provincial: "Did you have a dozen maids before you entered the congregation?" She admitted that she had none; she was of humble origin. I pursued the point: "If your Mothers did not have maids before entering, there is no need to maintain two classes of sisters." By then the good Mother Provincial was so incensed and angry she reproved me saying: "But, Father, tell me. How could I communicate with such an unlearned sister if I had to be seated at table with her all my life?" At this point the donkey of Balaam interrupted saying, "Mother Provincial, I think you could talk to her about the humility and love of Christ, and perhaps the humble sister might outrun the learned one."

Two or three weeks later when I was to address the clergy in a convent of the same order, the sisters pointed me out as the young man who had said all those things to Mother Provincial. Word had spread through the provinces and at the next General Chapter all class distinctions were abolished; they decided for one equal family. There was a little confusion and turmoil at first, much talk against the innovation, but in the end, when the issue was resolved, all realized that not one drop of blood had been shed.

A similar example concerns St. Charles Borromeo, the cardinal nephew who disregarded the established rule of the Curia and decided to dismiss about fifty of his seventy servants. All the cardinals of the Curia went on strike because the cardinal nephew dared to humble himself to the point of living with only ten or twelve servants; this was contrary to the dignity of a Prince of the Church. At that time, no one could foresee that at a later date the same Charles Borromeo, as Archbishop of Milan, would have no servant at all and would carry his bed on his own shoulders to the poorest man of his diocese. Yet it was a great step in the right direction when Charles Borromeo decided that ten servants sufficed for the household of the cardinal nephew. We must note that these changes took place gradually in the Church; even in the lives of saints there was a gradual growth.

Now that we have seen how a negative view can be transformed into a positive one with the help of God's grace, let us see what the true meaning of fidelity is.

God's Fidelity to Abraham

God's fidelity, the prototype of all loyalty, manifested itself in his unwavering patience with his people beginning with Abraham, the father of promises. Abraham was a man of faith, and God did not forsake him in spite of the fact that he had two wives and proved to be quite harsh toward one of them. You may recall that after a quarrel between the wives, Abraham sent Agar and her son Ismael away into the desert.

It was over a long period of time that God, through the mouths
of his prophets, clearly pointed out the evil of divorce. Step by
step he led his people to a fuller realization of the injustice of
dismissing one's wife chosen in early youth. The prophet Malachy
said that even the altar of God weeps when a man dismisses the
wife of his youth. Yet it took hundreds and hundreds of years
for the Chosen People to look at divorce from the socio-moral
point of view. In a similar way, as the result of a long series of
events, God purified his Chosen People's ideas about other matters.

God's Fidelity to the Primitive Church

God always was and still is patient and long-suffering. Christ's
fidelity to his Church is not that of the legalists: "Now you know
everything that is prescribed; do not change anything." At the
Last Supper when Christ addressed his disciples, he said: "There
is still much that I have to say to you but you cannot yet bear it.
When the Holy Spirit comes, he will teach you everything and
will call to mind all that I have told you" (Jn 14:26).

Only step by step did the Lord lead the primitive Church to
understand that his message was intended not only for the Jews,
not only for Galilee, but was to be proclaimed to the very ends
of the earth. It was difficult for Paul to realize that he would
have to be a Jew for the Jews, a Greek for the Greeks, and everything for everyone. This is the fidelity of the living God; it is the
presence of the living Word. God speaks to the people in their
present situation and constantly leads the Church on to repentance and to growth. The Second Vatican Council explicitly says
that the Church is always called to renewal and a constant effort
to improve herself.

In a way, the Church can be said to be the victim of her self-
righteous members. Vocation directors do poorly if they set up
the rich young man as the patron for religious vocations. The rich
young man responded to the Lord's invitation with "All this I
have done since my youth." People who make such claims feel

that they have nothing to change. They will leave the Lord as did the rich young man who refused to follow Christ because he failed to grasp the meaning of "If you wish to be perfect." The better translation is: "If you wish to go the full way" (Mt 19:21). He did not wish to go the full way because he had become complacent, convinced as he was of his own righteousness. God's fidelity does not allow this; it urges us to continuous growth and to growth in depth if we are to witness to a living God.

We have made our commitment to the living God, not to Latin. A bishop said of one of the arch-conservative men of the Curia: "He believes in Latin and probably also in God." The crux of the issue is belief in a living God who does not need to be protected by a dead language and dead formulas. It is an expression of unbelief to say that unity in the Church can be guaranteed only if all priests speak the same language at the altar. Was the gift of tongues at the first Pentecost "divisive" for the new Church? Unity of the Church cannot be dependent on and cannot be served by lack of communication with the People of God. All of us should deplore the fact that in the past, we proclaimed the Gospel to the workingman and the humble housewife in Latin. If I mention Latin here it is because it still stands as a symbol for so many dead issues requiring enforced conformity.

We remain faithful to the Church of the Word Incarnate if we follow the example of the primitive Church when in trouble and subject to tension. She grew out of the Hebrew language, Aramaic, and all the customs and rules of the Jewish people; she grew out into the world surrounding the Mediterranean Sea. Today, the Church is still growing and eventually will be ready for a journey to the stars. What kind of growing pains may await us when we have to adjust to people possibly inhabiting one of the other planets, who may be of another species, yet having the same heavenly Father? What adjustments and what changes will be called for? God alone knows. Why should we be afraid of growing pains in the Church when they are a sign of life and therefore basically good?

Fidelity in Creation

Fidelity implies the Creator's continuing interest and presence in the world which he brought into existence billions of years ago. Creation constantly depends on God who directs the course of history; it proclaims the dynamic presence of the Creator in history.

St. Thomas Aquinas expressed this idea in his writings, although he did so with great caution because he was under the constant surveillance of the authorities in Paris. His books were placed on the *Index of Forbidden Books* by the bishop of that see. There was particular grumbling over his idea that creation was not something that had just happened at a certain time but instead was something which continues to happen. It could be that the world did not begin in time but has its beginning totally with God, remaining always totally dependent on God. St. Thomas' book had the wonderful title: *De Aeternitate Mundi: Contra Murmurantes* (On the Eternity of the World: Written Against Grumblers). For the complaining People of God creation had happened five or six thousand years earlier; for them, the fact that God had made everything was well established. The forceful book of St. Thomas opposed this static conception of creation; he explained creation as more than a one-time happening. God did not take his leave from the world once created but was constantly present in it.

We fail to honor God the Creator if we consider the world as changeless and immobile. We honor God if we adore him in his work in history. In praying the divine office, we notice that in the psalms for Lauds God's praise ascends from his creation while the psalms of Vespers exalt him for his marvelous work in history.

God the Redeemer assists the world by taking upon himself its burdens with a view to changing it for the better. Christ continues to proclaim: be renewed in spirit and believe in the Gospel. If we are faithful to the Gospel message, the privilege of our vocation will keep us from being self-righteous or immobile. In

1959 when we began our work in the preparatory commission, Pope John exhorted theologians—and he had very good reasons for doing so—"Please, never forget that the Church is not a museum of musty antiques." Some of the sisters' ostentatious garb would undoubtedly be categorized as a museum piece. Blessed be God if it is only the garb!

One of my dear old confrères destined to become a professor of Holy Scripture was sent to the Biblical Institute in Jerusalem. At that time the Moslems would not tolerate a man without a beard. Consequently, all who went to the Holy Land had to grow beards. On his return, in an audience with Pius X, the pope laughingly said: "Please show your beard to your friends at home." Although the Redemptorist Rule does not permit beards, Father Schaumberger was still showing us his beard at the age of seventy-two. In reality, his beard had become a matter of past history.

Preserving the Image

While traveling recently in the company of an aging religious priest, I noticed that the good old man had tears in his eyes when he spoke about the constant changes being introduced at his college. One of the most unheard-of things was that the college president had not forbidden the students to wear long hair; he even allowed a beard! It reminded me of another incident. When I was in Russia I met an old Russian priest and inquired how things had been for him over the past years. He replied: "Everything is fine with me; I am very privileged, I have been imprisoned and released only four times. However, I did suffer in prison: once I was obliged to eat meat on Friday, and they cut my long hair." Evidently he considered the cutting of his hair a horrible experience. It can readily be seen that whereas one man lamented his short hair, the other protested the long hair of the students. When I tried to explain to the first old priest that perhaps Our Lord wore his hair long—it was the custom of his time— he vehemently objected: "No, Father, no! It is a question of the

image of our college! We want to preserve that image." Poor old
man! Is this a great question for the spouse of Christ at a time
when the Church is entering a new era, to preserve a certain
kind of public image of one's college? Short hair or long hair,
well-shaven or bearded, why should these things bother us?

When replying to some nuns' excited letters about the scandalous things going on with regard to experimentation with garb,
such as allowing the hair to show, I always quote a verse from
Matthew (6:25): "Why be worried about clothes?" The Lord
tells us in the Sermon on the Mount not to worry about clothing.
Have we nothing greater to talk about? There should not be great
anxiety about this, but it would be another matter if we were
thinking about introducing vanity as a symbol of Christian living;
that would be wrong. Yet there could be as much vanity in hiding one's hair as in exposing it.

Fidelity, Not Minutiae

Fidelity to the Creator, to the Redeemer, requires that we focus
our attention on the great problems of our times and not become
scrupulously observant of trivia. Are we alert and concerned
about how best to proclaim the message of the living God to the
men of our times? Are we preoccupied about counteracting the
"God is dead" trend in modern theology?

I am aware that there are many fine monsignors; yet some of
these take pleasure in their titles of "The right and very reverend
my-Lord" (Mon-signor means "My Lord"). This concern for titles
and for privileges and position is an escape into minutiae. If
we believe in the living God, in the living Christ who died for
us, our great concern must be for humble service in simplicity.
How, then, can we continue to have this concern for trivialities?
How can we fill our hearts and be content with the thought that
change is to take place only in small, irrelevant areas? Our concerns must be far greater. "Our God is a burning fire" (Heb
12:29). We must yearn for the salvation of mankind. Salvation

is brought as the message of God who is a faithful and a living God, whose love is everpresent in all ages.

Virtues for Times of Change and Renewal

The time for growth, adaptation, renewal, and reform in which we find ourselves calls for essential Christian virtues on the part of all of us: priests, theologians, good brothers and sisters, as we experience the "growing pains" of the period. Attention will be given to the most important among them, notably: readiness to change, continuity, spirit of prayer, patience, willingness to engage in dialogue, and charity.

1) *Readiness to Change.* The first virtue, readiness to change, relates to growth in humility. One of the conservative cardinals, who had been invited to engage in dialogue instead of persistently opposing the Council's efforts, reacted by saying: "Dialogue? Father, I tell you in all honesty: do not think that I ever intend to change anything that I am and that, in full allegiance to the will of God, I have to be." The Johannine concept of "world" is very well reflected in the negative attitude of this closed mind; it constitutes a refusal of Christ. People operating within this "closed system" of thought thank God for having no need to change. On the death of Pope John, this same cardinal brashly asserted that fifty years would not suffice to make good all the mistakes of this pope. When the Council ended, he felt that even a century would prove to be inadequate for undoing or counteracting the blunders of the Council. When questioned whether he did not owe any obedience to the Church, his response was that the Council did not oblige at all since it issued no definite dogmatic statements. May the progressive element in the Church not be seduced by resentment over extremism such as that manifested by these "rightists."

Should we follow this line of reasoning what child would be obliged to obey his parents? No mother makes infallible statements and yet there are very good reasons to support the child's

obedience to his parents. If the Church speaks infallibly it has
a divine guarantee. Yet the Church does not always speak infallibly. Nevertheless, there is greater assurance in the action of
the Holy Spirit guiding 2500 bishops than in one person's inspiration.

Therefore, in our readiness to change, let us beware of our
own "infallibility." None of us is infallible save the pope on a
few solemn occasions when acting according to the special charism and assistance of the Holy Spirit. In our readiness for
change, let us make allowance for each other's mistakes, being
ever willing and ready to correct them—not the mistakes of
Pope John, but our own.

Our readiness to change must not represent an eager desire for
innovation, but rather a keen vigilance and open-mindedness for
the real needs of our times, alertness as to how to proclaim the
message and how better to become a witness for the living God.
Our flexibility and sensitivity will attune us to the signs of the
time and lead us to study the needs of the moment with a warm
heart, without however disregarding sociological or psychological requirements. Contemporary problems, such as the difficulties faced by youth, are best approached with the tools of sociology, psychology, and anthropology; the social sciences shed light
on problems that elude the average layman. Vigilant virgins
should portray the image of the Church in their alertness for the
coming of the Lord even now, not merely at the end of time.
Once more there is a real danger of escapism into apocalyptic
expectations.

In this regard I recall two of my confrères who engaged in a
very spirited argument one evening at recreation; one of them
is already in heaven, I am sure, because he was a pious man although he was a burden to many people, and the other is a very
likable old man. The issue revolved about whether either of them
had any definite information from nuns' visions of things to come.
The one stated that the Lord's Parousia or Second Coming would
occur on Easter 2000, while the other violently insisted that the

Lord's Second Coming would stop the Council business before it ended. Such speculations are far from vigilance.

The Lord prepares us for his Second Coming. It is important to use the present opportunities to the utmost so that we will be found standing at the right place when the Lord comes. This present hour is given as a preparation for that final hour. The wise virgin does not sleep but is always alert and eager to serve the Lord in the best possible manner, thereby preparing for his final coming at the hour of death and his final manifestation to all the world at the end of time.

2) *Continuity.* The warp and woof of change must reveal threads of continuity, a continuity of life. One of the objectives of the Council was to distinguish carefully between what is of divine revelation, what is abiding, and what is evolving or changing, namely, human tradition. In no way do I intend to play down human traditions. However, to be of value, human traditions should link the present with the past in a continuity of life—a life that is developing, seeking nearness both to Divine Life and to life in the world today, a life full of responsibility toward future generations.

We must not throw away the baby with the bath water. I am aware that many great problems are agitating theology today; sometimes I find myself wondering what part of the problem is child and what is bath water? In such cases I keep both together until a common effort enables us to distinguish one from the other. As a rule of thumb I suggest: think first and then act; too many people find the reverse order more expedient.

3) *Spirit of Prayer.* In this age of change, a better and stronger prayer life is a necessity. Our prototype for fidelity and continuity should be Mary, our Mother. Luke's praise of her as the one who "treasured all things in her heart, pondering over them" indicates that her prayerful attitude must become ours in this critical period of change; we must make and take time for meditation. Religious who claim that it is no longer meaningful

to spend time in prayer, who believe only in *action,* will not bear
witness to the action of God, to the presence of Christ.

Since we are involved in such great undertakings we need
prayer even more than formerly, but not more prayers. I strongly
favor a reduction in the tremendous number of vocal prayers. It
would be far better for many sisters to spend their "rosary time"
in meditation on one mystery, treasuring it up in their hearts,
pondering over it, speaking to and with the Lord, or approach-
ing him with Mary, the Mother of God.

In 1949 I participated in a rosary devotion presided over by an
auxiliary bishop who has since been made a cardinal. The whole
rosary was "run off" in less than eight minutes. While the leader
had barely started with "Ave Maria," the first voices from the
congregation chimed in with "Sancta Maria." Although they may
have counted their Ave Maria's well in order to gain all the indulgences, I doubt that God's arithmetic corresponded to theirs.
Never trust in numbers!

Human beings need time for recollection in order to ponder
over God's work, to treasure up his gifts in their hearts. More
than ever before we have to aim at a depth experience in our
prayer life; it requires prayerful reading and meditative praying
before the tabernacle in order to permit Christ's gaze to penetrate
our innermost being and his grace to shine upon us. We should
not cut down on time devoted to prayer, but rather the quantity
or the number of prayers. We could improve our prayer formulas
with a greater emphasis on community singing. The future
Church, even in our own lifetime, will undoubtedly be a singing
Church. More importance can also be attached to spontaneous
prayer even in community experiences where we profess together
our faith and enrich our encounters with prayerful meditation.

4) *Patience.* Patience is recommended for everyone but especially for religious who are called to be exemplars of this virtue.
Christian patience should not be misconceived as a lack of initiative or action. It consists in the collected energies of a deep love
—a love channeling all its vitality toward the achievement of a

goal and thus permitting no dissipation in daydreaming, futile worries, anger, or bitter criticism. All the energies of love are gathered together, forestalling any dissipation, so that fully collected and perfectly directed toward a goal, they enable one to witness more effectively for Christ.

In a masterful way St. Paul uses picturesque language to convey his message: "Let yourselves not be conquered by evil, but use good to defeat evil. If your enemy is hungry, feed him. . . . By doing this, you will heap live coals on his head" (Rom 12:20). At first reading, the full significance of these words may be missed. Even Max Scheler, the great philosopher, exclaimed: "There we still see the old Jewish temper and attitude ready to burn the hair of the adversary." St. Paul's reference is to the ancient housewife who carefully gathered the fiery coals remaining after cooking her meals; she kept them well covered in order to insure her hearth fire for the next meal. In this sense, St. Paul uses the housewife's solicitude over the live coals that kept the fireplace ablaze to intimate that, like her, we should use every occasion and all our energy and vitality to warm up the heart of our enemy or adversary.

Similarly we may paraphrase St. Paul's exhortation with reference to the superior who may be a little "old-fashioned" or conservative. If you forever give him the cold shoulder, how can you expect him to reciprocate warmth? If, on the contrary, you collect all your energies to give him your confidence, using every possible occasion for patience and the expression of sincere love and concern for the sake of genuine renewal in Christian living, you may be certain that your fraternal charity will sooner or later bear fruit.

The same patience should characterize all your dealings, whether with superiors or fellow religious. As far as my experience with superiors is concerned, they have proved to be my best friends. Should I waste my energies in anger against others who are overly concerned about every word I utter or write? Why should I? In my best moods I believe that they are exerting themselves for the love of God and therefore I say: God bless them for this! It may be that they help me without knowing it.

Patience is the price we must pay for discipleship and unity. If on the highway we cannot move at the greatest permissible speed, such as 65 or 70 miles per hour, due to the fact that all the other cars are moving only at 20 miles an hour, we must adjust our own speed. There will be moments when the highway will be clear. Trying to speed through at 95 miles an hour on an overcrowded highway would be disastrous. Recently when speaking to a whole community I happened to say: "It is better that you move in unison at 15 or even 10 miles an hour and remain on the move in the right direction than to move at higher speeds in different directions. It is better for you to move smoothly together with regard to external changes. As regards love and kindness, no speed can be too high."

Immediately following my talk a group of young sisters approached me saying: "Father, please do not speak to our older sisters this way. Tell them to move, *move!*" I found it necessary to explain the point once more: "I want to see things on the move but I do not want to see you all crushed." I told them about a warning on one of the superhighways that reads: "Go slow. Death is permanent." If we fail to move at all, this will lead to a permanent state of death; however, let us move only after reflecting. We must move in the right direction and move together. We are all agreed on the principle that the Church should not be trailing behind society at large. Since we are to be outstanding witnesses for the living God, the God of history, the God of the living and not of the dead, it is not fitting that we be the "last stragglers" on life's journey.

5) *Dialogue.* There is great need for a structural dialogue in religious communities. A genuine exchange of ideas and opinions becomes possible only when members of the community steer clear of factions or cliques. A clever French Jesuit, speaking to a group of bishops and theologians before the Council, was asked what he would especially recommend in view of the forthcoming

Council. His advice was: "Never form an alliance; always keep yourselves open to all groups. In case of differences of opinion among groups, you will find that one group may be right in one respect and another group on some other point." Resist alliances and factions; instead, keep the doors open by communicating with all. Keep your minds open and do not retreat into little cliques that try to maneuver things. We do better by keeping our ears and hearts open, trying to understand, listening patiently and responding in mutual respect while offering reasons and arguments. The art of listening is indeed the first condition for a fruitful dialogue; then comes the even greater art of addressing the other in a language clear to him or to her.

Genuine dialogue is effectively initiated when common interests, ideals, and goals are brought to the foreground; these are elements that unite us. We should never lose sight of this common ground in the process of clearing away differences. Dialogue will be fruitful so long as no one poses as omniscient and in full possession of the truth; we can always learn from each other. That is why true Christian dialogue cannot insist on the "unconditional surrender" of the other party.

6) *Greater Charity.* Some people hold the mistaken belief that charity may be violated for the sake of reforms, but the truth is that reforms must be rooted in charity. Karl Marx thought that through a growing class hatred, through mounting tensions, we would come closer to the final paradise of brotherhood. We are Marxists in thought and deeds if we fight one another in order to achieve Christian renewal; in fact, we are worse than Marxists or Communists if we act against our great rule of love. Renewal cannot be accomplished apart from charity because renewal means greater love and better structures to promote this greater love. Consequently, it behooves us to use the appropriate means to achieve truly Christian renewal, namely, kindness and charity.

In our times marked by growth and tension, there must be readiness to compromise. The greatest mistake in American history was perhaps the demand for the "unconditional surrender" of Japan. The dilemma was whether to kill 152,000 by one atomic bomb or expose American soldiers to the dangers of further combat. The army itself questioned the wisdom and justice of an unconditional surrender instead of a compromise; Christian charity would have suggested the latter course.

Therefore, one should never impose "unconditional surrender" on the other side, e.g., the old on the young; they simply will not accept the terms. You will be throwing atomic bombs of dissension if you demand this unconditional surrender. Neither should the young religious impose a similar unconditional surrender on his seniors. Allow room for both groups to develop their ideas and let the older members become the leaders in the renewal. An old veteran of conservatism told me some months ago: "Now the time has come for me to apply the brakes."

"Your Excellency is well known for having used the brakes all your life," I replied. "You would serve the Church better now if you became a locomotive."

The senior religious should really have an understanding for the younger members. The future of the congregations belongs to the young. If you impose old ways of thinking and feeling on the young, you do great harm to the Lord and to the state of the Church. The young religious must also show understanding and leave enough room for the older religious to live and pray in their own way. These older religious should not be blamed for their devotions as long as they do not impose them on others. We should always be ready for a workable compromise, one with a promise of future development, and not a compromise that locks doors forever, rolling a big stone before the tomb. Christian prudence and fortitude forbid compromises that close the door to future improvement.

We may have to renounce or postpone the implementation of legitimate plans if by imposing them now we would cause a break in unity or charity, or would block future developments. I know that some great people do not like the connotation of the word "compromise." Yet old and young, conservative, liberal, progressive, or regressive would do well to ponder the inadvisability of unconditional surrender. Never should it form a part of Christian politics, which requires mutual respectful listening and at times yielding on minor matters.

The First Council in the Church at the time of the apostles led to a workable compromise. James finally conceded that those from non-Jewish lineage need not, after all, submit to circumcision and to the law of Moses. The terms of the compromise included the Jewish custom of kosher for all Christians of that time: "to abstain from anything that has been strangled and from blood" (Acts 15:20). Paul later gave a very broad-minded explanation of the other condition for which James held out: "to abstain from things polluted by contact with idols" (Cf I Cor 10:27-29). What James finally asked for included some minor unnecessary restrictions, yet Paul, Matthew, and Peter, the progressive ones, accepted such a compromise. They even complimented James that the imposition was not greater. It was a compromise that placated both parties and in the course of time unnecessary restrictions were dropped.

The prevailing attitude toward conservatives at the Second Vatican Council was not one of unconditional surrender; men promoting the renewal did not strive for that. Very little sophistication in psychology is needed to understand that the other party needs some satisfaction if a good working relationship is to be maintained. Pope Paul is serving unity and progress when he constantly asks for patience on the part of progressives, openness and acceleration on the part of the conservatives. Would not this service be more effective and beneficial if some old ultraconservatives would dedicate the remaining years of their life to prayer instead of blocking renewal and clinging to office or a career?

Christian Maturity

Christian maturity implies a well-formed conscience, a keen sense of discernment between true values and the sham, between abiding truths and the transient. How can we expect today's youth to accept the whole heritage from past centuries, the decisions of past General Chapters, if the latter are in opposition to the real needs of today? Granted they had a meaning in past German, Irish, French, or Italian days. Young people will lose faith even in eternal truth and will turn away if we expect them to enter "faithfully" our musty museums and live in the midst of antiques. In the Constitution on the Church in the Modern World, the Second Vatican Council indicates that we are to redeem the times by making use of present opportunities (GS, 52). This, however, can be accomplished only if we discriminate between immutable principles and evanescent values, between eternal truths and mutable forms of expression, patterns, and customs. Our present age requires Christian maturity based on depth of insight. In a static age or in a closed, self-contained society, it seemed sufficient to establish a pattern for conformity to rules. Today's dynamic and pluralistic society demands a knowledge of principles and an appreciation of values. It requires of religious a deeper knowledge of Our Lord and of his intentions. Christ manifested his expectations of maturity in his disciples when, at the Last Supper, he said: "I call you servants no longer, for the servant does not know the intentions of his master. I call you dear friends, since I have disclosed to you everything which I have heard from my Father" (Jn 15:15).

It is a blessing that most American major superiors have understood the importance of the study of theology for sisters and brothers. It is time for each congregation to prepare some of its members as well-trained, well-informed theologians who can transmit the best of theological thought, particularly in the areas of prayer and the apostolate. What is needed more than anything else is the study of theology in the spirit of prayer.

During the past ten years the American sisterhoods have taken gigantic steps to improve the professional training of their members. Similar and even greater effort should be exerted to give all the sisters a better spiritual, theological, and psychological formation. More scientific knowledge is needed; we can no longer be content with mediocrity. We are moving away from an age characterized by a closely controlled society and away from the cloister with its two thousand pounds of iron grilles behind which the best daughters of the Church were kept under tight security and control. These restrictions can be understood only in terms of the mentality of a past age. The present age calls for responsible persons to live a religious life in depth. As mature persons they should be able to give reasons for their actions. They should have a deeper understanding of both moral and religious values. Most of all, religious must be persons who act rightly not because they are under control, but because of their fidelity to principles and to their own conscience.

A timely example of excessive control is the censorship of mail, although in most of the congregations this question has been resolved. A few years ago I scandalized some of the provincial and general superiors in Europe when I appealed for abrogation of the censorship of letters. I begged them not to control the dialogue between a daughter and her parents. Today we realize that such control violated the right to privacy of communication between parents and the son or daughter. Such regulations are sins against gentleness and good manners. Why should the superior have to know what a father tells his daughter! These controls befitted an age when only the superior could read and write, and consequently, charity demanded that he or she help with the drafting of letters and perhaps even the reading of letters. For American nuns, free to write to anyone before they entered the congregation, even to their boyfriends, the censorship of mail, particularly to a brother, has been an unnatural and unnecessary control.

It appears that some sisters are still controlled for telephone

calls. It is a time-consuming procedure to go first to the superior
to inform her of who is calling whom, and then to notify the
sister of the call. Besides the considerable waste of time involved,
the caller is left with the impression that spies are at work in the
convent. These are unnecessary controls. However, the removal
of excessive controls is not sufficient; the religious should learn
early to use letters and all forms of communication in the spirit
of the apostolate. Letters may become witnesses to charity, especially if we respond kindly to a spiteful letter.

Christian maturity is inconceivable without a strong sense of
humor, especially in a time of change and upheaval. Christian
humor is the flower and fruit of humility, wisdom, and fortitude.
It helps one distinguish between comedy and tragedy. A good
joke, a hearty laugh can resolve problematic situations better than
long inquisitions or discussions. Humor holds our self-importance
in check and thus deters us from taking ourselves too seriously.
The gift of humor sensitizes one to the incongruities of certain
situations; it enables the Christian to laugh at everything except
sin. Errors committed inadvertently can be corrected with a
smile.

FIVE | PROGRESS IN MATURITY

Conscience is the most secret core and sanctuary of man. There he is alone with God, whose voice echoes in his depths. In a wonderful manner conscience reveals that law which is fulfilled by love of God and neighbor. (GS, 16)

In the light of the Pastoral Constitution on the Church in the Modern World, every Christian is duty-bound to study the characteristic features of the present historical period. The rapid pace of technological advances accounts for the blurred vision of so many as to what constitutes real progress; the value of the human person has been relegated to the background. Unless scientific development and cultural innovations are counterbalanced by progress in personality integration, our civilization is en route to chaos. Religious men and women need to be alerted to the problem because of their apostolate.

The better professional training of religious is indeed a heartening phenomenon, but for religious to counteract an unintegrated understanding of progress, they must receive a deep spiritual formation, i.e., one firmly grounded on the Bible and directed to the "treasuring up" of the Word of God. If a formation program is to result in the development of an integrated person, a mature religious personality, it must blend the professional and spiritual training of the candidate into a meaningful whole. This holistic approach focuses on the life of Christ, his life in us, our life in him, the great reality of his love in us and of our dwelling in his love. Primacy must be given to prayer, to the love of God and of neighbor.

The propensity toward superficiality is a feature of our times; one need only consider the amount of time wasted in viewing useless television programs and cheap movies. If there is to be sound training in the proper use of time, serious attention must be given to values and motives while young religious are in the novitiates and the juniorate. They need formation of conscience in depth so that in all things they ask: "How can I please the Lord? How can I, here and now, render unto the Lord all that he has given me?" Such formation is absolutely necessary for religious if they are to offset the increasing pressures toward collectivism and conformity.

Conscience Formation

Of paramount importance for all Christians today is the achievement of a *synthesis* in their whole outlook on life which will result in their relating all things to the living God and the great vocation of fraternal love. This synthesis can only be achieved through a deeply formed conscience. If commands are issued continually from the right, from the left—commands from a thousand sources—no allowance is being made for the development of a sense of values. More value may be attached to fish on a Lenten Friday than to charity, to the smallest point of the holy Rule (a seventeenth-century antique destined for the museum) than to sisterly love. By mere external conformity, some religious fail to witness to what is most urgent among Christians today, namely, the right kind of freedom, the freedom of the sons and daughters of God. Religious must learn to use their freedom intelligently, to give an enlightened obedience; they must live by a well-established hierarchy of values. Values are the language of love, reflecting the splendor of God in the personal confrontation, the loving encounter of God and man. There must be vision and synthesis in their religious formation for them to live with the true freedom referred to in the Constitution on the Church, the "freedom strengthened by obedience" (LG, 43). Obedience calls for an intelligent response, one that always sees the true values involved.

Religious men and women have the beautiful mission of giving testimony to the universal call to holiness for all Christians. This mission constitutes for them a sacred obligation to form their own consciences into that of outstanding Christians so that all may learn, by their example, the authentic character of a vigilant Christian conscience. Consequently, religious men and women must live their lives in a way even more thoroughly in accord with the dictates of conscience than is expected of the ordinary Christian; otherwise, they will fall short of "being the salt of the earth." It would be catastrophic, indeed, if in convents and monasteries only superiors were to live conscientious lives while subjects, like automatons, would simply follow printed rules, regulations, and the precepts of superiors.

Some time ago I gave a conference to a group of brothers, very fine and intelligent religious men. At the end of my presentation an elderly brother remarked: "We have always been told, 'A perfect brother is the one who keeps the Rule on every point.' From what you have said, this would be incorrect, would it not?" Such a concept of religious life is certainly erroneous for it reduces the whole of perfection to a life of "observing the Rule." Where is there any room for conscience? The Rule becomes a substitute for conscience; the whole wealth of "Thy Kingdom Come" is confined to a book. If seen in proper perspective, however, the conscience of a religious ought to be most vigilant, delicate, and tender. The "experience of conscience" must be deep-rooted, strong, and able to endure strain; otherwise, a full Christian life cannot grow and fructify in this time of stress and tensions. The *leitmotiv* of religious should be to live their lives according to the richness, the wealth of a conscience formed in such a way that it can serve as a model for a truly Christian life.

What Is Conscience?

Conscience is the totality of man where one's deepest being cries out toward oneness—oneness between the good or ideal one recognizes and the level of behavior one strives for. It is a oneness of the powers of the person, a being-one with the world of the good, the true, and the beautiful. The more one grows toward wholeness and oneness, the more one matures, and the more deeply aware one becomes that all the impulses of his nature are summoning him to the good. Conscience attracts mind, heart, and will to the world of values and finally opens the person to the One who is alone good; the intellect can be open only because the heart is open, because one is a loving person. In true conscience, one is obedient ultimately to one's own knowledge of the good and tries earnestly to understand the good in order to fulfill it. A man who does not obey his conscience feels that his innermost oneness is endangered. He suffers from a wound caused by the opposition between intellect and will.

Worse than a mistaken judgment of conscience in an individual case is the loss of vigilance which deprives man even of the awareness of the need for unity. The non-vigilant person thinks and speaks about the good and the true without feeling a thrust to follow through on his thoughts and words. This is perhaps the worst form of loss of conscience: a schizophrenia, a disintegration of the personality or splitting of man's intellect and affective life to the point where a knowing being no longer can exhibit the appropriate emotional reaction, where his actions are prompted by outside forces. The intimate appeal to wholeness is what makes conscience the summons to honesty; it calls upon us to serve untiringly for the truth and for the good.

The analysis of conscience is often based on such a negative experience as remorse of conscience, though its essence is a positive appeal to wholeness in goodness and truth. When man does wrong, when he has failed to cooperate with the inspiration to do good, he experiences compunction, provided that he still has a conscience. The dynamism and value of his pain of soul depends upon the degree of conscience. After wrongdoing, a cry pierces the human heart, thereby revealing exactly the worth of one's personality, one's nearness to wholeness. One feels this acute pain which leads to contrition, i.e., the state in which the will of man unites itself anew in a humble way with the value which he had recognized but shamefully violated.

It would be misleading to see the essence of conscience merely from the viewpoint of sorrow for wrongdoing. Conscience is active also where man does good and does it gladly, where he follows the promptings of grace without long hesitation, where with joy and gratitude he dedicates himself to the good. Moreover, conscience is an ability to listen and to hear; it shows its strength in setting the whole person afire with a passionate urge toward good. Where there is conscience, there is fire; its glow and heat depend upon its quality. When the inspiration to good enkindles the person to a holy enthusiasm, then conscience is alive.

Conscience includes allegiance. The wholeness of conscience is a reality only if man gives this total allegiance to a living God and to brotherhood. Man can truly be himself by total openness to God and neighbor; he comes to fullness by a response of love, by giving his own self to God in a deep response. Conscience, then, finds its expression in faith as a responsive reality.

Conscience and Faith

The greatest development in history was the coming of the Son of God. His life epitomizes the history of conscience in his attitude as the Son of God and brother of man. He does not wish to have slaves or blind followers; he wants loving disciples and faithful witnesses. The Father discloses everything to his Son (Jn 15:15); the Father does not reserve his knowledge and wisdom to himself. Indeed, he alone is good, he alone knows everything, but he has also communicated with us in his visible image, in Christ and his life and in the message which Christ explained to us. He has answered our *why;* he has shown the values. He leads us through the joyous news of his love, showing us the characteristics of true love, helping us to distinguish unselfish, heavenly love from an egotistic, self-centered variety.

The Christian conscience confronts the living God, the God who continues to operate in the world and, above all, in the Church and in our own heart. Therefore the Christian conscience is never totally concentrated on the abstract; it is always the living person, the loving person confronted with God, our Thou, the God who calls us. The final question remains: how can I please him? How can I understand all his words? This calls for a thorough understanding of the intentions of God, for a constant meditation on the theme: what does God mean? A Christian conscience comes under the law of faith illumined by Christ, by the teaching office of the Church, by the example of the saints, by deep insight into God's wonderful message and law.

Faith demands the fullness of conscience. In faith man accepts gratefully the self-manifestation of God and opens his deepest nature to God. Faith has the divine power to arouse and deepen our conscience, but it must be faith in prayer, a faith that adores, a faith in which we surrender ourselves to God and joyously accept his dynamic presence.

An example will help to make the point with regard to a conscience that does not manifest the full vigilance expected of a Christian. It concerns a priest belonging to a religious order, a pathological case; in many ways he was very kind but he was a sick man. He ran away with a seventeen-year-old girl, was captured and imprisoned for two years. During his incarceration, none of his fellow religious wrote him a line, nor did his confrères or superiors visit him once; "he was unworthy"! In this instance, we fail to find a conscience modeled on Christ, the good Shepherd seeking the lost sheep. Is it not a serious indictment that people of other faiths were kind to him and helped him get over the crisis? We must, in the world of today, where laymen look to us for holiness, bear witness to a personal loving encounter. We must reveal a conscience that confesses faith in the living God in great openness, watchfulness, and deep knowledge of the values that are at stake.

Only the true and moral Christian conscience with sensitivity and vigilance for values, for goodness in the other person, guarantees the authentic freedom of the Christian. We must face one reality, namely, that none of us here on earth has a fully developed conscience where everything is desirable in the sight of God, because none of us has the highest degree of freedom possible as sons and daughters of God. We have to grow through the painful process of self-denial, constant watchfulness for the needs of our fellow men, and vigilance as regards our motives.

It is not uncommon, even among many priests, brothers, and sisters, to detect "growth" in the art of rationalizing whatever they please. All religious know that commitment by religious vows is the most solemn act of religion; then we are offered to and with Christ, our life is put on the altar to be united with the heavenly liturgy of Christ. They also know that it is a horrible deed to withdraw our offering from the altar out of selfishness. Of late we hear rationalizations about a temporary vocation; one may say: "I have had enough; I have served the Lord for fifteen years and now I want to have something for myself." These religious have failed to integrate values in the personal encounter of faith. Conscience is based on love, whereas rationalization is based on the selfish defense of one's actions. Brotherhood becomes impossible for those who hide their self-seeking behind plausible alibis; the ties of brotherhood can be cemented only by genuine persons capable of fidelity to God's love and fidelity to themselves.

Law and Value

A mature conscience experiences God as Father, friend, wisdom, and only ultimately as legislator. God not only teaches principles; God manifests himself in love and he opens up the whole man— intellect, heart, and will—to seek good and truth. In which form does man take cognizance of the good? Awareness of the good can come in the form of a mere law claiming literal obedience, or it can come to man's knowledge in the form of a deeper realization of the value of the good.

There are various degrees of knowledge in relation to law. St. Paul speaks of two types of laws, similar to the antipodes. In one instance, the apostle writes that "the letter (of the law) kills" (II Cor 3:6), but in the Epistle to the Romans, when referring to the law, he intones the hymn of our Redemption. First the outcry of man, conscience-stricken: "Who shall free me from this dead body?"—a dead body, a human being without true life! Then the jubilant song: "Praise to the Lord, for the law of the Spirit of the life in Christ Jesus has delivered me from the law of sin and of death!" (Rom 8:2). The Lord gives us his word which is joy and life for the conscience of his friends. "The words which I have spoken to you are both spirit and life" (Jn 6:63). Christ's example and words can then be understood by men as a life-giving law since God himself sent the Spirit from above.

How, then, must the law be presented if it is to be functional in the formation of conscience? We can profit by listening to Christ himself as he takes leave of his beloved Twelve in the Cenacle: "You are my friends if you do the things I command you. No longer do I call you servants, because the servant does not know what his master does. But I have called you my dear friends, because all things that I have heard from my Father, I have made known to you" (Jn 15:14-16). There is no more unworthy knowledge of the law than the casuistry of the rabbi who, with a hard-boiled conscience, instructs his pupils (according to the "scrolls of Qumran"): "If a man falls into a well, you must wait until the evening of the Sabbath before bringing him help by means of a rope or ladder." Such an explanation of the law actually turns man into a being without conscience. The priest and the levite hastily passing by the wounded man who had fallen among robbers knew their rubrics perfectly well and followed scrupulously every minute detail of the law; but how could these legal sticklers find time to look after the bleeding victim by the roadside? It might have interfered with some of their strictly binding rules.

Knowledge of the law must contribute to conscience development and therefore the law must be worthwhile. Unless the value of the law is self-evident, its existence cannot be justified. St. Thomas, for example, teaches that a law that is not necessary or not very useful for the good of the community is unjust, and for that reason it cannot bind in conscience. To make an impression on conscience, the law has to manifest its worth. It is understandable that not every order of a superior or every law can at once clearly reveal its underlying motive to everyone concerned; its value, however, must be discernible in relation to the whole, and especially by the type of command given. Parents need not always give their young child a detailed explanation of the "why" of a certain request; nevertheless, the child ought to be able to say: "My parents are good; they mean well; therefore their orders are good." Superiors themselves ought to present individual orders as well as the whole body of laws and regulations in such a way as to inspire confidence and lead to the conviction that these requirements are good because the authority behind them is good.

A child goes through a period of seemingly endless questioning; the "why" is forever on his lips. It is a sad fact that many a child's conscience is stifled, even killed, by repeated scoldings. "Do as you are told; Father knows what is best." Naturally, doubts are awakened: does Father really know best? When, by such procedures, the will of the child is finally broken, when his inquiries are silenced, there follows as a logical result the typical infantile type of conscience. A normal development calls for a gradual explanation by parents of the reason for an order, revealing the motive, necessity, and value of the command and the good to be produced. Children are critical. The fundamental trust, "the order is good because Father and Mother are good," will begin to waver since parents are not good *ipso facto*. In spite of this hurdle, the child's conscience can and will be formed if,

for example, the father is humble enough after an uncalled-for outburst of anger to admit simply: "Child, this was not right. I
should not have been angry with you. God is far more patient
with me than I have been with you today." Then the child learns
that the parent is striving for goodness; he does not impose his
own will as something absolute. The parent indicates acceptance
of his human condition by his admission that he is correcting
faults and striving for greater goodness. The conscience will remain childish if one does not learn to distinguish, to discriminate
the partial goodness of those in authority from the absolute goodness of God.

The Rule and the Law

In religious orders, knowledge of the law has to be imparted and
acquired on a high level, intellectually and motivationally. The
Constitutions of an institute must yield first place to the Gospel,
which is the supreme law for all Christians. If the Rule of the
order merely regulates the mechanical aspects of exterior conduct, if no information as to the underlying motives is ever sought
or relayed, if postulants and novices no longer ask questions, one
can clearly see that the members of the order have stagnated at the
very lowest level of infantilism and that their questioning has been
suppressed. Young people are perceptive and critical; they want
to know the "why" and "wherefore" of expected behavior. Provided they ask questions politely, humbly, sincerely, the superior
or novice master should never hesitate to answer, even though
this might at times require a humble admission that certain points
of the Rule are antiquated, as for example: "This particular regulation which puzzles you dates back to the seventeenth century.
At that time, it proved necessary and useful. Today it no longer
serves its original purpose. New customs and new Rules will have
to replace it. We may and we should seek lawful ways to repeal
such a law." The written letter may reveal the gist of a law, but
we must also look to customs which help explain the spirit of a
law. Superiors must be able to distinguish between the essential

and valuable points and other non-essential aspects of religious legislation. At no time should they snuff out genuine life and progress because of a written law.

It will be helpful for us to focus our attention on the splendor of the divine law, the expression of God's freedom and fatherly love. The law may never be allowed to stand as a barrier between God and man, like a dead wall; it must always remain a living voice of God, revealing the One who is calling, the Lord. The law serves to bring man face to face with God, with his goodness, his authority, with him who is the living God of Abraham, Isaac, and Jacob, the God of Our Lord, Jesus Christ. It must lead us to see God. Hence, grave danger is involved if there is a stereo-typed, impersonal presentation of the divine law.

The Lord gave us his law not in the naked form of an obliga-tion but in an act of deepest humility, after first having washed the feet of the apostles, at the conclusion of a life of complete abnegation and the beginning of its culmination on the Cross. "And after Jesus had washed their feet and put on his garments, he said to the disciples: 'If I, the Lord and Master, have washed your feet, you also ought to wash the feet of one another. For I have given you an example, that as I have done to you, so you also should do" (Jn 13:14-16). The Twelve understood clearly Christ's new command to love one another as he had loved them. Here we have the promulgation of an all-embracing law, made known to mankind in the lustrous beauty of its divine origin. In truth this law is not a mere letter; it is a visible reality. All the evangelical counsels, all the standards laid down by the Gospel, all are tidings of joy; each conveys to man a message of the un-ending love and wisdom of God. Contemplating this overwhelm-ing truth, man cries out: "Your laws, O Lord, are my delight. Beyond all measure I love your law, O my God!" The law of the Lord is not a dead letter; its intrinsic worth is revealed by the Lord himself. He teaches us by his word and example and by the grace of the Holy Spirit how to understand his loving will.

Divine Law and Human Responsibility

The integration of personality proceeds along definite lines in the course of development. Frequently man comprehends the divine law only partially; in order to come to a better understanding of it, he must learn to humble himself and acknowledge his total ignorance in comparison to God's infinite wisdom. As man comes to an ever-deepening realization of the beauty of the divine law, to that extent will his confidence and trust in the Divine Lawgiver increase. Moral teachings are of no avail if they remain restricted to individual cases and solutions; only if they provide clearer and deeper insight into the totality and the beauty of God's loving design do they serve the Legislator's intent.

Defining limits and boundaries for these laws is preposterous; their excellence lies in their boundlessness. An elderly religious once told me about a professor who, after giving a whole year's course in ethics to a group of Catholic workers, asked his audience after the last lecture: "What did you learn in this course?" He received for answer: "We found out that until now we have done far too much; the moral code does not oblige us to do so much." The reply indicated that the professor had failed the course. He had transmitted only precisely measured and narrowly defined information. The dynamism and beauty of its wholeness and its value had been passed over. Of course I do not deny the importance of clear-cut prohibitions, but they are not the essence of a law given to friends.

Knowledge of God must first of all awaken in us the love of God; the knowledge of man and even of earthly goods, and above all the experience of genuine love, convey God's message of love to us. Therefore nothing may be excluded from the formation of conscience. Once again I emphasize the importance of the beautiful, of opening the human mind to an appreciation of its message so that it can become absorbed in meditation on a tiny violet, a beautiful rose, on the impressive countenance of a mature personality, the lovely features of a mother, the sorrowful, pain-filled eyes of a sufferer. Neglect of the beautiful in the formation of conscience may prove to be hazardous; man will consider the good mainly as a "must" and will fall into the trap of a "payroll morality": how much do I get out of it? The good then becomes synonymous with opportunities for earning merits of some kind, and joy, which should be the natural accompaniment of the good and the beautiful, vanishes simultaneously.

Openness to Values

Values are among the strongest motives of behavior; they are attractive conceptualizations of what one considers good and worthwhile. That is why all values should be made visible. There are certain religious who labor under the mistaken impression that they can better guard their virginal chastity by minimizing the value of the married state. In reality, the special worth of virginity is fully comprehended and appreciated only by those who, knowing of true bridal and conjugal love, pay to the God of their hearts the voluntary, wholehearted avowal: "Lord, you alone are worthy to receive my very best." If the values of the matrimonial state are disdainfully underrated, suspected and ridiculed, the scoffers living according to the virginal state offer to God but "lame animals, sick animals," according to the saying of the prophet Malachy (1:13).

The formation of conscience requires time: time for meditation, time for the loving contemplation of values, time for singing the praises of the Creator and Redeemer in all his works. A clearer understanding and insight into the beauties of the Psalms will teach us these necessary lessons, provided we have a good translation and an enlightened introduction. As a side issue, let it be said that praying the Psalms in Latin by religious who lack even a fundamental knowledge of the language has but one tragic result: the breaking of their conscience. All lights are extinguished; nothing is being learned from such a meaningless recitation of the words of these glorious hymns of praise and adoration.

Values are not the outcome of a single act of acquisition; they can only be acquired and internalized as part of an overall personality development. Conscience, as an unfolding of the whole man, evolves from an initial, rather shallow knowledge of values, leads gradually to an intimate understanding and awareness, and finally to a real and truly enjoyable taste for values. "Behold and taste how good the Lord is!" The same gradualism holds with reference to the appreciation of all his works. One must behold with patience, take time and taste the wisdom inherent in God's creation and in all of God's laws.

Christ instructs his apostles: "If you dwell within the revelation I have brought, you are indeed my disciples; you shall know the truth and the truth will set you free" (Jn 8:31). Personal involvement in promoting values and virtue, doing it joyfully and lovingly, fosters integration because of its worth, its intimacy with the good. One who is dedicated to love recognizes the good in a totally different way from another who is enslaved by his moods. Apply this maxim to a superior who finds himself obliged to admonish a subject on an important point of the Rule. If the warning is given with surliness and obvious anger, a sullen outburst will be the echo. If, on the contrary, the superior approaches the difficult situation in a friendly spirit, if the culprit is made to feel the understanding, compassionate heart of his monitor, at once the ominous horizon is made bright by the light of the good perceived in the valuable advice and in the adviser. This light is a reflection of the goodness of a loving God. Goodness and sympathetic guidance in love will unfailingly lead to a deepening of the appreciation of true values.

In the process of conscience formation through a correct explanation of the law, when providing intimate contacts with the good, the beautiful, and the true, we need to pay attention above all to the personalization of values. The great beauty of all created things consists in their being the language of a personal God.

Values are not abstract, dead things; they are not without a close relation to the rest of creation. "In the beginning was the Word, and the Word was with God, and the Word was God. . . . All things were made by him, and without him was made nothing that was made" (Jn 1:1-4). Man is created after the image and likeness of God so that creation can speak to him and so that he can hear God's voice in creation. In the formation of conscience, it is of far-reaching importance to relay this message so that one can hear the voice of God and recognize his call, recognize the caller as God, the wise and loving Lawgiver.

It is true: the written law can be dead, but it can also be a call, a vocation, a personal appeal. As long as life is solely concentrated on the law and the letter of the Rule, the law will never be a personal call to man, for God speaks through all things in creation. He speaks through his Divine Providence, through world affairs, through individual and universal joys and sorrows. God's voice speaks in every human heart.

The Law of Grace

Christian formation of conscience and, above all, religious formation ought to be based principally on the "law of grace." Grace means the gracious presence of God's love, the promptings of the Holy Spirit. Christ's Sermon on the Mount, the farewell prayer of the eternal High Priest at the Last Supper—these correspond to the work of his Spirit in the human heart. If St. Thomas teaches that the most original, most fundamental aspect of the New Law consists in the workings of the Holy Spirit, certainly the Christian formation of conscience ought always to strive toward viewing all exterior requirements of God's law in the light of this interior reality. Only then will conscience be a "meeting God in faith and love."

God's law becomes binding for us because he touches the human heart; he bestows his knowledge and gives the impulse to obey, to respond with love to his love. In an urgent way God reveals his law to us by his countless benefits, graces, and blessings, both spiritual and material. It seems logical and self-evident that a mature conscience will face all questions from this one perspective: "How can I best please the Lord?"

A certain abstract sophistic casuistry has attempted to prove that the whole Sermon on the Mount, particularly the verse: "Be ye then perfect as your Heavenly Father is perfect" (Mt 5:48) merely has the meaning of a counsel not a command, and that it becomes binding only for those who by a voluntary decision enter the "state of perfection." Theological tradition, however, is in agreement with St. Thomas. In his later years he kept repeating over and again that the great command of love, "Be ye then perfect as your Heavenly Father is perfect," is addressed to everybody. It is the all-important command to imitate God in his own divine way, in his own compassionate love. The Second Vatican Council speaks clearly of the universal vocation to holiness in the Constitution on the Church (LG, 5). Legal-minded man, because of his innate selfishness, carefully determines: "How far must I and how far may I go?" The law of grace provides the answer: "Everyone according to the gift of grace which he has received from the Lawgiver, Christ." The dual command to love God and neighbor cannot be interpreted and enforced like a state law. Man must be taught to pursue his goal step by step. Having received the gift and heard the call, he must know what step God wants him to take at that moment. If God favors him with great graces, confronts him with needs and appeals to his heart, he knows that God is expecting him to take a big step. Thus, ever faithfully cooperating with the Divine Will, he no longer argues with the Lord: "Am I obligated or not?"

This form of conscience development should find a prominent place in the schools, in all postulates, novitiates, and juniorates, in the whole system of religious education. Instead of staking out the outer limits of the law, we should concentrate on pleasing the Lord now, on repaying him for his bounties.

The Bridegroom's Voice

If only religious would learn to hear in everything the divine call! To attain that goal we need a special virtue, one of the great evangelical virtues: *vigilance*. Virgins are those who are alert, watchful in the service of the Master, who keep their lamps trimmed and supplied with oil; listen to the Bridegroom's call; keep a wakeful eye upon circumstances and events that relate to their service; intuitively feel the arrival of "their hour." Christ frequently speaks of "his hour" and he rejoices when "his hour" is near. Vigilance is one of the great eschatological virtues of the New Testament.

Allow me a practical application. Presuming that the Rule of your order contains quite lengthy and detailed regulations that possibly claim 90 per cent of your memory and attention; assuming also that, unfortunately, your superior scrupulously adheres to the favorite topics: the Holy Rule and condemnation of its violations. Then there might remain, at best, 10 per cent of your attention for the practice of vigilance. Psychologically, the result cannot be other than spiritual mechanism; the Rule is observed, but we overlook completely the crying need of neighbor and millions the whole world over. It so happens that in a "religious machine" of that type, the letter of the Rule supersedes everything else, even Christ's first and great command: *charity*. It also happens that these sticklers for the Rule condemn, without the slightest qualm of conscience, their poor fellow religious to a lifelong, bitter suffering of heart and soul.

It is not sufficient to know about God's greatest command. A true Christian, especially a true religious, blessed with a correctly formed conscience, is immediately alert whenever God touches the heart with a special message of love. All of life's circumstances are so many opportunities provided by God to give him thanks by returning his love while serving our neighbor, preferably the one who galls us, the one who is ever a stumbling block for us—or we for him.

Religious life has the privileged function of demonstrating to the Christian world in general the real meaning of a Christian life—more specifically, the call to holiness. It follows naturally that the main accent must be on vigilance. Vigilance points to situations demanding an absolute, unquestionable obedience to the law of charity; vigilance suggests the ways and means to a more perfect fulfillment of the commandment; vigilance enables us to see clearly how all things in life can and do lead to love. The Rule, therefore, must be so formulated and judiciously chosen as to be a help not a hindrance to the practice of charity in vigilance. Thus every religious will be firmly convinced that keeping the Rule is a service of love. When in isolated cases observance of the Rule violates charity, responding to the appeal of love takes precedence.

Several conclusions to be drawn from this truth have not been absent from traditional ethics; nevertheless, they have often been given little or no consideration when educating the conscience of the younger generation in various orders and congregations. It is imperative to see and be convinced that the positive divine law is the expression of God's plan of salvation and that the natural law is written in every human heart. Man-made rules, on the other hand, have no absolute, lasting validity; they are restricted to time and place. Whatever is the expression of our innermost being in the order of grace is always luminous, always lovable and worthy of love. Anything formulated as a result of temporary necessity can become meaningless and futile, even within the same generation. It is either idolatry or fanaticism to believe that positive rules and laws have an absolute validity and demand absolute obedience. If this is insisted on, by keeping the Rule we will often find ourselves transgressing the sacred commandments of God; especially the most sacred law of love.

The Letter and the Spirit

Moral theology acknowledges that numerous reasons can automatically exempt one from observing man-made laws. Some reasons excuse one from observing the letter of the law but hold that one is obliged to observe the spirit of the law and its intent in a different way. This is quite obvious in certain gross situations, e.g., if someone is called to assist a dying person, it would be rather unthinkable to offer as an excuse: "Sorry, but right now I have to go to Particular Examen." Unfortunately, similarly ludicrous and uncharitable reasons are not infrequently adduced to justify a multitude of minor violations of the law of love.

As regards dispensations, the superior has a right to claim in important matters that a formal request for a dispensation be presented to him together with the reasons prompting the request. In such instances the religious should manifest willingness to abide by the superior's decision. If in these cases the reasons are sufficiently weighty, the superior is under obligation to grant the requested dispensation. It may happen that certain dispensations involve serious obligations. If so, one should try, through a reasonable, benevolent, constructive handling of the situation, to open the way to sensible new possibilities. In cases when a point of the Rule cannot be observed and there is no chance to ask for dispensation, we ought to avail ourselves of the virtue of *epikeia* (self-decision according to the Spirit), for, according to St. Thomas, the fulfillment of the letter of the law *can* be a vice. All this entails risks; subjects can easily draw wrong conclusions to their own advantage. Life also exposes us to countless dangers, but no sensible man will, on that account, remain idle simply to avoid what may be a possibility. One must foresee the danger, guard against it, face it courageously, or, as regards the formation of conscience, awaken to a live, vigorous conscience by presenting it as a real confrontation with a loving God, explaining what is comprised in the liberty of his sons and daughters.

Love and the Law

A final point relating to the topic of conscience formation is that no law on this earth can be absolutely perfect. There are times when one would do well to observe a law out of love despite its lack of special relevance. Charity, peace, and harmony require its observance, at least occasionally and for the time being. However, charity would also require that one make known to local and major superiors the reasons that call for a change or the abolition of such an irrelevant and obsolete law. It is possible that some laws and regulations cry out for an immediate change in order to forestall, in time, the harmful consequences of bitter criticism. For example, a religious wrote to me recently: "Our Rule still contains the following, which is also communicated to candidates: 'Lay sisters may not be taught either reading or writing as such learning would lead them to pride.'" The reason for the division into castes and classes has to do with former historical situations which no longer exist. We are living in a democratic era. Such antiquated provisions must be eradicated as soon as possible, but with patience. Many subjects will go too far in revolting against blameworthy situations. To cope safely with such cases, it is imperative to make concessions, not weakly but with tact and flexibility, always retaining mastery of the situation and of oneself.

Finally, conscience presupposes a correct concept of family spirit, cooperation, solidarity, a noble *esprit de corps*. Conscience is that innermost aptitude of man to become one, a unity in himself through being one with the good. How, then, can we achieve that inner unity of all psychic powers and ultimately, that inner being-one with God? Only through constant striving for union with one another in community life. This endeavor must be a mutual recognition and realization, a joint search for the good, the true, and the beautiful. Formation of conscience convinces man that in spite of sincere efforts in the past, he still stands in great need of curbing his pride and acquiring humility. Step by step in the course of his self-evaluation, he becomes aware of his limitations; this insight renders him more willing to accept counsel gratefully from others and to appreciate the support offered him by the community. In final analysis, the community itself by its very structure must be a help, never a hindrance, to the individual member's conscience, and in its totality must express alertness, vigilance, charity, and loving kindness.

The Place of Obedience

What should the relation be between conscience and obedience? Conscience does not render obedience superfluous; neither does obedience eliminate the necessity for conscience. To have any value at all, obedience must consult conscience, prove to conscience its necessity and usefulness. Rules and regulations must testify before conscience that they are valuable and necessary for the general good, that they encourage the striving for holiness in the Church, as well as aiding the work of the various vocations and apostolates. Should these essential purposes be non-existent, subjects are not to be burdened with additional laws and regulations. It would only further delimit the psychological possibility for alertness and vigilance in living a life patterned after the Gospel. Let moderation be the imperative requisite of the Rule. Let the Franciscan spirit once again pass like a cleansing, vivifying breeze through our Rules, and may the Testament of the Seraphic Father, who implored his brethren not to obscure the Gospel by countless laws, once more be accepted as the authoritative norm so that each religious will be fully convinced: the Gospel is my Rule; our Rules help us to understand the Gospel better.

Moderation with regard to the Rule includes moderation relative to orders given. An authority that tries to rule out all possibility for mistakes to occur is not helping us to grow; it leaves no room for initiative. A child showered with commands from dawn to dusk will never be given the chance of realizing how he can please his mother specially. Similarly, if the Constitutions and the superiors wisely moderate the demands of laws but proclaim in words and example the beauty of the Gospel, the joyful tidings of God's love, then the subjects will not only obey gladly but will ask themselves spontaneously: How can I best please my superior and all my fellow religious? Joyful obedience and a living, wide-awake conscience go hand in hand. It would be fatal, moreover, to see in the establishment of external order the real purpose of the Rule and the chief function of the superior. External order can also be maintained in concentration camps and army barracks. The manner of issuing orders ought to be such as to evoke a joyful and willing "yes." It would even be preferable to overlook many minor transgressions than to risk choking the joy of obeying and the ready, spontaneous "yes."

A good superior will be imbued with great reverence for the feelings of his subjects. His main function is meant to be charismatic: he is to lead others on the path to sanctity. This charismatic function applies to all superiors of religious men and women. Superiors are *not* primarily administrators; rather they are pastors of souls, called to create joy and enthusiasm in daily living according to the Gospel. They are expected to recognize values, to cause the good, the true, and the beautiful to emerge in full splendor. The whole religious household benefits far more if the superior spends less time and energy on criticism and fault-finding and more on the constructive promotion of an enthusiastic and willing obedience in response to a vigilant conscience.

Maturity and Personal Fulfillment

Superiors must not expect initiative and responsibility to emerge if there is no allowance and no respect for such development. Where everything is begun and carried out mechanically, according to the Rule, there will be no maturity. As a reaction against failure to respect the sacredness of the human person and his God-given potential, we sometimes find too great an interest in maturity and its one-sided fulfillment; this represents a misguided concern often prompted by a wrong kind of personalistic psychology. Christians and religious who seek only their own self-realization are looking too much to themselves, are too self-centered. Superiors must be concerned to provide for growth toward fulfillment, maturity and a responsible life, but the real maturity of a Christian consists in going outside of himself, extending himself by an interest in and service to others. Those who sacrifice themselves according to a true love find their true selves. It is in this practice of daily love and charity, in the loving exercise of obedience and authority that we establish the image of maturity. From daily, watchful love of God and neighbor there will come maturity, with true discovery of oneself.

SIX | FREEDOM IN OBEDIENCE

... Let them bring to the execution of commands and to the discharge of assignments entrusted to them the resources of their minds and wills, and their gifts of nature and grace.... Religious obedience will not diminish the dignity of the human person but will rather lead it to maturity in consequence of that enlarged freedom which belongs to the sons of God. (PC, 14)

The twentieth century conceives of freedom as a passionate interest or concern for the political and civil liberty of nations and individuals. We find this hunger and thirst for freedom among the colored population of America, and we hope that there will finally arise among white people enough of this hunger and thirst for involvement in the promotion of civil rights to ensure the dignity and freedom of the underprivileged of every minority group. Implied, then, is freedom from every kind of unworthy dependence upon human persons as well as degrading conformity to the prejudices and pressures of an environment.

Civil freedom involves the whole structure of society and the state where every person and everyone's freedom is respected, where he is not manipulated, where he has a dignity, a value of his own. The political health of a nation exists only if the nation grants freedom to its citizens, and mere civil freedom is not the only kind of freedom. There is also freedom from undue dependence on a social pattern; in freedom of this kind we can encounter truth, can allow ourselves to think and seek the good.

There is freedom from a blind and slavish obedience, but we should not limit freedom to these few negative ideas.

Moral Freedom

We are morally free when the active power of the will and heart prompts us to follow our own conscience, to do what we have recognized to be the good here and now. Moral freedom, then, means the internal energy to seek constantly what is true and what is good. The freedom of a Christian consists in docility to the Holy Spirit; in the light of the Gospel, it becomes the liberty of the sons and daughters of God. By it we share in God's goodness, kindness, and love. It is the total dependence on God's saving will, freedom under the law of the Spirit that gives us life in Christ Jesus.

Moral freedom means that we have the internal power to love the good. If man's total energies are channeled into wrongdoing, he is not free; he is enslaved by his idols, by his selfishness, by an ideology. We are free if we grow in the understanding of what is good and have a choice, the internal possibility of loving the good. A serious desire for the good is significant in itself even if there are psychological and social barriers which, from time to time, hinder its realization.

In the realm of moral freedom, we are permitted to act even if our knowledge is imperfect. You may have heard of the famous principle of Cardinal Newman, "I have always contended that obedience, even to an erring conscience, is the way to gain light." There is no other possibility open to us except to be obedient to conscience. As Cardinal Newman expresses it, a true conscience always tends toward growth in knowledge.

The blessed freedom of the sons and daughters of God presupposes a deep insight into faith, a knowledge of Christ and of the exigencies of a living faith. The condition for this blessed freedom is that we look totally to God, that we be fully aware that we come from God, that we can develop our own personality, that we can reach fulfillment in a total surrender to him and in a loving service to the family of God. Religious obedience introduces us to the spirit of the Gospel and the community.

Conciliar View of Obedience

The Second Vatican Council regards the state of evangelical perfection as a compelling witness to the call of all Christians to sanctity. It is precisely this lofty view of the Council that must be adopted as the norm for an ever more profound understanding of the meaning of obedience in religious life. In order to penetrate to the essence of obedience, we must uncover the full beauty and great challenge of the ideal of obedience and free it from notions once prevalent in the days of feudalism and absolutism. Only then can we move on to a renewed conception of its practical role in Christian life.

Among other things, the Second Vatican Council acknowledged the fact that the Church no longer pursues her mission in a closed society according to forms of control and power typical of such times. The contemporary Church finds herself in an open, pluralistic society with ever greater demands for personal responsibility. Shamefacedly the Church acknowledges the fact that there has been a disgraceful misuse of obedience under totalitarian regimes. But if she is now to counteract the trend toward collectivism, she must conduct herself in such a way as to manifest respect for the dignity of the human person, promote a genuinely personal sense of responsibility toward the community and society, and in this way protect both. The religious who complies only when confronted by constant supervision is at best a museum piece, at worst one of the "submissive" subjects typical of totalitarian regimes. The modern world needs mature personalities who live according to the convictions of their own consciences. If the Church is to offer the modern world the liberating example of a real ethic of responsibility, then religious communities must be outstanding models of this particular ideal.

The Second Vatican Council, while calling for a greater sense of personal responsibility and freedom in *aggiornamento,* always glances back at the Gospel and seeks to revive the Gospel witness in the new world. The Decree on the Appropriate Renewal of the Religious Life mentions the historical context and ways in which obedience was formerly exercised; it maintains that there has been a constant and clear continuity in this regard (PC, 14).

Christ: Our Exemplar

Christ perfectly exemplifies obedience: his divine person is a gift of God which he gratefully acknowledges by rendering to the Father the fullness of the love of the Spirit. Christ also derives his human nature from the Father: "But thou hast prepared a body for me" (Heb 10:5); that is why the Father has full authority over him. "Here am I . . . I have come, O God, to do thy will" (Heb 10:7). In his obedience, Christ admits that the Father is the beginning of everything and that all things must return to him. Obedience to God lies in docility, deepening our understanding of God's gifts and the consequent demands of his love.

In the First Epistle to the Corinthians, the history of salvation is viewed according to the following terms: "And when all things are thus subject to him, then the Son himself will also be made subordinate to God who made all things subject to him, and thus God will be all in all" (1 Cor 15:28). Christ subjected himself to his Father's love in the Paschal Mystery, and he continues to subject his body by the grace of the Spirit. The history of salvation will find consummation only when this submission is perfect.

Salvation history, then, is nothing less than the record of submissiveness to God in humility. "No one has robbed me of life; I am laying it down of my own free will" (Jn 10:18), i.e., in a willingness totally dependent on the gift of the Father. Christ awaits the "hour" appointed for him by his Father; he lovingly keeps his Father's commands. His whole life is one of dependence on his Father who desires the salvation of mankind.

If we grow in the love of God, we will perceive better the meaning of his love and his authority. Continual growth in God's love sensitizes us to the unfolding and increasing exigencies of that love. If one says, "I have kept all those things since my youth" (Lk 18:21), he admits that he has failed to take a decisive step for the Lord. Those who are making progress understand well that the path leading to God is infinite: "So may you attain to fullness of being, the fullness of God himself. . . . Now to him who is able to do immeasurably more than all we can ask or conceive, by the power which is at work among us, to him be glory in the church and in Christ Jesus from generation to generation evermore! (Eph 3:19-21). Therein lies the dynamism of the law of the Spirit.

St. Paul describes for us the attitude of unredeemed man who recognizes that the law is good but, due to his self-centeredness, is unable to appreciate its goodness and blessedness. To him, the law appears as an imposition. Concluding his dramatic description, St. Paul cries out: "Miserable creature that I am, who is there to rescue me out of this body doomed to death?" (Rom 7:24). He answers his own question: "God alone, through Jesus Christ our Lord! Thanks be to God! (Rom 7:25) . . . because in Christ Jesus the life-giving law of the Spirit has set you free from the law of sin and death" (Rom 8:2).

We have received in abundance the fullness of the Holy Spirit. If we accept the Spirit as our law, if we recognize all his gifts —natural and supernatural integrated within the economy of salvation—as the expression of his benevolent will and his authority, if our whole life becomes a living expression of the eucharistic prayer of the Psalmist: "What shall I return to the Lord for all that he has given me?" (Ps 116:12), we shall be set free and we will come to know the blessed freedom of the sons and daughters of God. One can speak of true obedience only when it is lived according to the law of the Spirit. God's authority reveals itself in his gift of a new life. Our obedience must spring from this gift and find expression in a grateful response of service.

Obedience: Service of Freedom

The goal of religious obedience lies in modeling oneself more thoroughly on Christ in his obedience (LG, 42). Christ's obedience is simultaneously perfect humility in the form of a servant, the expression of the love and freedom of the Son, and our redemption in the blessed freedom of the sons and daughters of God. When we conform ourselves to him, we are redeemed from the pride and the slavish conduct of Adam and truly become free children of God. He who is called intends "by the profession of the evangelical counsels in the Church, to free himself from those obstacles which might draw him away from the fervor of charity and the perfection of divine worship; thus he is more intimately consecrated to divine service" (LG, 44). "Religious obedience will not diminish the dignity of the human person but will rather lead it to maturity in consequence of that enlarged freedom which belongs to the sons of God" (PC, 14).

How is one to understand the assertion that religious obedience is especially capable of increasing Christian liberty, and what practical consequences flow from this? One of the first answers to this question is to be found in the scope of the vow of obedience: ". . . religious offer to God a total dedication of their own wills as a sacrifice of themselves; they thereby unite themselves with greater steadiness and security to the saving will of God" (PC, 14). Obedience is a dedication to God; we are not confronted by the image of a human superior who can highhandedly dispose of the will of his subjects. Rather, superiors and subjects must both stand together before God in humility. They are likewise both striving to offer themselves in Christ and with Christ to the loving will of the Father in heaven and in such a way that obedience becomes a sacrifice of praise, thanksgiving, reparation, and intercession for the salvation of the world.

God himself, in turn, is not introduced as a sovereign will, but his saving designs, "salvific will," are clearly brought out. In this way obedience is understood as a loving, faithful reply to God's

loving appeal and to his own love. Love, however, and, all the
more so, God's saving love, is a liberating force. When obedience
is understood in the religious sense it has this power ultimately
to liberate because it is viewed in conjunction with Christ's sacrifice and offered freely to God. The criterion for our obedience
should be: offer it in such a way that we can bring it to the altar
and be united with Christ's sacrifice.

Obedience is, indeed, given to human superiors, but always
with a view to closer union with the loving will of God. In a
certain sense, superiors are the "representatives of God." The
expression could erroneously lead to idolatry, i.e., in cases where
superiors set themselves up "in the place of God," but this interpretation is absolutely impossible in the context of the decree.
Rather, superiors must render God present in such a way that
they completely make room for him. This point is clarified in a
twofold way: first of all, superiors are to be completely spiritual
men, "docile themselves to God's will in the exercise of their office" (PC, 14). Secondly, they are to exercise their office in a
spirit of humility, service, and brotherly love, so that they "manifest thereby the charity with which God loves them" (PC, 14).
It is not said that they must exemplify God's sovereign rights;
rather, they are themselves witnesses of submission and service.
Superiors must understand the Lord's saying: "As the Father sent
me, so I send you" (Jn 20:32), in the sense of the humility with
which Christ served the brethren and by which he is a perfect
image and witness of the love of the Heavenly Father for the
redeemed.

Spirit of Love

Religious obedience is offered under the influence of the Holy
Spirit. Hence, superiors, for their part, must be "spiritual" men,
i.e., they must be fully docile to the grace of the Holy Spirit and
open to the "signs of the time" that can be rightly interpreted
only according to such a docility. In this process, superiors are
not granted a monopoly of the perception of God's loving designs;

on the contrary, it is stated that a superior "should listen willingly to his subjects" (PC, 14). Hence, all must strive in unison and in humility for an ever greater docility to God's operative grace and for an ever better knowledge of God's will. When necessary, the superior indeed has the right to say the last word, but in such cases we rightfully expect from the superior the gift of "discernment of spirit." This can certainly be counted on, all the more so if we humbly seek knowledge of God's will together with our brothers and sisters.

Therefore, religious obedience represents, in an exemplary way for all Christians, a surrender to the "life-giving law of the Spirit in Christ Jesus" (Rom 8:2), which frees us from selfishness and fatal solidarity with sin. When interpreted in this light, religious obedience comprises the notion of the freedom of the sons and daughters of God.

This freedom and its witness, however, must not be sought independently. Instead, it must become the determining motive of one's whole life and its structures must express a genuine concern for fellow men. Psychological and sociological factors must be oriented toward the promotion of the freedom of the sons and daughters of God. Only in a spirit of humility and brotherliness in the exercise of authority and in the practice of obedience can this be achieved. Arbitrariness must be completely ruled out here. Obedience and authority must serve the same goals: the building up of a community of love that bears witness to Christ and an ever greater readiness for humble service in the Church. In so doing, obedience and authority incorporate that love, maturity, and readiness to accept responsibility that are the way everyone grows "to the full stature of Christ" (Eph 4:13).

The superior, therefore, will exercise power in such a way that by the example of his own humility and brotherliness he strengthens his fellow religious in these same virtues, and in turn is strengthened by them.

Enlightened Obedience and Initiative

In the realm of obedience Christians today are expected to exemplify, to a much greater degree than formerly, the stability
and clarity of their own consciences, as well as a spirit of spontaneity and initiative. Obedience and the exercise of charismatic
authority must not build a wall around freedom or intend to exhaust it completely. Instead, they must remain within the limits
that allow openness for personal initiative and the spirit of
eager acceptance of responsibility; furthermore, the limits must
promote this openness. Only in this way can the Christian in a
religious state be an exemplar for modern man. Activity directed
by his own conscience and a spirit of initiative are demanded if
the religious is to be the "salt of the earth" (Mt 5:13).

Expressions like "blind obedience" or "cadaver obedience"
not only have no place in the Christian vocabulary; all customs
that remind contemporaries of such impersonal behavior must
be scrupulously avoided. Regarding the historical background of
such terms, much could be said apart from the fact that a former
officer (St. Ignatius of Loyola) introduced it into religious par-
lance in the sixteenth century, before modern militarism caused
such expressions as *"militia Christi"* (war service under Christ's
banner) to be viewed with disfavor. We must always avoid
the blind obedience of a person who surrenders his conscience
to another and permits the other to decide on the deepest matters affecting his own life.

The Decree on the Appropriate Renewal of the Religious Life
emphasizes clearly that obedience must be enlightened and eager
to accept responsibility, and that humility should characterize
the Christian in religious life. "Realizing that they are giving
service to the upbuilding of Christ's body according to God's design, let them bring to the execution of commands and to the
discharge of assignments entrusted to them the resources of their
minds and wills, and their gifts of nature and grace" (PC, 14).
It goes without saying that this is psychologically impossible if

Rules and superiors have already minutely prescribed everything, and if superiors regard themselves chiefly as watchdogs for a depersonalized uniformity. Superiors are expressly told to make joyful obedience easier by a humble love; they are also directed to encourage a spirit of responsibility with respect to obedience and beyond it. "Let him [the superior] give the kind of leadership which will encourage religious to bring an active and responsible obedience to the offices they shoulder and the activities they undertake" (PC, 14).

Rightly understood, authority and initiative are inexorably bound up with love and service. Authority within the Church is likened to God's authority only if it shares in the creative love by which God brings things into being and conserves them. At the same time, the initiative of subjects is comparable to that of the obedient, love-filled Christ, but only if this initiative and obedience can be said "to look forward to the celebration of God's love." It is in Christ that we find the perfect example of both authority and initiative because of Christ's loving dependence on the Father. He is the prototype of initiative and authority, of creativity and freedom.

Authority must not be understood as something apart from the subjects which it serves, the People of God. To be rightly exercised, authority must bear witness to both—the familial relationship of the whole Church and docility to the inspiration of the Holy Spirit. Authority must not exclude encouragement and stimulation, nor must obedience exclude initiative and courage. Neither authority nor obedience precludes Christian love and harmony which promote Messianic peace.

Open Dialogue

The norms for the implementation of the decree on religious life moreover stress that all religious are to take a responsible part in the renewal of their religious communities. The decree also stresses that the principle of subsidiarity is applicable to the powers of superiors at various levels. Since the Holy Spirit works in all and through all, it is only right that all, according to the measure of their competence and docility to the grace of the Holy Spirit, should be able to make a contribution to the common goal and hence, even constitutionally, be allowed to use their charismatic gifts. "The superiors of all degrees may be provided with the powers for this purpose, so that useless or all too frequent recourse to the higher authority can be avoided as much as possible" (ES, 18). Along the same line, it will be only logical to conclude that mature, educated religious men and women must not waste their own and their superiors' time by too frequent requests for small permissions which are merely established customs or routines. On the other hand, the superior's door should remain open for anyone concerned about more important things involving the good of the whole community or personal decisions of some moment.

One of my confrères happened to become superior of a large community and among his subjects were four "eternal Fathers," religious priests who had been superior for twenty-five years or more. Each one came several times a week to inform the new superior what he was supposed to do; it was quite embarrassing: how was he to get along with all four of them? One day he called them all together and said: "You are dear confrères and each one of you tells me what I have to do; however, your advice is often very conflicting and sheds no light on my problems. Therefore, since I already have three men who are officially my advisors—and I always consult them—you are my secondary advisors. You should all meet, put your heads together, and then send me your spokesman; I assure you I will consider your recommendations very seriously." They never came back because they were never able to arrive at a consensus. Therefore when we have advice for superiors, we should remember that the superior also receives advice from thirty other persons; we cannot impose our views. Let superiors listen to us, but let us all take thought for the common good, recognizing that the superior must make the final decision.

Spontaneity and ease should mark our approach to the superior for the purpose of talking things over with him; dialogue should be frank and spontaneous, but the superior must have the last word if there is to be one. We must love and listen to each other and agree if possible without a decree. This is always best. Authority is a service of love and salvation, but superiors are also human beings; they need to be helped by our love. Authority above all connotes mutuality. Much is being said today about "horizontal authority" but our authority is really horizontal if we dare to offer good ideas to the superiors without making dictates of them. Religious superiors and subjects have but one great goal: to be docile and obedient toward the life-giving law of the Spirit, to see all things with a view to the gifts of God which always are given for the building up of a community of love.

The welcome directives of *Ecclesiae Sanctae* point in this direction. According to this document the juridical prescriptions that are always to be adapted to spiritual structures must not be too numerous. The book of customs must not become a *carte blanche* for immobility and meaningless traditionalism, but it should be the witness of the truly spiritual man who understands the signs of the time and who wants to use to the fullest, in community life, the present "saving" opportunities.

Obedience and Authority in Love

The development of the human person is bound up with the power to love. The more freely and spontaneously love is received and given, the greater its illuminating force and its witness value. Love is not a mere command externally attached to the total conception of man. In love the mature personality articulates itself and grows to maturity in Christ. In all documents relating to the religious life, the Council describes this state as a striving for perfect love (note the opening words "*Perfectae*

Caritatis" of the Decree on the Appropriate Renewal of the Religious Life). It is obvious, therefore, that those who are truly called, who grasp and live the meaning of their vows, experience love again and again. They interpret the denial involved in the vows as opening the way for greater love; it "does not detract from a genuine development of the human person. Rather by its very nature it is most beneficial to that development" (LG, 46).

This attitude must be the norm for the exercise of authority, for the kind of obedience expected, and for the reform of religious Rules. Rules which do not help build up a genuinely Christian community of love, or serve apostolic activity or "pastoral love," must be correspondingly changed. Likewise, superiors must not feel obliged to apply Rules mechanically, but should interpret and follow them according to the criteria of fraternal love and, hence, in a *spiritual* way. Superiors are expected to endorse gladly and not to block those new endeavors and customs that express and encourage genuine love and reflect an alertness to the needs of the Church.

The decree relative to the renewal of religious life very clearly states that superiors are appointed to serve their brothers. "Thus did Christ himself, out of submission to the Father, minister to the brethren and surrender his life as a ransom for many" (PC, 14). We must not be enslaved by selfishness, by narrow concern for our own self-fulfillment; this can only lead to frustration. We are to learn together the great concern for each other and for the common good. The superior must exercise his power in such a way that by the example of his own humility—being a brother among brethren, a sister among sisters—he (she) can strengthen his (her) fellow religious in the virtues of humility, openness to the will of God, openness to the needs of our neighbor. Religious obedience must never be a blind obedience; Christ, having proclaimed the great command: Love one another as I have loved you, did not say: "And now, you must obey blindly." No. He said, "I call you servants no longer; the servant does not know what his master is about. I call you friends, because I have dis-

closed to you everything which I have heard from my Father"
(Jn 15:15). We must study our Rule, our lives as religious, not
as a kind of anachronistic hold-over; we must see that every
article of the Rule is linked to the great commandment of love:
love of God and fellow man.

Synthesis of Love

It is precisely in this area that superiors as well as subjects must
see the great synthesis of love of God and of neighbor in the
Paschal Mystery. Christ's obedience to his Father is not something peripheral to his mission as Redeemer. The will of the
Father is love, the complete disclosure of his love for men, and
thus the revelation of his own mystery of triune love. As Christ
remains in the Father while fulfilling his great mission, so all
Christians remain in him while loving one another after the manner of Christ. All commands and virtues are included in this one
great mission of brotherly love. Religious obedience must not be
the obedience of an army of hired soldiers; it must be a loving
and illumined obedience. Hence all concepts of religious obedience which suggest that it is like that of a military barracks must
be ruled out. The authority-obedience relationship concerns the
practice and exercise of brotherly love in the fullest sense. Obedience must not set itself up as a competitor with love, but must
serve love. Religious obedience and the exercise of religious authority are also a real means of honoring God, but only insofar
as they find their true integration in love.

The spirituality of marriage today reveals that the sacramental
grace of marriage bears its most precious fruits if the spouses, by
their love, cause each other and their children to acknowledge
enthusiastically, "How good, then, God must be!" It is evident
that the religious life and especially religious obedience are
meaningful in a similar—not inferior—service of love. That is why
an altogether special charism is expected of superiors, viz., that
of manifesting the love with which God loves his sons and daugh-

ters. If superiors fulfill this vocation, everyone will be encouraged to recognize God's love happily and hence to grow in love for each other.

Should this outlook be adopted widely by all religious when revising their Rules, or in the formation of conscience or in the humble use of authority, then there will result a unified and unifying force among communities that will augur well for the future. Only thus can the Christian in a religious state continue to be generous and face daily trials. Life in a community ruled by a charismatic superior necessarily becomes one of eagerness to accept responsibility as well as growth in the capacity for responsibility. In such an atmosphere much external control can be eliminated. Formerly numerous restraints made sense, but today they only obscure the essential witness of Christians in the religious state. Consider, for example, the restrictions and supervision imposed on letter-writing; is not more to be attained when each one, on entering the religious life, learns that correspondence is to form part of his apostolate and witness?

Where a climate of the common quest for God's will prevails, superiors as well as subjects may speak openly. Excluded of course is idle, cowardly criticism behind a superior's back. We should cover our face in shame if we hear the words: "Why don't you speak openly to the superior about this? His door is always open to you. He is always ready to listen and learn, even if, in certain instances, the final decision rests with him."

Only love will give the strength and insight to conduct ourselves properly with regard to useless and antiquated Rules. Depending on the circumstances, one should be prepared either to disregard those prescriptions which lack any intrinsic binding force and thus accept certain hardships, or else to follow them in a spirit of generosity as long as this serves unity and avoids the risk of immobility. Love is the goal and fullness of the law. The preservation of what truly serves love here and now can never be dismissed as mere legalism.

All enlightened Christians know only too well that at times

they must pay for this atmosphere of love. This means abandoning all arbitrariness; it implies a readiness to consider the feelings and convictions of the other, to listen to him, to shoulder his burden with him, and to demonstrate kindness and patience even when the narrowness and fanaticism of others make it especially difficult. Renewal in the spirit of the Second Vatican Council also suggests a revitalized determination to follow the Crucified Christ and to commit oneself to the spirit of sacrifice. This renewed determination will come all the more cheerfully, and will appear all the more credible, if it is not misused to justify or perpetuate what is merely antiquated and meaningless.

Conscience and Obedience

When I was once giving a series of four conferences on authority to an institute for religious superiors, one good sister superior asked me: "What are you implying? Are we to renounce our authority and never raise our voices?" The good superior, a well-intentioned sister, was confusing authority with raising her voice. She had never read the book of Isaiah where it is prophesied that Christ would never raise his voice, and yet he had the highest authority. From another sister came the question: "Do we then have to give up our opinions, our consciences, if a superior tells us something?" This sister was confusing mere opinions with conscience—an opinion not yet examined, one that has not yet gone through serious meditation and prayer but is just an uncertain effort, a way of looking at things, a certain preference, perhaps a prejudice. Conscience means that one has exhausted his or her means for determining what is good here and now, what is absolutely immoral here and now and therefore can never be done; it does not mean merely superficial opinion. One cannot claim to have a good conscience if he has not done his very best to understand God's loving will.

There must be room in the Church and in a religious community for varying opinions, especially as they relate to ways of carrying out apostolic tasks, but nobody should impose his own opinion. An opinion, to be worthwhile, needs to be tempered in prayer; one should discuss it lovingly, respectfully with superiors and with colleagues on different occasions. It can happen at times—it has been my own experience—that we occasionally have to renounce our best ideas temporarily (at least what seem to us to be our best desires and ideas), but it is my deep conviction that if these thoughts really come from the Lord, they will bring us deep contentment nevertheless. We must trust in him; we must do our best and then let it depend on him whether or not the idea is worth promoting.

We all need a constant prayer life and a serious examination of our motives if we are to avoid confusing conscience with obedience. Care must be taken also not to confuse conscience with the process of rationalization: reference to conscience for a believer presupposes that he knows he is faced with a living God and that he should never dare to appeal to his conscience if he does not dare to kneel before him asking: "Lord, is it true? Am I doing this only in order to please you?" It is unworthy of a religious to insist "it is my conscience" if one cannot bear to tell the Lord, "I am doing it in order to please you." Ours is a difficult time, one of transition in which we have tremendous opportunities to become more mature, when the whole reality of the Church and the Word calls for more mature consciences, based on a strong living faith and on deeper insight into the Gospel and the message of the Church.

Let me conclude these few words on obedience and conscience with a story about Pope John. A monsignor was telling the pope how difficult his life had been: he had to fight for so many things, others did not understand him, he had to work on all things by himself because nobody else could do it, and so on. Pope John's comment was: "I had exactly the same temptation, but during the night my Guardian Angel came and told me: John, don't take yourself so seriously!"

The Realm of Obedience

Here is where the first responsibility of superiors lies. Our times require a change to more democratic ways intelligible to the younger generation; the style of command must be adjusted. In all humility, we must accept help not only from members of the council, but also in important cases from other truly wise religious in the ranks. Superiors and older members of the community must listen to the criticism of the young in spite of their tendency to exaggeration. When young people realize that they may state their opinions simply and openly, the venom loses its sting and clandestine criticism practically ceases to exist; it expresses itself in the open. The question then arises: "What is wrong with us that criticism has become so hostile?"

In difficult situations of this kind we Catholics are always inclined to look for the enemy in the opposite camp. Recently I asked some students of theology, priests in the thirty-to-forty age bracket studying for their doctorate: "What can be done in Italy or in Spain to stop anti-clericalism among the workers?" The first reaction was typical: many pointed out what others had done wrong and what the devil had inspired. It did not occur to them that we priests had done a few things wrong ourselves; this is the point at issue.

Realism demands that superiors ask the right questions, not "What are the subjects doing wrong?" but "How did we superiors fail to adapt ourselves? Did we foster genuine service and willingness to obey?" Superiors must not remain in the groove of trivialities. Are we not sometimes overly concerned with the small matters that critics point out? We should develop enthusiasm for an obedience that is not aimed at fulfilling our own will, our own way of living the religious life in keeping with our personal temperament and inclination, but at fidelity to the call of God that comes through the orders of higher superiors, the demands of the moment, the Rule. A superior's efforts should be directed toward stimulating enthusiasm and spontaneity in the community. However, creating such a permissive climate in the household can be achieved only at a price: there must be relevant asceticism and an intensified prayer life.

SEVEN | RENEWAL THROUGH PRAYER

Drawing on the authentic sources of Christian spirituality, let the members of communities energetically cultivate the spirit of prayer and the practice of it . . . they should take the sacred Scriptures in hand each day by way of attaining "the excelling knowledge of Jesus Christ" through reading these divine writings and meditating on them. (PC, 6)

The most profound and enduring significance of the religious life is that it is above all else the best school for a life of prayer and fraternal love. If I had to advise a girl or a young man with regard to the choice of a right monastery or congregation, I would have her (him) go around to find out how the religious pray and the extent to which they appreciate prayer. The intensity of their prayer life can also be judged by their yield of the beautiful flower of mutual love and apostolic work.

Prayer is not only meant for religious; prayer becomes for man, created by God, the highest privilege and a highly existential question. Peter Wust, a great lay philosopher and one of the first Catholic existentialists, bequeathed to his students the legacy of wisdom accumulated during a lifetime: "If you would ask me now if I know the key, the magic key that opens the door to wisdom, I can tell you with absolute certainty: I know the key. And it is not what you expect from a philosopher, namely, reading and reflection; it is simply prayer. Prayer is the art of listening to

God's words, of opening one's mind to him, of speaking out one's own existence to God; this makes man wise. This opens to him the kingdom of divine wisdom." There is nothing more important for present-day religious than a deeper understanding of the life of prayer, nor is anything more urgent during this time of renewal. We will be able to go the full way with the Church only if we are prayerful men and women.

What Is Prayer?

Prayer is an expression of faith, the total openness of the human person to the Word of God incarnate. It is a knowledge of Christ given by the Holy Spirit, and through the knowledge of Christ, a knowledge of the triune God. Faith comes from hearing the Word of God, but hearing not only with one's ears; we always need the finger of God, the Holy Spirit, whose touch opens the mind and heart to God's message.

God speaks to man in many ways: he speaks to man in creation; he speaks fully in the final Word, in Jesus Christ, in the Redemption. He continues to speak to us in his Divine Providence, in the way he governs the Church. He speaks to us through the needs of our times, the needs of our neighbors; he speaks to us through the love and kindness we receive from one another. Our whole life is based on listening to God, and listening in a way that will facilitate our giving the right response. The very reason of our being is to listen to God and to respond to him.

God has made us in his image and likeness; not only does this mean that we can rule over the earth, but it signifies that we can be concelebrants of the triune love of God, that we can share in the dialogue between Father and Son in the love of the Holy Spirit. God celebrates the fullness of his own life, and his beatitude, his love, his wisdom is to utter his Word. The Word that returns to the Father is a breath of Love in the Holy Spirit. God is Word and Love, eternal dialogue in self-giving love. In creating man in his image and likeness, God made man free, not a slave. He can be free in his earthly work only if he shares God's Sabbath, if above all earthly tasks he is with God, i.e., he finds his repose, peace, fullness in God. Man is created by God to be a man of prayer, to listen to God, to hear his name when he calls him, to understand himself in the Word that is spoken by God.

God has created us for no other reason than because of his abundant love, for no other purpose than to have concelebrants of his own love. Therefore he has created us in such a way that we can understand him who is Love, and can comprehend his loving design on us. We are created in his Word: "At the beginning was the Word; the Word was God . . . and all things are made through the Word" (Jn 1:1-3). We are made for the Word in such a way that we can understand it; we can understand him who creates us and we can understand why he creates us.

Holy Scripture is explicit in stating that God created us in his Word; God uttered us; God calls us. Such is the origin, the foundation of our life. We become fully alive as persons to the extent that we understand ourselves as a calling, as being called, and are ready to give a total response. It would be a grave error amounting to a fundamental heresy to think that man is first a substance and then has an accidental relationship to God. It is essential that we come to the realization that we are what we are through the calling of God, through him who calls us. Therefore we can understand ourselves only insofar as we look to him who calls us, and as we try to surrender ourselves in loving response to him. Worship, a worshipful response to God, is the origin of all blessings, of beatitude. For one to look to himself without God, failing to look above all to him who calls us, is the beginning of sin and perversion.

Dialogue with God

The book of Genesis is not a chronicle but a wonderful and deep theology of God's original design for man. The Creator's whole plan is expressed in the symbols and way familiar to the people of that era of salvation history. The first chapters of the Bible portray man's dignity as he is placed in paradise. To Adam, called into being by God, was given the privilege of prayer, expressed in Oriental terms: God, on a cool evening, descending to paradise to take a walk with man—fantastic! Paradise is a place where man is allowed to walk with God, to listen to him, hear him, and speak out his existence, his whole life to him. When God came, when God descended to walk with him, Adam was hiding with Eve. They were not looking for God, who had called them into being for a dialogue of loving adoration. They were talking with the serpent, the inflated ego, and behind the puffed-up ego-serpent, Satan himself. This is the beginning of original sin (represented today by a prayerless life) when man started a monologue with the serpent beside him, seeking his own independent power, his own wisdom. Adam and Eve were hiding from God for the sake of discussing their own egotistical search for self-fulfillment.

By looking selfishly to himself, man had lost his dignity, his privilege, his paradise, his prayer life. Do we fully understand what it means to be created in the image and likeness of God? We exist: we have a real existence, subsistence; but we have value, dignity only if we are in the Word and Love of God, if we understand more deeply the great message, the great Word God speaks to us; in creating and preserving us, God speaks a Word. As St. John explains in the prologue of his Gospel: "At the beginning there was the Word, the Word was directed toward God, and the Word was God, and all things are through this Word." It is evident, then, that all things convey a message, all things speak to us of God, but we men who are created in his image and likeness are the most substantial product of love. We find our true selves not by turning selfishly within but by understanding ourselves, our whole being, our whole existence as a Word coming from God, as an appeal and an invitation to love him in return. We arrive at an understanding of this Word only if we make our whole life a response, as Christ made his, who is the final Word that speaks to his world: "And the Word became flesh."

Christ's first prayer, the prayer that reveals his whole way of life is: "Thou hast fashioned me a human nature. Behold, O Lord, I come to fulfill thy will" (Heb 10:5-7). Here we see the existence of Christ as he understands himself, his human nature, united to the Divine Word and coming from the Father, as a gift from the Father. Therefore his whole life is spent in fulfilling his Father's will and he breathes out his soul in prayer: "Into thy hands I commend my soul" (Lk 23:46). He came to redeem man from a life without prayer, to rescue man from his foolish monologue, from his talking and babbling with the serpent, the selfish chatter about himself. Christ shows us what the real man is, the final man; he is the Word, the message, and he is the full response, in our name. His response must become ours: "Behold, O Lord, my Father, I come to fulfill thy loving will" (Mk 14:36).

Gospel Message

The whole purpose of Christ's life is to bring a message from the Father; he is the message, he is the Word, and he is the full response. We are redeemed; we are sharers of Christ's life if our ears—our body, heart, and mind—are open, and if they understand in all things the Word coming from God. However, if we want to do so we have to look to Christ; he is the final Word. All things are through him and for him. He speaks to us as the Creator, the Word in whom all things are made; he speaks when the heavens proclaim the glory, the splendor of God's love. We have to listen to him who came personally, who became man for us and speaks to us in human words.

The Council advises religious, all religious, constantly to read the Gospel and to try to understand better the message God sends us; it also urges us to be zealous to celebrate a living liturgy. Christ spoke more than 1900 years ago; the event belongs to past history and his message has been transmitted to us through the Holy Catholic Church, but he speaks to us also now. His message is current history here and now. God speaks to us in his dynamic presence, through baptism; he really brings the message of the heavenly Father: "now you have become 'My Son.'" He speaks now in human words, and at the same time he engraves them in our minds, writing them in our innermost being through the sacramental character; it is a message and an appeal of lasting value and significance.

It is the task of the Church, and as the Council explains, the noble task of bishops and priests, to explain, preach the Gospel, explain what Christ himself has written in our hearts and minds. He speaks to us daily in the Holy Eucharist; he not only preaches his Gospel, the one he preached in Galilee and Jerusalem and Samaria; he speaks to us personally in the assembly, insofar as we are living members of that assembly. He addresses us: "Take this and eat; this is my Body which I sacrificed for you. I died for you; I lived for you. I have risen for you; I have ascended to the Father for you. I have sent you the Holy Spirit; I have prepared room for you in heaven in the communion of the saints." It is he who assures us that all his words, all his deeds are done for us. This is the foundation of Christian prayer.

"My Eyes Are Always Looking to the Lord"

Adam's monologue was the origin of all perversity for he no longer looked to God; he was concerned only about his own business of self-fulfillment and self-pleasure, but with little success. Unlike the serpent's self-centered or Adamitic personalism, God calls us to a different personalism which has its center in him, which looks to him and with his loving eyes, then finds the true self of man. St. Paul resumes the theology of the first chapters of the book of Genesis in the first chapter of his Epistle to the Romans where he says clearly that man, having been created by God, was capable of knowing him but refused to be a worshiper, to adore him. Then he shows how the perversity of the world, all the malice, all the miseries originate in man's refusal to worship the Creator (Rom 1:18 ff). Therefore it is obvious that renewal, genuine renewal, begins, goes forward, and ends in better prayer, with a life totally dedicated to prayer.

The whole of the Word of God teaches us to be men and women of prayer, to be deeply rooted in prayer. It is fundamental that our whole life become a life of prayer; it is the best antidote for the innumerable sterile worries that come from cold "activism." We can never find our true self if we are engaged in monologue with ourselves; we cannot have the maximum energy for our tasks and community life if we are not constantly and deeply united with God, if we are not looking to him.

On a visit to Germany after the last war I preached in the local church where my little niece was attending Mass; she was about three years old. After the Mass she told me: "I understood you; you were constantly talking on 'my eyes are directed to the eyes of my Father'"; she had understood the essence of my homily. Should this not be the message of every life, of mine and of yours, as dedicated men and women: "My eyes are constantly looking to the Lord"? When our eyes are open, they see what is going on in the world; we are no longer blinded by the futile chatter of the completely new nun who has no time to waste on prayer but who spends considerable time talking with frustrated priests about their isolated lives. We do not have time for prayer, we do not learn to pray, but we have plenty of time to worry, to be angry and dissatisfied.

Ultimately, it is a question of the self, of what we are; not only the nun or priest but man himself is called by God; this is his *raison d'être* in the sight of God. Man sins and fails to find himself if he does not develop this fundamental attitude of viewing everything as the Word coming from God. If you do not understand yourself as a calling, as a vocation, as a being called by God, as being called to intimate friendship with him, then you have not yet found your name.

Hearken to the Call

God calls us through his creation, through our own being; this is a real calling, it is uttered in a word. God calls us in Christ, and Christ is the Man whose whole life is prayer, the fullest prayer. Christ lived thirty years in the house of prayer before going out to preach, and when he set out on his mission, he made it a practice to withdraw from the crowd for whole nights, going up into the hills to pray. In the Bible, before taking decisive steps, for instance before choosing his apostles, we see him in prayer; before celebrating the sacrifice on the Cross, we hear him in his High Priestly Prayer in the Cenacle, we find him praying on the Mount of Olives.

Christ's whole life consisted in "looking to the Father," seeking his loving will, awaiting the hour appointed by the Father. He responded with his whole being, even unto the shedding of his blood. Prayer is not merely something additional in our lives; prayer is the soul of our life, the form of our life. We cannot separate religion and morality. We can distinguish different aspects, but we are faced with Christian morality only when our whole life is a listening to God and a response in love. It would be a grave error to think that we can set aside a certain time for prayer to adore God and present our petitions, and then spend the rest of our time in the business of seeking our own perfection, or as some leftists of today put it, seeking our self-fulfillment.

In this day when the heresy of self-fulfillment is the serpent that poisons the environment of priests and religious, we must give up the approach to morality that was never a Christian one, that introduced into our teaching the ideal of "self-perfection" as the central notion of Christian morality. This is the approach of Aristotle, a great pagan, and of the Stoics, also heathens. It is a natural ethics, natural with all the attributes congenial to unredeemed man, fallen man. Christian morality, on the other hand, consists in humbly listening to God's Word, to events, while trying to understand what God means by all this, how he is appealing to us, and how we, as his beings, are to respond by offering ourselves, our words, desires, affections as a loving adoration. Our final happiness must be to try to know him, to understand him ever better and find ever better ways of pleasing him. True self-fulfillment follows in the wake of openness to God and neighbor. It degenerates into a lowly selfish business if the perspective is one of self-enhancement for one's own sake.

Isolated questions like: "Must I do this?" or "Is it a mortal sin if I do it?" should not be among the concerns of a Christian; such a slavish attitude is unworthy of Christians and absolutely unworthy of a religious. It is no better than the lopsided concern for self-fulfillment. If our approach is that of conscience—How can I please the Lord? How can I thank the Lord for all he has given me?—then our life will be filled with joy. Our life will be like paradise where God on a cool evening descends and allows us to walk with him.

Initiating Dialogue

God does not wait for our weak attempts to babble out something; his graciousness extends to the initiation of dialogue with man; it is he who speaks first to us. He then invites us to listen to him, to receive his Word and to respond. The sacraments are a basis for Christian prayer; they are God's strategy for teaching us how to pray. The Holy Spirit inscribes in our hearts: "Abba, Father." Hence the importance of the liturgy as life. We must feel that it is the living Word of God, his living presence, and his great nearness in our neighbor. The Constitution on the Sacred Liturgy says that the whole People of God listens to the Word of Christ who still proclaims his Gospel; they sing to him, they respond to him.

The forebears of many American sisters came from Ireland, and the Irish were once a singing people. It was during persecutions that they locked the doors and celebrated the low Mass so as not to be heard; the situation was an abnormal one. The Irish people and the whole Catholic Church must become once again a Singing Church rather than a witness to the very saddening history of a persecuted silent Church. Shout your praises, sing to the Lord! Why be totally silent at Mass and not express one's joy? Sing your gladness, proclaim your joy. We are receiving the great tidings, the joyous news of the Gospel, and our response must be one of joy. This is prayer.

Our prayer must also include the admission of "my fault, my most grievous fault," but if we love Christ, we are redeemed; we are the People of God. We are the holy assembly with Christ among us. Christ's word is not transmitted to us in a vacuum or in activities marginal to our own way of life; it is an appeal that our whole life become prayer, but through others, not as isolated individuals. There are modern, worldly sisters who tell me: "Our whole life is prayer; therefore we do not need to spend so much time on Bible reading, conferences, and praying in chapel. Our life is the only form of prayer." If we rule out time to take a walk in paradise, to kneel before the tabernacle of the Lord, the great sign of his everlasting love; if we refuse to take time to treasure up his words and deeds in our hearts and to ponder over them, then it is an insult to God to say "our whole life is prayer." If we never visit parents when we could visit them, never write to them but keep telling them: "All that I do is for you," will the parents believe that everything is done for them? How can they believe in our sincerity if we assert our love while avoiding them, never talk to them, never listen to them? It is really true that our whole life must become a life of prayer and can become a prayer-life.

There is great danger in the heresy of activism today. I am not denying that we have to work hard for Our Lord, but we must beware of activism. We can never do too much for him, but we have to do it for him, with him, and through him. Indeed, our whole life should become prayer, but let us not be foolish and insincere by resorting to the activists' prayer; in many cases it amounts to nothing because we have failed to learn to listen to him, to be always with him. We need time day by day to recollect ourselves, to engage in dialogue with him: to speak, to read over his words, to meditate on the liturgy, to sing together, to pray together, but our prayer must be cultivated and intelligent.

There are still blessed men and women of our day to whom he has given the constant experience of his nearness, but one has to go through the patient school of prayer and prayerful reading first; one must use the free time day and night to make himself aware of God's nearness, of God's calling, before God graciously grants this experience of his nearness. We must also use all of our resources—resources of nature and grace—to understand the meaning of our life in this perspective. We will then truly come to understand Christian morality as a listening to the Lord and responding to him.

"Lord, Teach Us How to Pray"

Prayer should be the great missionary task of religious; everyone who experiences the spirit of faith should feel when he prays: "Here is the Lord." This is because men are hungry for each word coming from the mouth of God, and once more, in life, everything becomes meaningful. Those who pray "in Spirit and truth" do not view eventful happenings as isolated episodes of human experience. The sacraments are God's gracious word to us and our response; they illumine and sanctify our whole life; they bring us in contact with God's saving love, they teach us how to glorify him in all our life. Thus God opens our hearts, our minds, our eyes, our ears so that in all things we hear the voice of God.

An illustration of the foregoing point could be the following: You have a nervous headache; if you are sacramentally oriented you feel that the Lord is calling upon you in this affliction. Through his grace you are sharing in his passion and you will kneel down and say: "Thank you, Lord. It is a sign of your love, since by it I share in Christ's suffering." He speaks to you and you listen to him, responding in gratitude; but should you resort to monologue with the serpent of your selfishness, you have already lost the paradise of prayer life and failed to capitalize on the present opportunity. Of course, the spirit of prayer will not keep you from taking care of your health.

Let us open our eyes to the beauty of a mature person, a kind person, music, a flower; in all these things God speaks to us, reveals his beauty to us; in all His works he manifests an attractive love. Love alone makes beauty great and truly meaningful; we see in all things and events the loving design of God who speaks to us. All events bear a message. We are invited to respond in a concrete way.

We should come to the Lord as the apostles did: "Lord, teach us how to pray." If we ask him, then we will come to realize that he not only teaches us in the Eucharist, in the message engraved in our hearts by baptism and confirmation; he also instructs us in the sacrament of mercy when he himself conveys to us his message: "Peace, peace and joy be with you; you are in me." In all things his peace and mighty love call us; the most wonderful reality is that he teaches us through the very gifts of the Holy Spirit, the same who anointed the human nature of Christ and offered the holocaust, the same by whom Christ is risen. Through him we cry out with Christ: "Father, our Father." We should not trust to our human understanding and intelligence; though we have to use these gifts of God, we should not trust in them unduly. We have again and again to ask God for his greatest gift, the precious heritage of paradise, the wonderful path to heaven, the gift of prayer.

We never fully achieve his life of prayer, of course, nor do we ever possess him; but we can always receive him. If we become more humble and persistent in asking the Lord to teach us how to pray, we will grow in the understanding of his word in our lives. Finally, our whole life, our whole being, our whole way of thinking and acting, will become the loving response to God's word, to the living word of God.

Prayer in the New Law

More serious attention should be given to the words of the Lord in the Sermon on the Mount where he proclaims the New Law according to St. Matthew; this is a synthesis, a summary of the Christian life. It is in the Sermon on the Mount that Christ teaches us the Our Father, and he introduces his teaching with the words: "Do not go on babbling like the heathen who imagine that the more they say the more likely they are to be heard. Do not imitate them" (Mt 6:7-8). If you pray, pray like this: "Our Father . . ." The Our Father, as given in Matthew, is translated into all languages, but we should not think that the first concern of the Lord was to teach us a formula. If this were the case, St. Luke would have received a poor grade in his reporting of the Our Father; he has only half the words of Matthew. In spite of this half version, St. Luke nevertheless gives the full structure and meaning of the Lord's Prayer. Apparently, the message is intended to disclose to us how our prayers should be structured but certainly not as stereotyped formulas. The daily saying of the Our Father should be a test by which we prove our way of thinking, praying, and acting.

Each religious family must strive to become a better college of prayer life. As for directors of novitiates, I feel that they should be more carefully prepared than professors of chemistry or mathematics; it would be disastrous and dangerous for chemists and physicists to learn only about dry formulas. If teachers have to be well prepared professionally, the novitiate personnel should be even better prepared, and especially well prepared for the teaching of prayer life and Christian life in this perspective. Religious superiors must above all be teachers of prayer by their own lives, their example and work. If you love each other, if you help each other grow in the spirit of prayer, and if you know how to talk to each other in a respectful, cheerful way, this is already a great step in learning how to speak to God. We must learn how to reveal ourselves, our true names, our love for neighbor. If we daily learn how to converse with each other, we are learning how to pray. Thus we help each other and learn more and more from each other until eternal life; we will be living in him, understanding him, and our whole existence will be a joyful response to his love.

Prayer is, in its essence, vigilance for the coming of the Lord, listening to him in all the ways he chooses to speak to us, for he does not speak to us through the sacraments only—this is the most privileged way of addressing us and there we can be sure of his most efficacious presence. He speaks to us also through the many events of our lives, through our neighbor, through the signs of the times. If our prayer life is indeed what it is meant to be— an awareness that it is he who speaks to us, an awareness of his nearness—then we will be like the Blessed Virgin, vigilant for the needs of our fellow man. If our prayer is constant openness to the Word of God, whereby we not only return words but ourselves to him, then our lives also will be enlightened. Indeed, we have not only to return words to God, we have to return ourselves as being wholly called to him, by him and for him. Then we will truly understand all the details of our lives, particularly appeals coming from our neighbor, as a call coming from God. We will then be offering our faithfulness and making a real effort to respond in genuine love.

Prayer and Celibacy

It is timely to say a word about the relationship of a life of prayer to the special vocation of celibacy for the kingdom of God. Recent discussions not only confuse "facultative celibacy" with optional fidelity to vows and oaths, but they often fail to see that the free choice of such a vocation and fidelity to the commitment depend wholly on God's grace. He who believes in God's graciousness and sovereignty will believe also in the value of prayer through which we acknowledge our total dependence on him. It may well be that among those who condemn celibacy there are people who do not believe in the blessedness of such a vocation in the light of the Gospel. However, this point is specifically made by the Council of Trent (Sessio XXIV, Ca. 11, Denzinger n. 1810). Celibacy does not make sense from the bare viewpoint of a self-seeking fulfillment, but it manifests goodness and blessedness, brings contentment to those who view their whole lives from the viewpoint of everlasting happiness in the concelebration of God's own blissful love, in that loving service that reflects Christian faith and hope.

Celibacy cannot be appreciated by those who have lost the spirit of prayer. When the Lord praised those who for the sake of his kingdom remain celibate, he added: "Let those who can grasp it, grasp it" (Mt 19:12). It is a gift coming from God, one of the richest harvests of the Holy Spirit; it is given only to those who pray and it can be preserved only in the spirit of prayer. In his book on virginity, speaking of the prime importance of prayer, Romano Guardini says that the strength of celibacy and the apostolate will collapse if prayer is assigned only a secondary place. If in our daily lives, in the apportioning of our work and time, prayer becomes a subordinate thing, if colloquy with the Lord becomes relegated to a secondary place, then we will soon not be laboring for him; impure selfish motives will dominate our activities. Our lives will be fruitful and we will work hard in the vineyard of the Lord if we are anchored in him, if our lives are rooted in him through a prayerful life, through listening to the Word of God, through prayerful reading and joyful praise.

EIGHT | UNDIVIDED LOVE AND SERVICE

That chastity which is practiced 'on behalf of the heavenly Kingdom,' and which religious profess, deserves to be esteemed as a surpassing gift of grace. For it liberates the human heart in a unique way and causes it to burn with greater love for God and all mankind. (PC, 12)

In the last thirty years the Catholic Church has developed a very deep and rich spirituality of marriage. Since the sacrament of matrimony and celibacy are related to each other, both being related to the great mystery of the Covenant of love between Christ and his Church, there is an urgent need for a development in depth of the spirituality for those following the evangelical counsels of celibacy, poverty, and obedience. In his recent encyclical on priestly celibacy, Pope Paul VI makes an authoritative statement about the historical development of the institution of celibacy and its significance for the priesthood. Faithful to the desire of the Council Fathers, while opening the door for the ordination of mature married men as deacons, Pope Paul reaffirms the Church's stand on celibacy and attempts to add luster and strength to it by explaining the reasons and motives for the long-standing tradition. The same motives apply to the consecrated chastity of religious men and women.

136

Elements Human and Divine

In celibacy and consecrated virginity, we renounce marriage in order to consecrate our lives to the kingdom of God. Evidently part of the order of redemption, celibacy can only be understood by men and women of deep faith and lived by spiritual men and women. The order of salvation, however, is not separated from the divine providence of the Creator; when God wishes to prepare someone for celibacy in the kingdom of heaven he also prepares him naturally.

A life vowed to celibacy as a witness to the superabundant graces of God's kingdom must reflect a life of gratitude toward our parents. By their selflessness, spirit of poverty and humility, by their tender love as spouses, by their exemplary Christian parenthood, have they not contributed significantly to our preparation for a religious life? Those who follow the call to celibacy are thus obligated to exemplify, for Christian spouses, an unselfish love, fidelity, and spirit of poverty. How can religious encourage generous parents to assume their magnanimous responsibilities if they fail to be a witness to the spirit of generosity that marked their parents who brought up four, six, eight, or twelve children?

The vow of celibacy for the kingdom of God presupposes a greater maturity than that required in matrimony. If we rush into marriage without maturity, we will tend to use the spouse as an object, a means or an instrument, thus making impossible a real union; immaturity even jeopardizes the possibility that marriage may be a human success. As for virginity, it is even more demanding. A self-centered adolescent is not capable of celibacy even if he has no trouble with sex. One of the first and almost essential signs of a vocation is an openness to others: the capacity to feel with others, to share their joys, bear their burdens, be serviceable to others and grateful for every sign of goodness received from others. The art of receiving and reciprocating kindness and goodness is a part of that openness.

The vow of chastity in celibacy is theologically a witness to the liberty of the sons and daughters of God. The New Testament proposes celibacy as a free choice in grateful acceptance of a special vocation or a special spiritual gift (Mt 19:11-12). It therefore assumes a high degree of natural freedom and spontaneity, freedom from egotism with an inclination to do good spontaneously and not only under pressure from precepts, threats, or approval. We should enjoy doing good for others, doing more than one is obliged to do by external sanction; this is a truly human freedom. A cumbersome system of laws and precepts that leaves no room for spontaneity and initiative suppresses those psychological qualities that are essential conditions for the development of the supernatural character of celibacy.

Maturity means a rich and well-balanced approach to the whole of life. Whenever everything is reduced to mere external obedience we are preparing for infantilism because of the elimination of a scale of values. In earlier days a system of protection could have had beneficial results in preserving observance of the vow of celibacy. In the social life of today, however, there are so many distractions and possibilities for escaping from this kind of external protection; the dangers are all the greater because modern life is permeated by unredeemed sex. Therefore a much higher degree of psychological, moral, and religious maturity is required, but a minimum of protection is also at all times necessary. Concern for maturity does not mean that man should be exposed to unnecessary dangers.

We must behave normally. A minimum of common sense suffices to show that we cannot lead a truly celibate life if much of our off-duty time is spent reading underground novels or magazines of the *Playboy* variety, attending controversial libidinous movies or plays, or even constantly looking at mediocre television programs. There are sound psychological principles that should serve to protect and promote our efforts toward fidelity to our commitments. If we deliberately refuse to be governed by the psychological laws relating to human behavior, we cannot realistically expect to remain faithful to the law of grace. It is of utmost importance to relate the human and religious elements, because it is the same God who created us in his image and who redeemed us in the love of the Holy Spirit.

A Spiritual Unction

Celibacy for the kingdom of God comes under the guidance of the Holy Spirit. It is a spiritual unction meaning that one is anointed by the Holy Spirit, but we can grasp this only if it is given from above. The primacy of grace is fundamental and must always be uppermost in the minds of those consecrated to celibacy. "You did not choose me; I chose you" (Jn 15:16). Therefore our attitude must be aligned with the Gospel, the good tidings that everything is a gift of God; thus it must also be a reflection of humility. On the practical level this means continuous prayer; before we decide for celibacy we must pray to be given the gift. If we wish to be perseverant, to live in fidelity to this commitment, we must remain men of prayer. Gratitude and humility must mark our prayerful request for perseverance.

Unction means joy; where there is a gift or an unction of the Holy Spirit, there is joy. Joy is one of the fundamental fruits of the Holy Spirit; but sad people do not manifest the signs of this spiritual unction. We must accept joy, ask for joy, and cooperate in a joyful spirit. Of special importance, in my opinion, is the joyful celebration of the liturgy which expresses in the best way this spiritual unction, this consecration of ourselves to the glory of God. It opens our hearts for the divine unction, the joy of the Holy Spirit.

Christ is the Anointed One; the fullness of the Spirit has come over him, has anointed him. He is totally consecrated to the glory of the Heavenly Father and at the same time devoted to the salvation of mankind. The vow of virginal chastity is cultic and should normally be accompanied by the Eucharistic sacrifice. Celibacy for the kingdom of God must be understood as adoration in unity with the Eucharist. Those who freely accept celibacy as a calling consider this gift as a kind of glow or reflection of the glory and love of God. They will respond with a life of adoration, gratitude, and unity with the Eucharistic sacrifice, a life of reparation in union with Christ.

In the vow of virginal chastity, man is consecrating more than a thing; he is offering a person, himself with all his faculties, to the glory of God and for the redemption of mankind. He who does not sincerely intend to give himself totally, always trying to consecrate his whole heart, mind, and body to God and neighbor, should not dare to make the vow. Accepting celibacy for the kingdom of God is a contradiction if we do not wish to give all our love to Christ and to love others with Christ and in Christ generously and unselfishly.

Primacy of Love

It is generally true for all Christians that we cannot really love the invisible God if we do not love our visible neighbor. This is true in a very special way for those living under the vow of virginal chastity: the fulfillment and meaning of this vow depend on love of neighbor. As an essentially redeeming love, "as Christ has loved us," it must also be a warm human love, full of kindness and attention to the other. With regard to virginity, Johann Adam Möhler speaks of undivided service, but he himself shows the deeper meaning. It is not first a simple service or a cold ministry; first comes undivided love which makes the undivided service fruitful, possible, and gracious.

We can gain an insight into the deep theology of Johann Adam Möhler by an episode in his life. When Möhler was about to take holy orders, while enjoying the seminarians' usual three months' vacation period at home in Germany, he fell in love. One day he declared his love to the girl and expressed his doubt as to what his future course of action should be; he was considering renouncing holy orders for marriage. The girl was as much in love with Johann Adam Möhler as he was with her, but she reacted in a way that impressed Möhler greatly. She asked him: "Were you sure you had a vocation to celibacy and to the priesthood before you fell in love with me?" He answered: "Yes, I felt sure of it." So she firmly replied: "God is a jealous God. I would not dare take away from God a heart that he has consecrated for himself." The seminarian Johann Adam Möhler thereupon accepted this, and decided wholeheartedly to go ahead and renounce his love for a girl he considered to be the best imaginable. He was a man of warmth and love, capable of an unselfish love, capable of loving a girl with a noble and deep love, not one based on sex-appeal. He knew that celibacy meant sacrificing something that is deep and great, because God is worthy of the best sacrifice, not the sacrifice of sick and blind animals as stated in the book of Malachy. We must be capable of real love. A castrated man, a man psychologically sterile, one who lacks warmth of heart and therefore never falls in love because he cannot extend himself to others, such a man is incapable of celibacy for God's kingdom.

In the theology of marriage we see more and more clearly that the power to preserve fidelity and chastity is a mark of deep conjugal love. It consists not in a desire to use or exploit the other person sexually but in a real gift of oneself, a mutual giving and living for each other and in a way always open for the third partner—the tremendous Lover, God—and always open also for a parental vocation. This is the power that makes a couple chaste. The same holds true for the other kind of celibate love; it is in fact a deep, absolute condition for celibacy. There must be an enthusiastic love of God, the experience of nearness to the Lord, an awareness of the new and eternal Covenant of love, devotion to the Eucharist. It means faith that Christ is in us and we are united to him, and thus are aware of an unlimited love beyond mere attraction.

I admit to a special fondness for members of the French school of sacramental theology who have developed among themselves truly Christian friendships. Friendship is of the essence of virginity. Those who renounce the love of *one* man or *one* woman do not renounce all friendships, intimate and deep love purified by the Lord. Great harm is done to many priestly and religious lives because of too much insistence on the dangers of "particular friendships" during their seminary or novitiate days. I in no way mean to dismiss the dangers of sensual friendships for a real understanding of celibacy. However, it is imperative to realize that we must have true friendships bound by the love of Christ. A genuine friendship grows in the pursuit of fraternal correction. A criterion of true friendship is concern for the upbuilding of brotherhood; instead of monopolizing the heart of another it seeks to extend itself to others, especially to those in greater need of kindness and affection.

Celibacy witnesses to love, to the mystery of charity. "God is love" (Jn 4:7-8; 4:16). God loves us more intimately and more efficaciously than our good parents ever loved us. Those who are blessed with the charism of celibacy love Christ and remain in him. From their nearness to him comes their power of transforming the world: the power of the Gospel, the power of the love of Christ, the power of a love in the service of others. Religious men and women gain by daily renewing and deepening their personal gift to the Lord, thereby receiving the fullness of the love of Christ.

Fidelity to Celibacy

Fidelity to the vow of celibacy involves building up a community of true love and friendship, including both the natural and supernatural aspects of love of neighbor. The redeeming love for other people which belongs to the vow of celibacy would not be true and sincere if there were not first of all this love for one's nearest neighbor: the members of the same community. Those living under vows have the obligation to be witnesses of a warm heart, an undivided heart—witnesses that the total love of God means the greatest and most unselfish and warmest love for one's neighbor.

We do not protect and foster consecrated chastity by forbidding friendship but by promoting the right kind of friendship: friendship especially between and among the members of the same community in order to make everyone more capable of the love of God and a redeeming love for all men. It is not the apostolate alone, but even more so the undivided love of God and of neighbor that is the foundation of virginal chastity. The apostolate will be all the more blessed and efficacious the more it springs from a deeply felt friendship with Christ and his disciples.

Celibacy for the kingdom of God or consecrated virginity is a gift of God and means the blessed experience of the nearness of the Lord. Consecrated virginity began on this earth with the Virgin Mary's nearness to the Lord. She was allowed to live in absolute nearness to her Lord and to pray to him. She was filled with joy to be near him, even if it was in exile, in poverty, at the foot of the Cross. Celibacy is preserved by nearness to the Lord in the Eucharist and in all other ways in which we experience his dynamic presence. I have found a striking relationship between the loss of celibacy in priests and their failure to pray before the Blessed Sacrament, never enjoying his nearness, never exposing themselves, minds and hearts, to the sunshine of the Lord's love.

We draw nearer to self-realization in Christ as we consecrate ourselves to God's glory, rejoicing in the beatifying revelation of his love and devoting our energies to the redemptive tasks of the world. In this perspective we perceive the important relationship between the Eucharist as an act of redemption, consecration, and adoration. The recent Council explicitly stressed the desirability of having profession ceremonies take place in conjunction with the Eucharistic sacrifice (LG, 45).

Celibacy for the kingdom of God is doubtless a renunciation. It means that we renounce something which is vital, fundamental; it means offering to the Lord the first fruits. The fundamental reality of celibacy, of consecrated virginity for the kingdom of God, is the nearness of the Lord, bringing to the world the message that even on this earth God is near to us. God gives us the great experience of his joy, his kindness, and his goodness. The great sign of the new and eternal Covenant of love is the Eucharist—the Eucharistic sacrifice, of course, but also the nearness of the Lord, the permanent real presence of Our Lord in the sacrament, and his being among us where two or three are gathered in his name.

Once I was in a parish and I had a long talk with the sister of the pastor. She complained that he was an incorrigible drinker; every evening he sought consolation this way. Several of the parishioners told me that they would like to see their pastor at least once kneeling before the tabernacle. He would run into church for services, then run out; they never saw him praying before the Blessed Sacrament. This is one of the chief reasons for the crisis in celibacy. Consecrated virginity entered into the world when the Blessed Virgin experienced the nearness of the Word of God. In pastoral tasks I have found that when priests once more find the taste, the joy of the nearness of the Lord in his sacraments and in his word, they come through unscathed, even through difficult situations.

The great sign of the new and eternal Covenant of love is the Eucharist—including of course the Eucharistic presence of Our Lord in the tabernacle. Eucharistic devotion in the full sense of the renewed liturgy therefore, together with prayerful reading of the word of God, should be a pillar of virginal chastity. Our vocation to celibacy is best expressed by song, in the joyful celebration of the liturgy, and it thrives on the art of bringing joy to others.

Spirit of Poverty and Humility

God gives great gifts only to those who are humble and have "the spirit of the poor" (Mt 5:3). An undivided heart in total and immediate love of God and redeeming love of neighbor is not possible if man is seeking an earthly compensation for his renunciation of marriage. In an affluent society like ours, there is a dangerous tendency to look for such substitute gratifications. The use of modern means for the apostolate is not dangerous in itself, but a possessive attitude is; if the institute as a whole is possessive, unavoidably the members will be contaminated. The services rendered by such an institute will be significantly reduced in scope.

According to the definition of the Council of Trent, celibacy for the kingdom of God is described as *"beatius et melius"* (filled with special blessedness and value). *Beatius* is surely not used here unintentionally; it reminds us of the beatitudes in the Sermon on the Mount. There the Christian life is summarized in the nine-fold "Blessed are you"; those who can grasp celibacy, those who are living a life of celibacy are blessed—they have something that is a special sign of blessedness, a witness to the joy of the Gospel. You will note that the first "Blessed" is said to the humble: blessed are those who have the spirit of the poor, those who by the power of the Holy Spirit are humble before God. Also included, at least indirectly, are those who are not possessive, those who in all things see the gifts of the Heavenly Father and therefore transform them into means of love, of fraternal love. It is impossible to reach the state of *beatius et melius*, to experience it, if one does not follow the first precept of the New Law of the Sermon on the Mount, humility and the spirit of simplicity.

We must face the problem that priests and religious today have numerous temptations to seek compensations elsewhere; in this post-puritan period they are sorry for themselves for having renounced so much happiness and some decide to get something out of life, and so become possessive in one way or another. One depth psychologist told me about his analysis of certain priests. First he said that among the most wonderful and most mature persons he had ever met in his life as doctor and analyst were priests, but he also conceded that some priests had probably sublimated their sexuality 100 per cent into aggressiveness. Perhaps these men would not experience any temptation against chastity, yet they were not witnesses to celibacy for the kingdom of God. Celibacy always includes a warm heart, an openness, the "blessed are they . . ." There is a great danger of the wrong kind of sublimation or looking for inordinate compensations.

There can be good sublimations, however; in its deepest meaning, sexuality is the desire to overcome loneliness, to live in real mutual service. If we give our whole heart to Christ and with Christ, in Christ, to the poor, the old, the lonely—then we are *beatior et melior* in this condition. Of course, in today's society we cannot live as men of the Stone Age. We have to adopt modern means for the greater effectiveness of our ministry, but nevertheless I think one of the greatest appeals which the Church of the Second Vatican Council made was for us to become the Church of the poor. Christ is the witness to celibacy: he is totally given to God and neighbor in poverty unto his death on the Cross. There is no other way to understand the mystery of celibacy except the way of Christ. It is unreasonable to renounce married love if we intend to fill our hearts with earthly things and pleasures. Some religious are frustrated by celibacy because they are too self-centered and possessive; they try to be chaste but at the same time they do not make the sacrifices that are necessary for the protection of this treasure. The keystone of our sincerity is this spirit of simplicity and self-denial.

Covenant Between Christ and the Church

Christian marriage is a holy but transitory sign of the love of the new and eternal Covenant between Christ and the Church; in heaven they will not marry and be married (Mt 22:30). Celibacy must be viewed even more than marriage in the light of the blissful Covenant between Christ and his Church. Virginal love anticipates in a more visible way the everlasting Covenant; it is a final reality. Virginal love is therefore a more immediate and blessed expression of belonging to the Covenant through baptism, confirmation, the Eucharist, and Holy Orders than through sacramental marriage. However, an expression has value and meaning only to the extent that it is true.

Pope Paul adopts this line of reasoning when discussing the more fundamental motives underlying and justifying the practice of priestly celibacy. "These can be brought into greater evidence only under the influence of the Holy Spirit, promised by Christ to his followers for the knowledge of things to come, and to enable the People of God to increase in the understanding of the mystery of Christ and of the Church" (*Sacerdotalis Caelibatus*, 18).

Celibacy, as a state of life, must be a credible sign of a supernatural reality; it must be a witness. It must be in the highest sense a witness to the Covenant of love between Christ and the Church. Virginity is vital to the full image of the Church, the virginal spouse of Christ. The celibacy of the priest has, apart from this, a special significance: to represent Christ in his sacrificing and redeeming love for all mankind, without exception. From this it follows that celibacy obliges us always to be ready for all people, to suffer with them, serve them, bring them the good tidings with a loving and merciful heart. An aggressive man or woman—a hard, unmerciful, rigorous type—may have sublimated his or her sexual desires into aggressiveness, but his or her chastity does not represent Christ; it is not a witness.

Eschatological Reality

Celibacy without frustration, lived joyfully with a warm heart and in a spirit of self-denial linked to greater love of God and neighbor, is a sign of the fullness of the final age! It is life not under the mere law but under grace. Therefore it is not proper to view religious life primarily as a life according to a rule which concentrates on restrictions and meticulous external points. The great Rule remains the grace of the Holy Spirit and the Gospel. It finds expression in the spirit of gratitude: "How can I render to the Lord all that he gave me?" The gifts of the Holy Spirit and, generally, in the same light the gifts of God are fundamental Rules "written upon our hearts" (Jer 31:33). The role of the superior is not that of a policeman but of a charismatic leader, guiding his charges toward sanctity in joy, gratitude, and enthusiasm. The secondary Rule of the institute must serve the primary goal.

Celibacy is a witness of Christian hope, and to this extent, an eschatological reality. However, hope must take hold of the present opportunities, of all those manifestations of the love of God which reveal that the final time, the kingdom of the beatifying love of God has already come. Only joyful gratitude in view of the present goodness gives Christian hope its power. Hence the necessity for an approach to celibacy based on the Gospel, on the Good News, on the joyful celebration of the liturgy, on songs and hymns, on the art of bringing joy to others.

Finally, eschatological witness means the blessed freedom of the sons and daughters of God: allowing ourselves to be guided by the overflowing grace of God, to be docile to the Holy Spirit within us and working through the Church. To be enslaved by all too human traditions and thus be trailing far behind the dynamic Pilgrim Church, to resist as long as possible everything new that the Church and Council propose, is to be a witness against celibacy and against the true freedom of the sons of God. The structures of the Church and of congregations must express this constant openness to the *kairos*—present opportunities—and must foster the real freedom of the sons and daughters of God.

The lively witness of the evangelical counsels, especially celibacy for the kingdom of God "foreshadows the resurrected state and the glory of the heavenly kingdom. To all men it shows wonderfully at work within the Church the surpassing greatness of the force of Christ the King and the boundless power of the Holy Spirit" (LG, 44). We understand what it means to renounce something attractive; we understand better what it means to be chosen by the Lord. It is a sacrifice, but not one that drains the heart if we carefully protect the treasure. It then will become a participation in gratitude, a participation in the heavenly liturgy.

Ascesis and Chastity

Essentially, virginal chastity is a method of attaining greater freedom and paschal joy. If we truly live according to the vow that deprives us of marriage for the sake of the kingdom of heaven, we shall never become cantankerous old maids or irritable old bachelors. It is an error to think that genuine chastity makes us emptyhearted, bitter, and sour. Should this happen, then the meaning of celibacy has escaped us.

The vow of virginal chastity demands sacrifice, namely, the rejection of everything that might endanger our undivided freedom to belong to the Lord in the service of those who need us. If we wish to have a certain sister or brother all for ourselves and are not open to others, then we are not yet open to God. Friendships which lead to selfishness must be given up; this means spurning excessive liberties in our contacts with others. We must not be prudes, of course, but we must renounce all familiarities which may become a scandal to the weak; we must likewise deny ourselves everything that causes too much distraction. Again I do not believe that virginal or religious persons ought to sit too long before TV sets. We may use the mass media for education, for an understanding of the world, but we must do so with interior detachment and temperance as to the use of our time.

All this merely represents the battle on the outer ranges. Deep down there must be concern that we have been chosen by Christ and exist for him alone. For this reason we must reject everything that impinges on the true freedom of being for Christ alone. In our times this freedom is hampered more often in communities of men than of women because of a desire for everything sensational. News cannot be missed; stacks of newspapers and the radio seem to be a necessity of life. It would be well to resolve: "On Fridays I will not read the newspaper unless professional work requires it; I will not listen to the radio or watch TV." This will help to dampen excessive desire and preserve interior freedom; it is a practical but genuine form of *ascesis*.

Pope Paul VI in his recent encyclical on priestly celibacy also stresses this need for asceticism: "It will be a demanding asceticism but not a suffocating one which consists in the deliberate and assiduous practice of those virtues which make a man a priest: self-denial in the highest degree—an essential condition if one would follow Christ—humility and obedience as expressions of internal truth and of a guided liberty; prudence, justice, courage and temperance, virtues without which it is impossible for true and profound religious life to exist; a sense of responsibility, of fidelity and of loyalty in the acceptance of one's obligations; a balance between contemplation and action; detachment and a spirit of poverty which will give tone and vigor to evangelical freedom" (*Sacerdotalis Caelibatus*, 70).

NINE | MEANINGFUL ASCETICISM

The fact that they are in God's service should ignite and fan within them the exercise of virtues, especially humility, obedience, courage and chastity. Through them they share spiritually in Christ's self-surrender and in his life. (PC, 5)

———◦◦◦———

The pluralism of our democratic society has a legitimate place in the Church of the Second Vatican Council. Diversity strengthens the unity of any social group provided the various entities comprising it strive for a common goal. Our goal is to live the whole mystery of Christ, the great mystery of life through salvific death. St. Paul gives us definite directions for achieving this life through death in his Epistle to the Romans: he speaks of putting to death the deeds of our selfish nature (Rom 8:13). Ascetic discipline, then, is a condition for attaining the freedom and maturity of the sons and daughters of God and for the formation of a truly Christian conscience.

Asceticism addresses itself to the actions of the person but not in terms of self-perfection or self-liberation. On the contrary, it poses the question: Am I really and entirely open to God and to my neighbor? A qualified but negative answer will compel the Christian to exercise more self-control but control that is neither destructive of self nor turned in upon oneself. Self-discipline helps the self achieve a fuller expression of *faith* through listening and response; it expresses man's *hope* to give completely of

151

himself to God, and it bespeaks man's *charity* as a glorification of God through selfless service to neighbor and community.

Conciliar Directives

The norms for implementing the decree on religious life lay down the guidelines: "Religious should devote themselves to works of penance and mortification more than the rest of the faithful. However, the special penitential practices of institutes should be revised insofar as it is necessary so that taking into account traditions, . . . and modern circumstances, the members may in practice be able to observe them, adopting new forms also drawn from modern conditions of life" (ES, 22).

All ascetical practices must be for the service of life. Holiness and self-perfection are not synonymous terms. There is a danger in self-perfection in that it can be valued more than perfection of love, that is, more than openness to God and neighbor. Asceticism for self-perfection often betrays a reflexive viewpoint; by turning back on ourselves we can reduce our ability to live spontaneously and can encroach on our openness to others who justifiably expect loving services from us.

There is an asceticism of numerous individual acts, mortifications, and penitential exercises that runs the risk of regarding them as goals in themselves. Asceticism must remain true to life, i.e., its authenticity must be reflected in a self-denial related to a life understood as an adoring love of God and selfless service to neighbor. Renunciation must be oriented to the blessed freedom of the sons and daughters of God and must nurture an openness for God and fellow man. From this freedom for God and neighbor, the fullness of the individual self develops.

Ascetic discipline must never become an end in itself but must always be related to the vital values at stake. Training for combat, not routine practice, prepares one for the battle in which "the old man," the self-centered man dies in order to live the new life in Christ. Training must be tested constantly on the battlefield of daily events. The renewal required for a more vigorous religious life calls for serious reconsideration of asceticism in terms meaningful for this day and age.

Archaisms

How can we practice asceticism today? We must first detach ourselves from habits and forms of life irrelevant to the spiritual combat, for example, concern about clothing. It is not fitting to be too attached to past relics, closing our minds to new practices and new forms of life. Sometimes we fail to appreciate the insights of youthful members of the community; we refuse to recognize what attracts them and moves them because we have a fixed pattern in mind.

The differences between generations constantly make new demands on ascetic discipline. This mortification cannot be required first from youth; those who have been in the spiritual combat thirty, forty, fifty years can be expected to be more advanced. Furthermore, the future does not belong to the old ways but to the new. It may be worthwhile to look about in the convent or monastery and ask yourself: what are the things to which we have become particularly attached? They are so numerous! Even in a general chapter it is possible to become excited with the holy zeal of prophets to the point of cursing (using verses from the Psalms!) and disowning members of the community regarded as unfaithful. In reality, there is no connection with the Gospel; we are sentimentally clinging to habits and customs proper to the seventeenth and nineteenth centuries when most religious congregations began. We must seriously consider: Are we truly animated only by zeal for the Lord and his purposes? Each age manifests its own spirit. If we burden ourselves with museum items from a previous age, we will be unable to fight with the Lord against the spirit of selfishness.

The Gospel Message Today

At the present time theology is engaged in the task of investigating what is firmly rooted in the Gospel and what is merely an expression of past centuries (consequently, additions), and what in the Bible is intended as a directive for all ages and what is a concrete appeal intended for "that time." Religious congregations must go through the same kind of examination. They ought to draw inspiration from the Gospel in a realistic, dynamic way for the needs of our times. In the Gospels forms of ascetic discipline are mentioned that apply not only to the individual religious man and woman in the ranks but also to superiors, the Council, and the entire community.

Activities and aspects that are no longer relevant, classes and privileges that are deterrents to our present witness, must be eliminated. A realistic examination of conscience will also cause us to admit our tendency toward sloth. Asceticism must be true to reality; this means that we must not demand too much of the weak. We must be aware of our own weaknesses as well as those of others, including a fragility in spiritual matters. There must be a clear distinction between the highest ideal toward which we must strive "according to the measure of Christ," and the minimum that needs stressing in the form of a written law.

The "Old Man"

Strenuous attacks must be launched against pride, self-centeredness, and spiritual sloth which also affects the body. An effort should be made to counteract routine. The requirement of numerous ascetic practices leads to an unhealthy state of affairs; many religious consider themselves mortified if they faithfully observe these practices. According to the law, they are judged just and thus protect themselves from battle against the real enemies. It is true that certain demands must remind us of the need for asceticism, but this should be done realistically. For example, to acknowledge as a fault the breaking of an object that happened to fall because one was overtired is contrary to truth; it is a form of distorted humility. Our practices must be true to life; they must be genuine acts which cut deep into the "old man" and "old woman."

Loving Service

From the truly Christian viewpoint, all ascetic practices that do not result in greater willingness to serve and greater sensitivity to the needs of others are untrue to life and bypass life. Willingness to serve is an *ascesis,* and this willingness to serve must be manifested in community. Rules intended to provide protection against the world, to prevent our contact with visitors and strangers whom we ought to serve, are meaningless prohibitions and unrealistic as ascetic discipline. A religious institute must be true to life; it must discontinue activities and practices no longer of actual service. The real ascetic battlefield is that of love which offers plenty of room for practice or exercise every day.

The young will need much practice in asceticism in order to avoid offending older members. If older members want to show the genuineness of their *ascesis,* they must outrun the juniors in sensitive concern for the feelings of others, a sympathetic yielding to personal peculiarities whenever charity is involved. It will often help to consider the example of St. Paul, who was long-suffering, who bore many a scar but still was not always able immediately to adjust himself to others. When his young assistant Mark became weary after a few stonings and imprisonments and returned home, Paul was angry with him; instead, he should have reflected: "Mark is not yet as well trained as I."

When Mark returned the following year, moved by admiration for Paul, the latter told him he could not use cowards. For the same reason, Paul and his best friend Barnabas parted ways. In these matters, even a St. Paul was unsure. One of us may be quick to say: "I was right!" Paul, however, later wrote to Timothy: ". . . bring me my dear Mark for I find in him a useful assistant" (Tim 4:11). Communities and elders of the Church had received Mark well; he became a distinguished soldier of Christ. Paul had not been right, and he uses every opportunity to admit his shortcoming. Of course, it is a mortification for a superior to admit that she (he) was not right, that she (he) did not have sufficient confidence in a sister (confrère), but such humble, charitable admissions help build up community spirit.

Collegiality

Mortification must take place within the sphere of love, or at least prepare for action in this sphere. There is need for increased willingness to go along with others, to cooperate with people, be more sensitive to their way of thinking. Whenever common action is being planned, there is a call for mortification. Collegiality, a central preoccupation of the Council, makes it clear that neither the pope nor the bishops are to consider themselves as self-sufficient sources of commands. The pope takes upon himself the highest office of service, but he treats all with love in order to bring all together, always remaining open to advice and constructive criticism from the bishops. For bishops, it means abandoning many favorite ideas of their own in order to carry out common pastoral programs, both in their own country and in the Church as a whole. Collegiality cannot function without self-denial on the part of individuals and groups.

Collegiality also affects religious life. Every congregation must ask itself: How can we contribute to the pastoral aims of the Church today? How can we do more in the parish, in the diocese, in our country, in the entire world? For the community as well as for the individual religious, this will often entail much self-denial.

Unity in Community

Community spirit is a sign of whether or not we are ready for the things of Christ. The mystery of unity was at work at Vatican II. We Catholics may not say to others: "You damned heretics, go home!" We must beg forgiveness for having mortified ourselves so little; we must admit our own faults, but not in the manner of a false humility akin to lying. We must continue to praise God for all the good he has performed through his Church while, at the same time, examining our consciences thoroughly: "Are all the things to which we cling really from God? Do they really serve unity?" Even if we are emotionally attached to them, when we realize they are hindrances, we must part with them. This conviction must permeate the entire Church, being most typical, however, of the dedicated sons and daughters of the Church, namely, religious. Whatever makes it difficult for others to approach the Church must go.

Today we would sin grievously if we wanted to adopt only what causes no trouble, by considering only "What can I say so as not to be misrepresented?" Our one concern should be that nobody's salvation is unnecessarily endangered, no one is scandalized. Instead of basking in a false security, we should seek liberation from human accretions in order to facilitate access to the Church and the reunion of the churches. Do not think that this is the business only of theologians; the same attitude must be adopted by the entire Church. We must examine ourselves carefully and ask: What promotes unity—unity in the house, in the province, in the congregation; unity among the religious orders; the unity of all Catholics? This will attract others to strive for unity. I mean a change of structures as well as attitudes. We must exert ourselves in that direction and build structures that express a willingness to serve the community with a view to the unity of all mankind.

Ascetical Realism

Let me suggest some ascetical practices that have a bearing on our real needs: Before criticizing a superior or other person, say three Hail Mary's for the person concerned. If this is omitted, say a rosary after a fruitless argument. After committing a fault in the eyes of others, we should profoundly humble ourselves and accept without excuse any comment from others. After an uncharitable word, we should perform a service of humble charity or at least attempt to bring some joy to the other person. This is being realistic. Meatless Fridays had practically lost all ascetical significance and the law was virtually abrogated. We ought now to find some appropriate substitute, for example, no TV or doing without something to which we are attached. The sacrificial element must always have a bearing on something related to life, inner freedom, love and service.

A certain amount of freedom must be left to provinces and houses so that each can discover what is truly best, what real mortification is. There must be genuine spontaneous mortification, not merely mortification according to the Rules. I cannot give numerous examples or any recipes. At best, I believe we should lay down only general directions. If we are realistic, we must face life squarely to see what has been learned in its course and ask ourselves: What is hampering our efforts toward a common, dedicated apostolate? What is hindering our full, generous devotion to the needs of the Church today? What diverts our attention from the demands of the hour?

Source and Goal

We must clearly understand what the moving force and real power of Christian mortification is. It is paschal joy. A Christian should not walk about with a long face. In the book of Nehemiah, we read: "The joy of the Lord is our strength" (8:10). If we celebrate the liturgy joyfully, if we are mindful of our status as redeemed men; if in addition to all this we are full of joy in our vocation as Christians and religious, which is such a marvelous gift of God, then we will more easily reject everything likely to lessen our joy or prevent its complete fruition. A well-prepared and carefully fostered celebration of the liturgy demands many mortifications. From older people, it means accepting liturgical changes gladly, trying all the while to understand how the younger sisters or brothers feel. If you comply only reluctantly, you show how little mortified and how full of self you are. If everyone enters wholeheartedly into the new liturgical rites and contributes his share, then hearts and voices will resound together and become a wellspring, a life-giving fountain of joy that prepares anew for daily mortification wherever fraternal love demands it.

Ascesis in Obedience

Heavy demands are made of religious men and women in the realm of obedience, whether they are superiors or in the ranks. When revising the Rule, the opinions of subjects must be considered. The superior cannot join with a few council members to place the Rule on the table like a trump card forcing others to withhold their opinions. Of course, there may be tendencies that could endanger true progress; if so, there is need for much prayer, good example, mortification, and open dialogue in charity. At any rate, there must be room for those who realize their responsibilities and accept them. "A superior should listen willingly to his subjects and encourage them to make a personal contribution to the welfare of the community and of the Church" (PC, 14). He should cup his ear to these calls for mortification every day.

Religious in the ranks must try to see and accept in self-denial the meaning of the Rule even when it hurts. One must not be too quick to say: "This makes no sense!" After careful, prayerful consideration and an unselfish judgment, we must honestly ask ourselves whether there is not, after all, an inner meaning and deep justice in the Rule. Such an honest striving for a deeper understanding and better appreciation represents mortification of one's subjective views. It is a mistake to think that there is no need to mortify our way of thinking as such; there is much pride in our thinking. What we state as a judgment based on reason is often merely a reflection of the Adam and Eve in us. For this reason, everything that flatters our own judgment and readily corresponds to our superficial inclinations must be carefully examined and scrutinized during prayer as we ask ourselves: "Am I thinking only of myself in this?"

Examination and purification of motives is definitely one of the great tasks in mortification. We are under obligation to keep a Rule even when we do not know the reason behind it, if keeping it is necessary in order to foster love of neighbor or a community spirit. Sometimes we must keep it to preserve peace. It goes without saying that we keep Rules and orders when they are just, and that we do not keep them when they are unjust or harmful to Christian life.

Between these two extremes, there extends the large area of action where the Rules no longer are suitable, no longer are truly meaningful, do not promote harmony and usefulness for the things of God, but on the other hand do not block the good. In this extensive area we must mortify ourselves and obey the Rules as long as obedience serves the greater goal of gathering a community of unselfish love around Christ. Of course, when the gap between the two extremes of good and obsolete Rules becomes too large, no doubt the spirit of the institute will suffer and love of obedience will decline. Therefore the responsible people are duty-bound to keep this in-between area as small as possible; however, these clouded areas will remain in spite of our efforts because we are still pilgrims in this earthly exile. If religious endure them for the sake of unity, love, and order, their opinion ought to be considered when they recommend changes.

When superiors and novice masters endeavor honestly to explain the significance and meaning of the Rules, they must sometimes admit: "I do not understand the meaning of this Rule. Still, let us try to keep it in a reasonable way according to the needs of charity and unity until it can be changed." The "yes" of obedience will thus gain new meaning, but we must be open and ready for new developments. For present-day *ascesis,* the following principle should be kept in mind: If a person is concerned about the shortcomings of a Rule, the limitations of superiors and of structures, and at the same time keeps in mind his own deficiencies, he will find himself involved in the double effort of improving things and bearing burdens. He will find strength for sustained effort in his prayer life.

Openness to the World and Poverty

The Pastoral Constitution on the Church in the Modern World lays down the basis for further development of the theology of material things. Whoever seeks first the kingdom of God gains at the same time an awareness of the nature of all of creation as the manifestation of God's fatherly love and the means of expressing fraternal charity.

The theology of material things and of the world has a very fundamental bearing on the direction of Christian asceticism. It is only when the world is fully understood in its true significance that the complete meaning of asceticism becomes manifest. The world is, before all else, the good creation of God inviting us to praise him and to be united in the bonds of brotherhood. However, the world is subject to man and he is a sinner. As God's good creation, and even more as creation redeemed by Christ, it cries out to redeemed man, for it is through him that it is destined to share in the freedom of the sons and daughters of God.

In Christian asceticism we seek a harmonious response to the world in all its aspects. Asceticism is a readiness to suffer in the struggle against a world that is God's enemy. It is readiness to give witness to Christ, so that those who are seeking the truth may be led to faith. It is above all warfare against one's own sinfulness and against the insidious forces in one's environment, so that the true meaning of created reality may once more be revealed.

A truly relevant asceticism is sensitive to the yearning cry of all reality for full participation in the freedom of the children of God. Asceticism will be relevant if it is not tied to immobile programs or involved in legalism, but is open to the realities of a given situation—if it is willing to go out and meet God's world.

A requisite for an asceticism open to the world is the spirit of poverty. By poverty we do not mean lack of possessions, but rather that attitude which is expressed in the first beatitude: "Blessed are the poor in spirit, for theirs is the kingdom of heaven" (Mt 5:3). Whoever is poor in spirit—and this is always a gift of the Holy Spirit—renounces an inordinate desire for possessions. He is able to acquire, but not without a struggle against selfishness, a purified love for all values and all earthly realities. Only in this way can he become involved in worldly affairs, eager to engage in genuine cultural activities, concerned about economic matters, open to the need for institutional reform, and all the while remain sensitive to the claims that his neighbor has upon him. The man who is poor in spirit rejects the use of things simply as a utilitarian means; he recognizes in them the gifts of God. He perceives in them the call of God. He is able to appreciate their true worth, for he sees them as a sign of the love of his Heavenly Father. Because of this, he understands as well that he is being challenged to give them up or to modify his use of them whenever the needs of his fellow man demand this.

A brief consideration of ascetical practices reflecting both openness to the world and renunciation of the world will follow the discussion of poverty in the next chapter. Attention will be called to full positive Paschal acceptance of the world as well as to willingness to practice restraint and self-denial in the interest of the salvation of all.

TEN | HUMILITY OF THE POOR

Poverty voluntarily embraced in imitation of Christ provides a witness that is highly esteemed, especially today. Let religious painstakingly cultivate such poverty, and give it new expressions if need be. . . . In discharging his duty, each religious should regard himself as subject to the common law of labor. (PC, 13)

There is probably no area of religious life calling for greater adaptation than that relating to the evangelical counsel and vow of poverty. Legislation which was once adequate under totally different conditions of life must now be discarded. However, a wise and courageous adjustment will be possible only if we have a better understanding of the essence of poverty and a greater readiness for renewal in the spirit of the Gospel. A deeper appreciation of the spirit of poverty must be attained before we approach the actual problems of *aggiornamento*.

Spirit of the Poor

According to the New Testament, law and obligation have meaning in the light of the Sermon on the Mount which summarizes the Gospel message. In the Beatitudes, poverty is not represented as a law to be enforced; it is a proclamation of the joy and richness of the kingdom of God. "Poverty in spirit" becomes the blessed gate to the kingdom of God, a blessed condition for entry into the joy of that kingdom. In the Biblical sense, it means hu-

mility. It means that in view of the richness of the heavenly kingdom, we must empty ourselves of selfishness, we must give up
an egotistic search for self-fulfillment. It may be understood in
opposition to the prejudiced attitude of the Pharisees toward the
underprivileged, the truly poor, the humble social classes, simple
country people. Also included by them were probably those who
did not have an opportunity to be trained in the science of casuistry, the knowledge of the "law," and who therefore had no
reason to boast. The poor and humble, humble in their social
condition, were more ready to accept the Gospel than the rich
and teachers of the law. Our Lord, and especially St. Paul later
on, showed a certain preference for the lower social classes because they revealed more open-mindedness to the message of
redemption.

In the Old Testament, the divine blessing is often described
in the form of earthly wealth; many pious Jews considered economic success a sign of God's preference for them, and as a
result they showed contempt for those who were poor. This attitude came to the fore in another context and with a different
emphasis in Puritanism. Even today it is a classical trait of the
Calvinists of South Africa. The evangelical counsel of poverty
reverses and corrects this attitude, but it does not mean that
poverty by itself, in the sense of misery, is a divine blessing. The
accent should be on the word "spirit." We cannot exclude the
fact that we have praised here, above all, a gift of the Holy Spirit.
It is not poverty as such that is lauded, but those who have the
spirit of poverty; blessed are they who stand before God as poor,
as beggars, fully conscious of their total dependence on him and
loving this dependence. They are able to renounce many earthly
things and without risk of frustration, because they are filled with
his love, his joy. They rejoice in being servants, in bringing kindness, goodness, and peace to others.

Every attachment to earthly goods becomes an impediment to
the joyful acceptance of the Gospel message. As indicated earlier,
the patron and protagonist of the people who seek only their

own self-fulfillment is the rich young man in the Gospel. Turning to the Lord, he asked: "Good Lord, what must I do in order to gain eternal life?" (Mt 19:16). The Lord enumerated the teachings from the Old Testament and finally said to him: "One thing is lacking to you; if you wish to go the full way [of the New Testament], then go, free yourself through detachment to earthly goods, and follow me." The Gospel then reports: "The young man went away with a sad heart" (Mt 19:22). He had not seen the Gospel as a joyous news because of his worldly and selfish concerns.

At the beginning of the second century, the so-called Gospel of the Nazarene—a commentary on this Gospel—quotes the Lord as uttering these words and then has the young man replying: "All this I have done since my youth; I have fulfilled all the commandments." Our Lord is then reported to have said: "You are a liar; your house is filled with earthly goods and nothing comes out of your house, whereas your brethren, the sons of Abraham, are dying from starvation." So the young man prefers his earthly goods to himself, perhaps to his eternal life, to the joy in the Lord, because he loved himself more than his brethren, "and he went away in great sadness."

Essence of the Beatitude

The essential elements in this beatitude seem to be the following: (1) Freedom from any kind of attachment that would impede man's joyful acceptance of the Gospel; freedom from a possessive attitude; humility in gratitude, the need for few earthly things. (2) An intimate relationship between the right attitude toward earthly goods and humility. (3) The freedom of the sons and daughters of God that makes them aware of the fact that everything is a sharing in God's goodness, that this freedom comes from God and therefore has to be returned to God. (4) Openness to the kingdom of God in the sense of being led totally by love of God, by the law of grace, to such an extent that the gifts of

God for which we humbly implore him and joyously thank him are also the rule of conduct. The kingdom of God becomes visible by the rallying power of His love, by the solidarity of all who allow themselves to be led by the love of God. Therefore poverty considers earthly goods, not only material goods but also our capacities and abilities, as signs of God's bounties and consequently as means of building up the brotherhood of the children of God. (5) A clear relationship to joy. The joy of the Gospel enables us, even in difficult situations, to perceive the joyous message more and more deeply and to find all our joy in the love of God and neighbor. (6) Christian joy, even in humble and difficult circumstances, and Christian charity, both bearing witness to the coming of the kingdom of God. All Christians should bear witness here regardless of the differing conditions of their lives; however, religious are called upon to give this testimony in an outstanding way through their state of life.

Those who have freed themselves from attachment to earthly goods experience joy in the Lord, the joy that is our strength. The spirit of poverty is included in the blessed freedom of the sons and daughters of God; it enables us to see the enjoyable aspects of our abilities and our earthly goods as gifts of God linked to the well-being of his whole family. Humility is the condition for the kingdom of God for all men, not only for religious, but religious should manifest the fullness of the times, the beatitude of the heavenly kingdom, by their total freedom for the Lord. Those who are attached to their own wills, who seek chiefly their own happiness and fulfillment, are not ready, are not open to the great blessing of the kingdom. Joy and the spirit of poverty are intimately related. The reason some people need so many unnecessary things is that they are sad; they do not know the joy of the Lord.

The Following of Christ

The Decree on the Appropriate Renewal of the Religious Life views the vow of poverty chiefly in the light of following Christ in the pursuit of perfect charity, and following him as closely as possible on earth. Religious life means "to follow Christ more freely and to imitate him more nearly by the practice of the evangelical counsels" (PC, 1). The religious "imitate Christ the poor man; . . . the more they unite themselves to Christ through a self-surrender involving their entire lives, the more vigorous becomes the life of the Church" (PC, 1).

Through the virtues, especially humility and obedience, the religious "share spiritually Christ's self-surrender and in His life. . . . Let religious follow him as their one necessity in fidelity to their profession and in renunciation of all things for the sake of Christ" (PC, 5).

"Poverty voluntarily embraced in imitation of Christ provides a witness that is highly esteemed, especially today. Let religious painstakingly cultivate such poverty, and give it new expressions if need be. By it a man shares in the poverty of Christ, who became poor for our sake when before he had been rich, that we might be enriched by His poverty" (PC, 13).

A Christocentric morality and specifically a Christocentric understanding of the spirit of poverty must not begin with the overt imitation of the external conditions of the earthly life of Christ. Following Christ includes a combination of the following elements:

(1) A spiritual sharing in Christ's self-surrender, a sharing in the mystery of Christ's self-immolation and thus in Christ's life. "The divine nature was his from the first; . . . He made himself nothing, assuming the nature of a slave. Bearing the human likeness, revealed in human shape, he humbled himself . . ." (Phil 2:6-8) and he died on the Cross—giving himself to his brethren.

Through sacramental assimilation with Christ, we share the spirituality which is revealed in the mystery of the incarnation, death, and resurrection of Our Lord. All Christians should be imbued with this same spirit, striving constantly to express in their lives the mystery of Christ's poverty as he manifested it in the incarnation and in his passion. This is the most demanding law; it is the mystery that must at all times shape our lives.

No specific form of economic or social structure is contained in this most fundamental requirement of Christian poverty. However, this is the most radical approach that urges the disciples of Christ, ever anew, to adopt those expressions of life that are here and now most appropriate for the total service and witness of the greatest possible unselfishness.

(2) The second element is a very personal confrontation of man with Christ himself, a loving look to him, following him on the way he has paved for us. Those who wish to follow him talk everything over with him; they implore his grace; they are docile to the Holy Spirit, the internal teacher. The follower of Christ is confronted with the living Person, with all the words and deeds of Christ; this confrontation is a real one through the Paraclete. It is a life in Christ and with Christ.

(3) The third element then is the imitation of Christ, which however has its true meaning only if it is integrated in the sacramental assimilation with Christ and becomes a part of the discipleship. During his earthly life, Christ expressed in a variety of ways the poverty that is the essential element in the mystery of the incarnation and passion: by his birth in a stable, by his years in exile in Egypt, by his life as an emigrant, his common life in a little town, his profession of carpenter, his forty days in the desert, his insecurity of a wandering preacher—"The Son of Man has nowhere to lay down his head" (Mt 8:20). None of these situations can be imitated literally, but the disciple must be ready to face *similar* situations and he should have a spirit of initiative to find an appropriate embodiment of the same spirit in a world different from that of the time of Jesus of Nazareth.

Christ does not wish us to be stereotyped copies, but real followers through whom his life finds an ever new incarnation in the history of salvation. One characteristic trait emerges both from the example of Christ and his teaching: namely, his closeness to the simple people in his way of life and language which appealed particularly to the poor, to the great mass of the people.

(4) The imitation of the saints is a fourth element. St. Paul appeals several times to the Christians to "be my imitators" or "be imitators of the Churches," but this is always in the light of his own discipleship in Christ. Christ teaches us through the variety of approaches adopted by his saints during the course of the centuries. From them we learn fortitude and humility in seeking new ways of humble service and witness in different circumstances of life. It is a great help for us to look for practical applications in the light of the Gospel, the pursuit of perfect charity through poverty. This pursuit of perfect love always looks to those in great need: to the poor, the underprivileged, those who need encouragement from us. General chapters and superiors cannot lay down minute rules covering the realm of poverty. Apart from structures that foster the spirit of poverty, we must leave enough room for pioneers, the charismatic members of our orders, men and women who courageously embark on new ways of self-denial and service.

Perfect Charity Through Poverty

The Decree on the Appropriate Renewal of the Religious Life begins with the words "perfect charity." This is the clue to understanding the essence of the evangelical counsels and it is the theme of the whole document. The holiness of the faithful consists in the perfection of charity. "For charity as the bond of perfection and the fulfillment of the law rules over all the means of attaining holiness, gives life to them, and makes them work" (LG, 42).

The decree on religious life speaks about all the evangelical counsels as a means or path in the pursuit of perfect charity. The dogmatic Constitution on the Church has a very explicit reference to poverty, which characteristically is linked with humility: "Since the disciples must always imitate and give witness to this charity and humility of Christ, Mother Church rejoices at finding within her bosom men and women who more closely follow and more clearly demonstrate the Savior's self-giving by embracing poverty with the free choice of God's sons" (LG, 42).

The Church is a mystery, a community of humble service and love. The vow of poverty is associated to this service of salvation. "By the charity to which they lead, the evangelical counsels join their followers to the Church and her mystery in a special way" (LG, 44). However, this fundamental relationship between the evangelical counsel of poverty and charity must not be understood merely in view of a loving use of the earthly goods in common life and in common service for the whole of mankind; this is certainly very important. It must also be seen as an expression of redeeming love insofar as it is a witness to the freedom of the sons and daughters of God which comes from their faith in eternal life. Since man in an affluent society is especially tempted to forget about the heavenly good, this aspect of poverty becomes an ever more pressing appeal for charity. The world needs this witness of poverty. "Freedom from earthly cares more adequately manifests to all believers the presence of heavenly goods already possessed here below. Furthermore, it not only witnesses to the fact of a new and eternal life acquired by the redemption of Christ. It foretells the resurrected state and the glory of the heavenly kingdom" (LG, 44).

The evangelical counsel of poverty should be seen in its very fundamental relationship to celibacy for the kingdom of God. Celibacy means undivided love for Christ and his work. By the vow of celibacy man promises to keep his heart perfectly free for the overwhelming love and joy of Christ, so that he may be able to love all men with Christ's own loving heart in the power of his Spirit. An attachment to earthly goods would destroy this freedom for Christ's love and his redemptive work. We must not only realize that an indiscriminate participation in earthly goods fostered by the modern welfare state endangers priestly fidelity to celibacy in many cases; we must also know that the world will not believe our witness of celibacy if we appear to be rich and seek unnecessary wealth. Earthly goods and a comfortable life can be a substitute for a marriage that one has renounced, or can at least give an appearance of such to others. Therefore redeeming love of neighbor obliges us, as religious, to be really free from all kinds of greed and to exercise caution so that our witness of the eschatological realities will be credible to men. This should be the great charism: to give witness to the freedom of the sons and daughters of God, the witness that we believe in eternal life, and therefore can renounce many comforts in this world. In the Constitution on the Church in the Modern World, the point is made that freedom from earthly cares more adequately manifests to all believers the presence of the heavenly good already possessed here below. Furthermore, it is not only a witness to the birth of a new and eternal life acquired through the redemption of Christ, it foreshadows the resurrected life and the glory of heaven.

Common Life

An essential element of the counsel and vow of poverty is the "common life" modeled on Christ's life in Nazareth; he lived the common life of the poor. The prototype of the common life of religious is the primitive Christian community in Jerusalem. "They met constantly to hear the apostles teach, and to share the common life, to break bread, and to pray. . . . All whose faith had drawn them together held everything in common; they would sell their property and possessions and make a general distribution as the need of each required. With one mind they kept up their daily attendance at the temple and, breaking bread in private houses, shared their meals with unaffected joy, as they praised God and enjoyed the favor of the whole people" (Acts 3:42-47).

In this description of the common life we see a marvelous unity between sharing in the word of God (including the Eucharist) and the communality of earthly goods. Faith, the hearing of the word of God, and the celebration of the mystery of faith had drawn them together. The solidarity as to their daily needs is a reflection of their oneness in faith and joy. The fundamental reality of the common life, then, is to be together in the celebration of the Word of God, in the prayerful praise of God, in the mutual strength of faith, sharing the charism, the supernatural gift. Similarly, in religious life, the solidarity of salvation as the common effort on the way to holiness should reflect itself in a loving solidarity in the use of the earthly goods and abilities of each and every one. A very important element of the "spirit of poverty" consists in not being proud of our abilities, thinking: my abilities were given primarily for my own self-fulfillment. All our capacities and abilities are destined by the Heavenly Father to serve the common life, the common apostolate.

Common life does not mean, at least not essentially, "common ownership," as the history of the order of St. Francis proves, where together they renounce all titles to ownership. Common life means chiefly total dependence on and service to one another, absolute renunciation of any selfish, individualistic claim of ownership and use. The modest use of common goods and generous service to one another should indicate that religious really are exemplary members of God's family, that they are, to a certain degree, the embodiment of the whole "family of God." From this angle, it becomes evident that "common life" should not only reflect the ordinary conditions of a modest life and family solidarity, but also express the solidarity of a religious family with the whole of the Church, with the whole of mankind, and especially a deep solidarity with all the poor.

Church of the Poor

The "Church of the Poor" was a favorite expression of Pope John XXIII. Since then, the idea has been repeated thousands of times, especially by some seventy bishops who during the Council examined their own consciences and discussed how they could live as humble, poor apostles of the Lord. Several theologians and bishops belonging to religious orders had an active part in this movement. Some of the fundamental questions raised by this group were: Does the Church of our time, especially in her bishops, priests, and religious, manifest to the world Christ's own simplicity, humility, poverty, his nearness to the simple people, to the lower social classes, to the hungry? Is it sufficient for the Church to organize charity drives when she herself, in her appearance, structures, titles, prelates, and even her religious orders, seems to be so wealthy?

It does not follow that all members of the Church have to belong to the lowest social classes. Poverty in the sense of the Gospel does not mean material or spiritual misery, but the Church of the Word Incarnate does mean a special *nearness to the poorest*. Her structures must manifest simplicity and humility. A chosen part of the Church must courageously "imitate the mystery of the incarnation": freely choose to be poor with the poor, to be simple and modest with the modest and simple. Religious, particularly, must not serve the poor while appearing to be wealthy aristocrats. They must, in today's way of life, be present *among* the poor, belonging *to* them. The mode of their service must not only be effective from a material point of view, i.e., in the struggle against misery, but it must above all be credible in the light of Christ "among the poor."

If the Church, because of the generosity of her members, disposes of considerable material means for the relief of the poor, and if she has the material means and facilities for carrying out her pastoral mission, then all this cannot necessarily be in opposition to her witness as "the Church of the poor." However,

dangers arise constantly and special care must be taken to avoid
the temptation to act or to appear like the rich man of the Gospel who seemed willing to give Lazarus scraps from his table
but little more (Lk 16:19-26). Proportionately, how much money
is being spent by our churches and our communities on modern
comforts in comparison with the help they are giving to poor
nations? How much goes for smoking, a rich table complete with
alcoholic drinks, and how much is effective help for the poor?
The answers to these questions become a source of anguish when
men of the Church appear too satisfied with the charitable stance
of the Church.

A recurring issue raised by the press during the Council ses-
sions was: Why does the Church, in so many of her structures,
hide her financial status? Every modern enterprise at least appears to be frank with the public on this score. Why does the
Church have a different attitude toward finances since Church
members and the world are not allowed to know what happens
with all the money and how much wealth Church institutions
really possess?

We cannot give a ready answer to all these questions, which
include both justified and unjustified criticisms. The matter is
complicated because during past ages, that of Constantine,
Charlemagne, Otto the Great, bishops and abbots were made
princes of this earth. Can we say truthfully that we have done
away with all those remnants of titles and styles of life? New
difficulties of a different nature have arisen in view of recent tremendous economic changes that have also altered the material
needs and means of the Church. All these problems are multi-
plied by the tension between the rich nations of old Christendom
and the newer nations now in development. It is a fact, however,
that the renewal going on in the wake of the Second Vatican
Council is bringing about a new, acute awareness in the Church,
a real examination of conscience that looks to Christ who characterized his mission in these words: "The spirit of the Lord is
upon me because he has anointed me; he has sent me to an-

nounce the good news to the poor" (Lk 4:18). The Church, as a whole, has the same typical mission, and religious have, on this point, their own special vocation. The future of religious orders taken together and of every order individually depends on the answer that is given to the question regarding an appropriate renewal in a spirit of poverty.

Corporate Witness to Poverty

"Depending on circumstances of their location, communities as such should aim at giving a kind of corporate witness to their own poverty. Let them willingly contribute something from their own resources to the other needs of the Church and to the support of the poor, whom religious should love with the tenderness of Christ. Provinces and houses of religious communities should share their resources with one another, those which are better supplied assisting those in need. To the extent that their rule and constitutions permit, religious communities can rightly possess whatever is necessary for their temporal life and their mission. Still, let them avoid every appearance of luxury, of excessive wealth, and accumulation" (PC, 13).

In these words the Second Vatican Council lays down one of the most important laws for renewal. The general principle that not only the individual but also communities as a whole are bound to give witness to poverty is a fundamental one as attested by the history of the religious life. An accumulation of wealth in religious houses or orders always marked the beginning of a decline in a truly religious life. The Council text, however, does not confine itself to generalities; it makes some very important applications and suggestions.

A legitimate distinction can be made between communities that can possess property and communities that want no ownership, but even these communities allow themselves the necessary use of things without owning them. Historically, the distinction often appeared to be different. It seemed that besides religious communities that were poor and wished to be poor, there were legitimately wealthy and rich communities that could possess more than was necessary for their temporal life and mission.

Many historical circumstances led to this situation, for instance, the old Germanic system of the *Eigenkirchen* or churches and monasteries erected by princes and belonging to them, which, because of their wealth, were reasons for boasting, a symbol of power, a social influence. All too literal, at times almost slavish respect for the will of deceased benefactors made the *beneficia* and endowments immobile, even under new circumstances when the property no longer served a religious goal. The religious communities became, at least in respect to a stable possession of property, a *brachium mortuum*, i.e., a dead arm that could receive more and more, but could not give anything away. As a result, the monasteries were the greatest landowners until the French Revolution and the Secularization (1806), and in some countries are still so even today. No doubt, a portion of these impressive holdings served many charitable and cultural purposes, but they also allowed the religious to live an all too easy life, especially in comparison with the really poor of the time; they constituted an even greater occasion for power and domination. Even in cases where the religious communities were generous in distributing the income of their possessions, they were regarded as rich in the eyes of the poor.

It is imperative that the religious life as a state of life bear witness to the eschatological reality of the Church, the witness of total freedom for the coming of the Lord and total service in humility. The spirit of poverty must be reflected in all the structures of the Church, and, above all, in the structures of religious communities. It is a sin against the mystery of the incarnation to expect the individual religious to maintain the spirit of poverty and bear witness to poverty within structures that betray a possessive instinct; how can we credibly be poor religious while living in rich communities? Renewal of spirit and reform of structures depend upon each other.

The decree on religious life refers to the extreme limits of legitimate possession in the words "religious communities can rightly possess whatever is necessary for their temporal life and their mission" (PC, 13). The Rules can even prescribe not possessing too much, but they cannot "rightly" allow possessing more. However, the answer to the question: "How much is necessary for the temporal life and the mission?" will depend on historical and social circumstances and on degrees of generosity.

One consequence seems to be clear: religious communities are obliged by the Council decree to liberate themselves from everything that is not necessary for the temporal life of those who have taken vows of poverty (necessity being measured with a view to the ideal of poverty and the poor in the environment where the religious find themselves) and for carrying out the specific religious mission of the institute.

Furthermore, it is important to realize that the Council not only forbids "luxury, excessive wealth, and accumulation of possessions," but also everything that would give the *appearance* of such a state of affairs. This is most fitting since religious life as a whole is to be lived in the perspective of a witness. Hence, simplicity in all external forms is an absolute necessity.

Poverty and Effectual Apostolate

It is certainly not easy to determine how much is necessary for "the mission" of a given community. On the one hand, the religious should courageously use everything that helps them carry out their religious mission. "All things are yours. You are Christ's." It can be against the spirit of religious poverty to impose on modern apostles time-wasting, old-fashioned methods of work or tools. Man and the real service of man are more important than things. At a time when the number of apostolic workers is insufficient, we are not allowed to waste unnecessarily the manpower we have by refusing more effective means of transportation and work. It seems to me to be against religious poverty for a community with its own scholasticate not to provide professors with the necessary library enabling them to keep up with the scientific discoveries of our time. Must a religious whose apostolate is the press have the worst kind of typewriter, thus diminishing his effectiveness by at least 20 per cent?

On the other hand, it must not be overlooked that the witness of poverty is one of the most fundamental aids to an effective apostolate. A practical case will illustrate the point: A community that is alive to the importance of modern methods in apostolic work could well provide other communities, for example, those in foreign missions, with the most necessary modern tools while at the same time using them only sparingly itself. This would surely not diminish the sincerity of their witness to poverty.

Another practical problem along the same line is the following: Must religious retain the ownership and administration of big hospitals or colleges in order to guarantee an effective apostolate? Or might the success of their apostolate, as well as the credibility of their witness, sometimes not be much greater if they would entrust the ownership or at least the administration to a corporation in which the laity would have a broad part? The response may depend upon many factors, but generally speaking, religious should not assume that they can be the most effective apostles by displaying their power or trusting too much to ownership. Possession of hospitals, high schools, and universities could be used as an argument for a privileged position in questions of administration.

All religious communities are bound to bear a corporate witness to poverty, but the limitations of property ownership, the use of earthly goods, and other forms of witness depend very much upon historical circumstances. On the one hand, our wealthy modern society makes it psychologically impossible to live the poor simple life of the desert monks in Egypt or even the life of religious in the seventeenth century. On the other hand, the modern world has developed new forms of ownership, sharing in wealth, and a much sharper conscience with respect to matters of social justice. What in the era of feudalism was considered normal would now provoke great scandal. In past eras it was sufficient to adapt the witness of poverty to the immediate environment in which the witness or the scandal took place. Today the world has come much closer together. We are visible to the poor nations of Africa and Asia; they watch us critically. Thanks to modern means of communication, we can give a visible witness to the whole world or scandalize entire continents.

The new circumstances impose a courageous revision of the system of the *beneficia* (especially in Europe), of begging alms on the part of mendicants and non-mendicants, especially if they are not really poor or do not really appear to be poor. A combination of older and newer forms of collecting material means can be particularly harmful to the witness, for instance, if those who keep revenues from endowments and collect alms do not accept any apostolic work without receiving a stipend or a salary. How much worse if those who beg, as mendicants, accept only the most profitable kind of commitment. Does work among the poor and for the poor have preference over other activities that pay well? Are we for the poor and among the poor chiefly in those places where the state gives grants or where public funds are available? This does not mean that we always have to refuse public grants in connection with our activities; this has to be judged on a case-to-case basis. The question remains: what here and now helps or harms our corporate witness?

New times call for new forms of the apostolate. Sometimes religious are not vigilant or favorably disposed to changes because of money invested in older apostolic enterprises. This is where religious can become slaves to their properties. The witness of poverty means the freedom of the sons and daughters of God in response to the real and actual needs of the apostolate and without concern for possessions where they no longer really serve.

Solidarity in Corporate Witness

The conciliar decree on religious life states clearly and in very positive terms that corporate witness cannot permit any kind of collective egotism. Religious must not let themselves be served by the Church out of self-centeredness; they are totally directed toward the service of the whole Church. They are not hired servants of the Church but spend their lives for the Church. This point warrants reflection in relation to the material needs of the Church and the poor. Therefore the decree admonishes communities to "contribute willingly from their own resources to the other needs of the Church and the support of the poor." No religious community should keep any superfluous possessions as long as there are other needs in the Church. The communities are not only asked to collect funds for the other needs of the Church, but also to give from their own resources. A spontaneous exchange must not only show solidarity between two houses of a province but also solidarity between provinces and even outside the institute.

The generous collaboration of different communities, for instance, in the field of the formation of members can also be a corporate witness to poverty. Those who are well equipped could offer their facilities to other communities. Others could merge their modest forces and thus obtain better results for the good of the Church with less expense. Why cannot the religious in many countries set aside many excellent members for countries that are less well provided with apostolic workers, if they exhaust all the possibilities for collaboration, for example, by having common faculties of theology and philosophy for their scholasticates?

It is true that poor people in many countries cannot properly take care of their sick and handicapped. From this, does it not follow that religious communities should do their very best for their own sick members, especially if sickness impairs the effectiveness of the personality? Could not religious communities offer a very effective corporate witness to poverty by erecting houses

for the proper treatment of alcoholics or other frustrated members of the Church? They could do it, of course, only by mutually
joining forces and efforts. They could even take care of diocesan
priests; a guest house in the archdiocese of Detroit has proved
the value of such an enterprise.

Personal Responsibility in Poverty

Renewal of the spirit of poverty demands a constant effort on the
part of the whole community and above all a wise cooperation
between legislators, superiors, and subjects. New stringent Rules
without a proper spiritual preparation for the members of the
community would be deleterious. On the other hand, it would
be unrealistic to leave everything to the spontaneity of the members. Renewal of the spirit, promoted by superiors and all members, and reform of structures must go hand in hand.

"Let religious painstakingly cultivate such poverty, and give
it new expressions if need be" (PC, 13). It is the will of the
supreme legislator that all members of communities participate
in and contribute to the new formulation of their Rules and constitutions. Toward this end, a common interest in the work of
renewal must be aroused, but before subjects are asked to express their desires, it should be assured in all possible ways (e.g.,
through retreats, study weeks, circular letters) that everybody
understands the spirit and goal of *renewal*. All too many are still
thinking only about adaptation to the style of life of today. If
there is not a very conscientious and lively concern for renewal
of the spirit, the adaptation will easily lead to a dangerous conformity with "this world" which means a worldly way of thinking.

All members should be enlightened as to the mutual relationship between renewal of spirit and reform of structures (juridical
norms and administration) and the difference between the two.
On the one hand, there is sometimes evident an unrealistic
"spiritualism," and on the other still a "legalism" that would try
to achieve everything chiefly by legal means. Consulting all the

members not only results in excellent ideas; it also prepares them for cooperation in implementing the new Rules. It gives expression to the great importance of "public opinion" in modern times, and fosters Christian solidarity, a spirit of dialogue.

Rules and Superiors

Rules and superiors have a double role to perform: they must arouse and encourage an evangelical spirit, serving the need for spiritual guidelines; they must also serve to "incarnate" the spirit of some (not too many) juridical structures and precepts. Between the two there should be a clearly visible bond; everyone should know what spiritual values are at stake and the need to protect them by some specific Rules.

Legislation must not only bear in mind the ideal, but also allow for present situations. An ideal Rule that might not be acceptable to the majority of the members might be less satisfactory than a less ideal Rule that would be followed willingly by all or almost all the members. The reform of structures must proceed gradually along with a growth in spirit. Our whole lives, reforms as well as spiritual renewal, are subject to the "law of growth"; we must proceed step by step.

There should be consultation not only for a general chapter, but also between provinces and individual houses. The local superior, especially, should try to get the whole community to take part by making practical suggestions and getting their agreement to the next step in the practical implementation of a spirit of poverty and corporate witness.

Renunciation of Inheritance

The decree on religious life proposes a new idea which, practically speaking, would abolish the difference between the simple and solemn vows of poverty; "In their constitutions, religious communities can allow their members to renounce any inheritance which they may have acquired or are due to acquire" (PC, 13). The instruction of the post-conciliar commission wisely says that this renunciation *may* be made compulsory. I think that it would be better not to make this obligatory for older members of the community, but only for those to be professed (on the occasion of their perpetual vows). They could renounce in favor of poor relatives, other definite poor persons, the missions, established charitable projects, or the community to which they belong. In the latter case, it would be prudent to return everything to those who later leave after receiving a dispensation from their vows. The constitutions may provide, at the same time, that the community should give away immediately (to the foreign missions or the poor) those inheritances which subjects bring with them and that the community itself does not need for its own mission. It is evident that in this case, any subject later asking for a dispensation could not expect to have returned to him whatever inheritance he might have possessed before taking his vows.

In view of the greater generosity expected of young religious with respect to a renunciation of inheritance, the same generosity should be practiced by congregations relative to professed members receiving dispensations from their vows. They cannot be satisfied to release a sister or a confrère with a bare minimum of clothing and a hundred dollars. Charity dictates providing adequately for the religious disassociating themselves from a congregation, such as help with job placement and adequate housing, helping them when possible to establish a credit rating. All this points to the necessity of providing letters of reference for employment, necessary transcripts of professional standing and continued advancement, and other helpful services depending on individual cases. In some cases, women's congregations have been remiss in this area to the point of callousness. For moral bodies like religious congregations to violate so flagrantly the law of justice and charity is nothing less than scandalous.

Human Dependence

It has sometimes been thought and even explicitly asserted that *the* very essence of religious poverty is dependence upon the will of the superior in the use of earthly goods, even to the extent that the substance is saved if a religious lives a comfortable life, but with the consent of the superior. The decree on religious life meets this problem head-on. "Religious poverty requires more than limiting the use of possessions to the consent of the superiors" (PC, 13). Often superiors are choosing a lesser evil if they allow what is not totally in conformity with religious poverty because the subject would not obey greater demands or would become bitter or excessively critical. The Council appeals to the personal sense of responsibility of the members of a community. Before asking permission of the superior, he must ascertain that he is fulfilling God's will by asking it. In other words, no one may ask for anything which does not correspond to the spirit of poverty. In case of serious doubt on this point, the religious should at least express his own doubts to the superior when asking the permission.

Undoubtedly, humble dependence upon superiors belongs to the essence of the vow of poverty, but this is not the whole essence. If the poverty of the members does not go beyond what the Rules and superiors impose on everybody, the witness of poverty will be very weak. It is part of the evangelical counsel always to try to do more than what is imposed by common rule and precept.

The members should not be expected to ask for those permissions that belong to the daily use of necessary things; this becomes mere formalism. Wasting time asking permissions for daily necessities is contrary to today's social conscience and the good use of time. The mature religious person should only be obliged to clear extraordinary or unusual permissions with the superior.

The principle of subsidiarity should be applied to the administration of material things. Those holding an office should be provided with the necessary permissions and faculties; however, extraordinary expenses should be accounted for. The evangelical counsels rightly understood do not hinder but should promote a growth toward full maturity and responsibility.

Common Law of Labor

"In discharging his duty, each religious should regard himself as subject to the common law of labor" (PC, 13). Most religious men and women of today are hard-working people and the good use of time belongs very much to the spirit of poverty. If the community provides the necessary things, this should not lessen but rather strengthen the energies of the religious to carry out his special vocation in prayer, in constant eagerness to deepen his formation and fulfill his task better.

As we religious are subject to the common law of labor, we should also study the common conditions of labor in our time. We should study its hardships, its progress in social and psychological terms. Above all, we should bear valuable witness to the spirituality of labor as expressed in the pastoral Constitution on the Church (GS, 34, 35, 67).

Religious must "make their necessary provisions for their livelihood and undertakings" (PC, 13). Their finances must be kept in good order. Why could not a good part of the necessary care of our finances be entrusted to laymen who are more competent than we, and who at the same time have a great awareness of the prime importance of our religious task and witness?

Labor conditions today mean that man lives not from a savings account but from his daily work. If we work for the altar, we are also allowed to live from the altar. Therefore a religious should not be ashamed to receive a stipend or salary, thus contributing to the common life, but he should be particularly happy if entrusted with a task for which he is not remunerated. There should

be no distinction at all between religious who "earn" and those
who do not.

Marxism holds that the economic conditions of the time are
the decisive "infrastructure" of life. Therefore Marxists view the
whole of human life from this one point of view. It belongs to
the essential witness of the religious in our time to acknowledge the relative value of money and economic structure, and at
the same time show how to subordinate these things to spiritual
values. Everybody, especially superiors and administrators, should
take care that no "undue concern" for earthly goods hides or
endangers the supernatural motivation of their work. There
should not be too much talk or writing about finances, no more
than is necessary, so that the whole mode of living manifests a
trust in divine providence and proper concern for spiritual riches.

Asceticism in Poverty

The Constitution on the Church in the Modern World contains a
forceful paragraph about the spirit of poverty as an absolutely
necessary condition for a courageous confrontation with the
world, for a magnanimous open-mindedness toward the world
(GS, 69). What does poverty mean in this connection? Not
misery; not a disregard for what God gives us each day, but a
firm detachment from a proud possessive attitude, from an unredeemed urge for acquisition and the desire to be important. Even
when we have but little, we are attached to it; we often go into
the world in order to acquire something for ourselves. We accept
certain apostolic endeavors because they will pay off in the form
of money or prestige or something else. That certainly is not the
spirit of poverty. The spirit of the first beatitude consists in being poor in the sight of God, realizing that everything comes
from God. We own nothing except our sins. Beggars, we must
ask God for everything. We must not aim at owning things for
self-aggrandizement but accept everything gratefully, consider-

ing: "How can I transform the gifts of God's love into ways of love, into expressions of love?"

Religious orders of today must courageously use modern means and should not cling to anything merely for the sake of keeping it. We can use new means only if at the same time we have the courage to give up the old whenever it has become useless for our witness. I admire the Polish episcopacy which never fought for ancient properties, forests, or estates. The bishops surrendered these with a light heart in order to fight with all the more courage for Catholic truth and morality. It was a great tragedy, before the French Revolution and afterwards, that the French episcopacy put up such a big struggle for earthly possessions and privileges. In Germany, also, we had many tragic experiences, possessed many things which like leaden weights made the bearers unable to engage in the real contest.

May I mention that it is an old-fashioned idea to accumulate dowries? This custom fitted into an entirely different social order when it was necessary to have certain benefices, certain monetary assets or income. Today, man lives by his work. Should our money be buried in alien enterprises when the missions so desperately need it? If a congregation has money, it should invest it where it is most needed for the advancement of the Church, in the missions, in the works of charity.

We may use modern means if we do not allow ourselves to become attached to them, if we remain humbly able to detach ourselves. In this connection, too, I believe it is necessary to consider how institutions, congregations, orders can practice poverty not only individually but also in community. Our houses may be beautiful and healthful, but at the same time they ought to be modest. Therefore, why accumulate what we do not need, what only serves as security for the future?

Even on the part of communities, there must be willingness to give. It is a personal sacrifice for religious not to be able to give something to a beggar; this is supposed to be the concern of superiors. Until now that is how the Rules were written. Yet when

I see a person in great need, the vow of poverty cannot keep me from doing good. Naturally one must know the limits; one cannot encourage imprudence. Nevertheless, there must always be a certain measure of readiness to help whenever a community is not poor.

An institute must never be a dead hand, one that can only receive but is dead when it comes to giving. There are those who accept donations and inheritances without ever having the courage to say: "We have enough." Many workers want to build a home; why not give them land for building at the price we paid twenty years ago or help the laborer's family by selling it at a cheaper price than we paid?

Truly, it is not the material fact of poverty that is at stake but the willingness to own nothing, the readiness to dispose of everything because we are no longer self-centered, the ability to detach ourselves. There are times when God is forced to send us the scourges of war or communism. Then we can say, "Thanks be to God! We lost everything and now we can travel more lightly."

ELEVEN | THE EUCHARISTIC EXPERIENCE OF COMMUNITY

[The religious] should enact the sacred liturgy, especially the most holy mystery of the Eucharist, with hearts and voices attuned to the Church. . . . Fed thus at the table of the divine law and of the sacred altar they can bring a brother's love to the members of Christ. (PC, 6)

————◦◦◦————

The farewell discourses of the Gospel of St. John synthesize the whole of Christian life as a summons: "This is my love: love one another as I have loved you" (Jn 13:34-35). This call is ideally expressed in the experience of the Eucharist, the community experience par excellence. Here we once more hear the echo of the Sermon on the Mount being delivered by the Word himself as he teaches his disciples gathered closely around him.

Humble Service

At the Last Supper the disciples once again sat around the Lord at the table where he, as father of the family, washed their feet. This was the Divine Teacher's way of further instructing them, correcting them, disciplining them, and keeping down the "old man" in them. "You call me Master and Lord, and rightly so, for that is what I am. Then if I, your Lord and Master, have washed your feet, you also ought to wash one another's feet. I have set you an example: you are to do as I have done for you" (Jn 13: 13-16). Accessibility to the Eucharist is conditioned by this prior experience of washing one another's feet.

A community of true disciples of Christ can never be built up if the superior does not genuinely seek humble service, if he does not expect sometimes to be humbled by the greater experience or greater wisdom of some of his fellow religious, if he does not dare acknowledge humbly that he has made mistakes: "This did not work out too well; let us try to do better." It is at the Eucharistic table that we learn to wash each other's feet and to appreciate true fellowship in Christ. We must perform the most humble services and do so genuinely, not merely symbolically. It was not a mere symbol at the time of Our Lord; the slave girl *really* washed the dusty feet of the man who came in from the dirt road. The superior, as well as everyone else, has to share with others this experience learned from the Lord. Love is wanting if we do not seek to perform the most needed, the most humble services for the brethren. Humility is the first step toward the altar. "I confess to Almighty God and to you, brethren." This is the first lesson of the Eucharist, and the experience must be part of our community life.

Humble Avowal

We must pay more attention to the chapter of faults. If we want to do away with phoniness and rid our lives of artifacts, it is high time that we stopped confessing throughout our whole lives that we have only broken a glass or interrupted silence for a few minutes. We must review our lives and face together the shortcomings of our community life, face our imprudence, our rushing into activities, or our reluctance to change. Let us encourage each other by a mutual and humble confession of our frailties.

Last year I ran into an unexpected experience, one to which I would have objected had I been asked beforehand. As our modest contribution that year, the professors of the *Academia*

Alfonsiana offered a four-week course to the clergy, religious, and laity of Mexico City. About six hundred attended the whole course which ended with a concelebration of the Eucharist. I was a concelebrant and was a little surprised, therefore, when at the beginning of Mass, the monsignor, who was Director of the Pastoral Center, informed us that we would introduce this Eucharistic sacrifice with a penitential rite; the concelebrants would confess the sins of their pastoral life, their conduct toward people. He began with such striking evidence of humility, and the other concelebrants who followed likewise evidenced such real depth of humility in the avowal of their misdeeds, impatience, domineering or routine attitudes in their pastoral life or in their attitudes toward the brethren, that all the other participants were inspired to make a serious examination of conscience. Such an experience may be disturbing to one's peace of mind at first, but he will be encouraged to do the same when he sees how everyone is expressing his own shortcomings sincerely and humbly. This is the first step toward the altar; it is also the first step, the decisive step into the new era. The old era means pride: Adam and Eve accused each other in a monologue. "This wife thou hast given me, she has seduced me!" Adam should have confessed, "I have been seeking my own self-fulfillment as well as she. I, too, am guilty."

Let us learn from the Eucharistic sacrifice to take this essential step of acknowledging our faults to each other. The Eucharist teaches us to pay the price of discipleship. Aware of this, we are always celebrating the glory of the Lord. It is good for us to remember the price paid by our Master which he expects us to pay also; the self-denial of the redeemed personalist must go beyond the painless mortification of eating fish on Lenten Fridays. Real mortification puts to death selfishness, pride, closed minds, impatience; even mortification, however, can become meaningless if it is not undertaken with a view to the real needs of our brothers, our sisters, or the community as a whole.

Community of Faith

The Eucharist is the mystery of faith which builds up a community of faith. Its celebration is not an event circumscribed by itself; it is the proclamation and humble, joyous acceptance of that faith which should transform the whole world. Through it we become ever more luminous in the Lord in order to let our light shine before men, who will then praise the Father in heaven. Only if we become hidden in the Lord, if we are paying the cost of discipleship, if we no longer seek our own light or our own glory, only then can we let the light of Christ shine; only then will men praise the Father in heaven.

The Church is a community of faith. As we listen to the Word of God, we are not only listening to an account in a book written centuries ago but we hear Christ himself proclaiming the Gospel. All the words in the book derive their meaning from the essential message which is today no longer pronounced in Latin but intelligibly proclaimed as: "This is my body, sacrificed for you. This is my blood shed for you." The words of the Gospel, the words of the homily receive their meaning from the essential message: "I died for you. I live for you." Acceptance of this most fundamental message, pregnant with salvation, is an awesome experience. Woe to us if we accept it as a "normal" thing. The Lord, the only-begotten Son, the perfect man has shed his blood for us. If we truly believe this, we are beside ourselves and shudder as we ask: "Did we, in our struggle against the sin of self-centeredness, resist to the point of shedding blood?" (Hebr 12:4). Do we respond with the same faith which is fitting for this message of faith: "I died for you. I live for you"? We will not dare to profane the blood of the covenant by which he was consecrated (Hebr 10:29).

In faith it is essential that we listen not only to words but rather to the One who is the Word, the messenger, the person who is the loving presence of God. We are looking to him and this is what gives meaning to all words. We are aware of his presence, but this lesson must be learned in the Eucharist. We will then not only listen to the words and thoughts of our sisters or brothers; we will listen to *them as persons*. How do we listen to a person? We look into the other's eyes, into the other's mind and heart with deep sympathy. We really empathize with our fellow religious; we feel that this person is suffering, that he is appealing to us as a person.

Humble Self-surrender

Faith brings one face-to-face with a living Person and demands the surrender of oneself as a person to this Person. If we celebrate the Eucharist as the great mystery of faith where God makes visible the full extent of his love and where we surrender ourselves to him in this message of faith, we will learn to look at the real needs of our communities and look, in the right way, at our individual gifts with relevance to the community. The community likewise should not be considered only as an institution in the abstract but rather as this *Us*, composed of you and me as persons. It is this perception of community that leads one to see others in their uniqueness.

If you read the farewell discourses you will understand this personalized way of talking. Christ is talking about the Eucharist, about the Paschal Mystery. He is seated at the table and is listening to Philip, Thomas, Peter. Everyone receives a reply from the Master. To Philip who has so naïvely asked, "Show us the Father; we don't know the way," Our Lord, astonished, replies: "Philip, have I been all this time with you and you still do not realize that I am the Way? Anyone who sees me sees the Father." Philip understood. "Now he speaks plainly; now we understand." There is kindness and goodness in Christ's reply as well as firmness and frankness with Peter who so boastfully tells the Lord, "If all these people here betray you, I will not. I am the rock. I am the appointed superior. I know it." The Lord is straightforward but good to him. He tells him, "If you will be converted, then you can give strength to your brethren." Does not the Eucharistic Christ sometimes tell sister superior, "If you will grow to greater humility, if you will be converted, not looking down on other people but rather looking to me and to others, finding others in me; if you arrive at full humility, you will give strength to your sisters"?

Openness to Joy

The Eucharist is the celebration of the mystery of faith and joy. Is not the daily celebration of the Eucharist a joyous experience? The joy of each one sustains the joy of the others! Our joy and gratitude for the message of joy increase as we join together in one hymn of praise. Let us take great care to make the Eucharist always a joyous hour. The humble sisters should discuss the situation with their chaplain if he rushes through the Mass in fourteen minutes as I once saw it happen. Why should they not be courageous enough to say to him, "We are not impatient people; we are not so hard pressed for time. We always have time for the Eucharist. Do not rush so to please us; we want time to listen to Christ's Word." A joyous celebration depends on the active participation of all; our openness, responses, and song constitute our offering to the one who is the Word, the Incarnate Word. Sing joyfully to the Lord because faith is the source of joy. Where there is neither joy nor an expression of joy that promotes even greater joy, faith is weak and love will be weaker.

At the Eucharistic table in the Cenacle, the Lord introduced his great command to love with these words, "This I tell you, that my joy may be in you and your joy complete. This then is my command, love one another as I have loved you" (Jn 15:11-13). We can celebrate the Eucharist joyously if we have prepared ourselves by bringing joy to our brothers and sisters, by being attentive to opportunities likely to foster joy—joy in the Lord, fully human and Christian joy. We keep ourselves open to the joy of discipleship by paying the necessary price of self-denial.

Where our attitude is one of emotional insulation, lack of openness to others, we do not facilitate the development of joy. Then we should learn from the Eucharist to promote a joyous approach to life, and this not only in spite of, but even by means of difficulties, for Christ paved the way for joy by suffering. We must have confidence in his ways.

Community of Hope

As genuine Christians, both superiors and brothers or sisters must show unflinching trust in the Lord. We can anticipate confusion and turmoil in a period of transition, but if we trust in the Lord, if we accept difficulties by offering them on the altar, they will be a source of hope and joy. This we learn from the great mystery of faith; it is knowledge imparted at the table of the Lord. There we find a community of hope but not that hope of sisters or brothers who still wish to return to the stagnant era when no changes were imposed on them. Nor is it the hope of those pining for the hour when they will go undisturbed with their "sweet Jesus" of the *Imitation of Christ* where it is said, "I was never less a man than after having been together with other people."

The Eucharist tells us what St. Paul wrote in his Epistle to the Ephesians: "There is one hope held out in God's call to you" (Eph 4:4). Our hope will be firm when we realize that it is the rallying call of Christ which assures us that all is going well and that our community will bear rich fruit to the extent that we accept and honor his solidarity. He did not come to please himself. Neither does he leave us with the anguished question: "How do I find a God merciful for me? How do I save my soul?" If we embrace the mystery of hope, we realize that he died for all and therefore nobody is allowed to live for himself. Hope lies in solidarity.

Power of Solidarity

Modern psychology and sociology emphasize the tremendous power of the environment on human development and behavior. Our surroundings exert a striking, molding influence on our behavior. A spiteful or impatient environment where there is an atmosphere of competition or contentiousness will affect us considerably. How can we be liberated from these "hidden persuaders"? How can we escape from this shaping power of our culture? Many seek the answer in a selfish way, in an individualistic philosophy of self-actualization. There is so much restlessness, so much superficiality in the tense business of self-fulfillment! But it is never possible to find liberation, freedom from domination, as isolated individuals.

The Eucharist shows us that Christ transformed the shaping force of history by his solidarity. He took upon himself the burden of the whole world. By the power of solidarity in Christ, we can reshape whatever is formalistic, legalistic, superficial, and selfish in our lives. What is a burden and a handicap can be reshaped to the extent that our solidarity implies cooperation rather than a distinct separation into opposing factions. In every one of our fellow religious, even in the most old-fashioned and conservative, we can find something that is precious—a deep desire for continuity, even though he may not appear to be concerned about continuity. There is some promise even in the most impatient, restless people. They are seeking life, true life, though they may not realize that it lies in continuity. Every one of us is old-fashioned and stubborn in at least one respect. In other respects we may be quite open. Let us help each other with our differences, never allowing the community to be split into sheep and goats.

In solidarity and hope we are gathered around the altar, around Christ in his solidarity. Therefore every celebration reveals to us his attitude which is expressed at the beginning of the Constitution on the Church in the Modern World: "The joys and the hopes, the sorrows and worries of men of our time are ours." Indeed, the joys can be ours only if the sorrows are ours also. We can rejoice with our brother and sister only if we can weep with him or her. Hope lies in patience, in gentleness; "How blessed are those of a gentle spirit! They will possess the earth" (Mt 5:5). In your patience, you will possess yourself. This we learn in this era of change. It is true that many changes are long overdue; they should have happened years ago, and now many are impatiently urging changes. Secession, however, cannot be the solution. The solution can only be patience—patience as realized in the collected energies of Christ on the Mount of the Beatitudes, on the Mount of Olives, on Calvary, and in the collected energies of John who outruns Peter and waits for him. Some religious wonder: "What will John do if Peter never catches up?" The solution is quite clear: "Love hopes everything." Just have enough love and you will have enough hope that he will catch up; but if you tell him that he is one of those crazy people who are always turning backward, he may adopt the attitude of the goat and operate only with horns because you treat him like a goat, i.e., with distrust. Let us trust each other, and let us trust in the power of the Spirit.

Community of Love

The Eucharist is a community of love and adoration. We can praise God only in our oneness. This does not mean, however, that we have no time for praise in the form of songs and hymns. Before extolling love in marriage, that is, before exhorting the husband to love his wife as Christ loves the Church, St. Paul appeals to the whole family of God to sing hymns and songs constantly, to praise the Lord always (Eph 5:18-33). The more we learn to praise God, the more we are aware that our whole life is to be this shining light that incites people to praise the Father in heaven, the more readily we will find that our oneness, our loving kindness, our patience, our love and our hoping constitute the praise that God desires. Paul urges Christians to "offer continually to God through Jesus Christ a sacrifice of praise, that is, a tribute of lips acknowledging his name, and never forget to show kindness and to share what you have with others; for such are the sacrifices which God approves" (Hebr 13:16). God approves our kindness and generosity in sharing everything with others; this is contingent, however, on sacrifice.

In order to assure this charity, Paul admonishes us to offer to God the tribute of our lips as something more than mere "lip service." It must be done by acknowledging his name. His name here refers to his countenance, his face turned toward us. His name is Father, Savior, Redeemer. We give such tribute obviously only if we say *"Our* Father." If we have in mind in our prayers our confrères and all suffering people, and if we include in our praise not only ourselves but also all who rejoice in the Lord, we are praising God worthily. Only if we train our voices to sing (apart from formal training), and only if we are willing to bear the cost of discipleship in oneness, can we worthily praise God in our life.

Cost of Discipleship

St. Paul says with reference to racing and boxing: "I am like a boxer who does not beat the air; I bruise my body and make it know its master, for fear that after preaching to others I should find myself rejected" (I Cor 9:26-27). In this passage Paul also employs a word which was only used by boxers, meaning "knock-out." One must be watchful and hit quickly where we find our weak point. In our asceticism we have often engaged in "exercises" marginal to life. There were Rules, and we could fulfill them all without ever hitting home. We must be vigilant if we are to understand clearly where we need humiliation, where we need a sacrifice in order to remain free, where renunciation should be practiced in order to be free for prayer, free and watchful for the needs of our neighbors.

Everyone must make a serious examination of conscience but with the eyes of love and under the eyes of the Lord. We so often find the wrong solution to our problems because we are treating them only with an abstract principle in mind, only in the light of a certain Rule instead of facing the living Lord. Keep in mind that Christ died for you and rose for you. If you are burdened with the problems of the day, the problems of the community, problems with a sister or a confrère, remember that Christ died for you. Then we are facing him and asking: "Lord, can I offer this solution, this desire to you in gratitude for what you have done for me?" This is the meaning of bearing the cost of discipleship.

It is easy at times to conform to some abstract Rule while forgetting about the more urgent rules, the precepts of the Gospel. If we face him searchingly, however, we learn to discern spirits; we learn to know the criteria of true love. This is not learned abstractly, but, rather, knowledge is acquired by facing him in prayer and life where he shows us what can and must be sacrificed in order to build up this adoring community, which with one mind and voice will praise God the Father of Our Lord Jesus Christ.

In the Holy Spirit

The Eucharist makes us truly a "fellowship in the Holy Spirit" (II Cor 13:14). Christ the High Priest is not a man of routine; he is not a functionary. He does not even belong to the tribe of Levi, of Aaron. His whole priesthood lies in being anointed by the Spirit in order that he might sacrifice himself. "Sacrifice and offering thou didst not desire, but thou hast prepared a body for me. . . . Then I said, 'Here am I . . . I have come, O God, to do thy will'" (Hebr 10:5-7). Only because the fullness of the Holy Spirit has come upon him can he extend his hands to all and offer his life: "Father, into thy hands I commend my spirit" (Lk

23:46). We must pray to the Holy Spirit for all the things we expect from him, above all, for genuine fraternal love.

When our Lord promised to institute the Eucharist, many were scandalized. Many even left him. His final words, his final response was simply: "The Spirit alone gives life. The flesh is of no avail. The words which I have spoken to you are both spirit and life" (Jn 6:63). Only if we trust in the Spirit, if we implore his help, if we ask him over and over again to make us docile, if we learn this docility to the Spirit in docility to our confrères and to our superiors, only then will the Holy Spirit open our eyes of faith by opening our hearts to the Word of the Lord in the Eucharist: "I died for you." The Spirit leads us thus to the life-giving Word.

Prayerful Support

Religious must also sustain each other in their efforts. In the future there may be less control over prayer life. However, we can renounce controls over prayer life only if each individual religious sustains the others by his prayer, that is, by the witness he gives to the prime importance of praying and listening to the Word of God. Before the Lord gathered his disciples around him in the Cenacle prior to the Paschal Mystery, he entered the temple to throw out the distracters, the men of business. He then said, "My house is a house of prayer" (Lk 19:46).

The Eucharist reminds us day by day that the whole Church must be a "house of prayer," and especially those who are called to be eminent witnesses. On several occasions I have suggested that larger communities, realizing that their members may become exhausted by too many activities, should open a house of prayer. If a sister, having come to the realization that she is exhausted and empty, asks for a year to return to a house where the one and only concern is to listen to the Lord, to study spiritual theology, and to ponder over the Word of God, she will come out filled with the joy of the Lord and will do more in one year than an "empty" sister can do in ten. This idea of a "house of prayer" will be further elaborated in the following chapter.

When questioned as to "how much prayer?" my response is, invariably: "Fewer prayers but more prayer!" Some communities have too many prayers, "duties of prayer." I suspect that some sisters face the same trying experience I had when I entered the novitiate. Without proper preparation, we had to say the whole office. I was so glad every day when it was over! I could once more begin to pray. I was only tired and "glad to have it over with" at the completion of the office. For the very busy religious, perhaps it would be better if they could just put their troubled hearts at rest and be seated for a half hour before the tabernacle instead of rushing through the office. There would thus be more time for prayer as listening to the Lord, pondering over his words, and expressing one's deepest being to him.

Let us not forget the new change: the half hour during the Mass which was formerly a time for individual private prayer has now become once more the common worship. The change is in the right direction, but time must now be found for another half hour of private prayer. Only if we have enough time for personal prayer in which, however, we meet our brothers and sisters before God, can we express ourselves to him and listen to him. Only thus can we sustain the common worship in the Eucharist, the spirit of faith and prayer in daily community life.

Community Prayer

In our common prayers we should also cultivate more spontaneity. Because of the all too accurate and meticulous nature of the rubrics, the celebration of the liturgy was anything but a joy for many priests. They were not able to relate their experience to real life and to express their lives. They were only worried about the rubrics; they were fearful that in spite of good will, they would transgress some Rule. So for many the Eucharist became a source of separation between religion and life. We have taken a great step forward, but other steps have still to be taken before our Eucharist will become part of our minds and hearts, part of the life of our community. Our lives must become filled with the warmth, light, and joy of a Eucharistic experience that is meaningful.

The problem of community prayers must be studied from various angles. May I offer a few suggestions? Leave open at least some days of the week for the younger sisters to prepare some of the prayers for dinner or lunch. This may be a song or a personal prayer. Begin your meetings with a spontaneous prayer; then there will be more creativity in the whole community life. If you have adopted the office, why not leave open at least some days and allow a group of sisters or brothers to use the Gelineau psalms, Somerville psalms, or something similar at Lauds or Vespers? Let fewer psalms be sung, psalms which express your heart and mind in joyous praise. The book on prayers by Michel Quoist may be helpful for other forms of prayer. I am not sure whether you can learn from *Are You Running With Me, Jesus?* but it may be helpful to some religious. At times it may have a wrong slant, but at least it is a great attempt to bring life to prayer and to make life prayer.

Day by day, let us bring our whole life to the Eucharist, but then let us also bring the Eucharist to life. This means that our whole life must be permeated by a spirit of prayer, faith, hope, and love.

TWELVE | CONTEMPORARY ISSUES

A life consecrated by a profession of the counsels is of surpassing value. . . . That this kind of life and its contemporary role may achieve greater good for the Church, this sacred Synod issues the following . . . general principles which must underlie an appropriate renewal of the life and rules of religious communities. (PC, 1)

The redefinition and renewal of religious life ordered by the decrees of the Second Vatican Council present new challenges and new opportunities for religious men and women today. The full impact of the Council cannot be assessed as yet; our nearsightedness accounts for much of the groping and grappling with the immediate problems of "rethinking" our role in the Church. Religious congregations all over the world are calling special and general chapters for the revision of Rules aimed at a more joyful personal and communal life in the light of the Gospel.

Since the conciliar decrees have laid down the guidelines for renewal and adaptation, I shall be content to suggest here only a few critical areas that call for serious consideration on the part of individuals and groups. I will limit myself to renewal in prayer, motivation to responsibility, primacy of conscience, priorities in the apostolate, and feminine spirituality.

I. RENEWAL IN PRAYER

Renewal in prayer is always a matter of the individual person and the community. Prayer must express life, therefore the style must be appropriate for our times. We should make allowance for more singing, more spontaneous prayer. Encourage some experimentation in the community; not everything has to be ruled upon once and for all. A minimum of time for prayer is guaranteed, but more time should be spent on prayer.

Reform is needed on the community level. The norms for the implementation of the decree on religious life recommend a renewal of mental prayer: "In order that religious may more intimately and fruitfully participate in the most holy mystery of the Eucharist and public prayer of the Church, and that their whole spiritual life may be nourished more abundantly, a larger place should be given to mental prayer instead of a multitude of prayers, retaining nevertheless the pious exercises commonly accepted in the Church and giving due care that the members are instructed diligently in leading a spiritual life" (ES, 21). All other prayers must be dignified, expressing what is in the mind and heart.

Allow me to state my position on an issue that is now on the agenda of many general chapters and that is one of the greatest hopes for an authentic understanding of Church renewal. I am referring to houses of prayer.

Prayer House

Almost every week I receive letters from religious who are intensely interested in the idea of a contemplative house in the midst of our active religious communities. Many priests, religious, and laymen support this idea by their thoughts and prayers. My reasons for endorsing such a project are many.

"My house shall be a house of prayer" (Lk 19:46). In our dy-

namic society where man organizes and manages almost everything, one aspect of humanity is greatly endangered: man in his
dignity before God, man in his receptivity and humble dependence on God's graciousness. The feverish pace of technical development, the quasi-religious belief in economic progress and
organization, threaten man's capacity to listen to the Word of
God, to treasure it in his heart, pondering over it. All mankind
needs to study the problem of prayer with a view to helping
modern man relearn what it means to pray. To achieve this goal,
it is not enough for some people to retire completely from active
life to the cloisters, giving up their contact with the "world." The
value and function of stable contemplative vocations must not be
overlooked, but an old-styled cloister must not be considered
the only way of restoring contemplative life or of witnessing to
the prime importance of prayer.

The era of the Second Vatican Council is marked by change.
In certain sectors of the Church, deliberate or unconscious re-
sistance to the approach of Pope John and the Council, even by
men and women in authority, is provoking an increasing impatience and restlessness. Changes are sometimes made in a spirit
of counterreaction against reactionary attitudes. All of this unrest
and ferment must be countered by a more contemplative and
tranquil approach to renewal. Only if we have brothers and
sisters *among us* who can treasure in their hearts the Gospel and
the salvific events of our time, revealing our needs to God in
prayer, can we begin to find that peace that bears fruit a hundredfold because the changes have been wise.

In our time, specialization and differentiation in society and
in the Church have reached a new stage of development, and
legitimately so. Our active religious communities have developed
a new style of effective and well-planned activity because of excellent professional training, and the like. For the integrity of
the person and the community, we must now stress the aspect
of synthesis or *integration*. It is not sufficient to have in addition
to active congregations a number of contemplative orders. There

is not enough exchange and sharing between these two different kinds of religious life, and communities tend to maintain the dichotomy. At least some of the contemplative communities could and should be deepened in their spirituality and broadened in their horizons. They could then serve as schools of prayer for others who are engaged for the greater part of their life in apostolic or professional activity. For the present it seems to me that, generally speaking, the more expedient solution would be, not a kind of federation between contemplative order or cloister and an active community—although this might work out well in some instances—but the opening of a house of prayer as an essential and integrating part of the active community.

A house of prayer in the midst of an active community would foster a different concept and style of prayer than a cloister composed of people who do not wish to return to apostolic work. Those who come from an active life and wish to prepare themselves for even more activity need a style of prayer and contemplation that manifests and fosters in a special way the integration of religion and life, of prayer and activity. A house of prayer should concern itself with the problem of how modern man can truly express himself in prayer so that genuine prayer will contribute to the shaping of life.

Just as there is a need for integration in every community, especially in the highly efficient active community, so there is also need for integration in the life of the individual person. We have tides in our lives during which we may need another type of community and another style of life; it may be the need for more contemplation. On the one hand, in an active community, some may well develop an authentic permanent vocation for the contemplative life; there should be provision for such a vocation within the congregation. On the other hand, many of us would like a sabbatical year that could be devoted to spiritual renewal within a zealous healthy contemplative community.

Forms of "Houses of Prayer"

Much consideration must be given to this question and experiments should be conducted in somewhat different ways. After listening to many religious who are interested in this idea, I am sure that the Holy Spirit will move us in the right direction, though perhaps with humble experiments and some mistakes. The greater mistake would be to sit back instead of trying to find a concrete solution. There must be an exchange of thought and experience.

In my opinion, a house of prayer should be, if possible, a center for the earnest study of theology, that mystical and ascetical theology that is needed so badly by the whole Church. Contemplation and meditation must be solidly grounded on a deep knowledge of Our Lord and of the brothers and sisters with whom we live. There should also be, as far as possible, a *stable* nucleus of sisters (or Fathers or brothers) with an authentic vocation for the contemplative life. Among them there should be at least one who is well trained in theology, and possibly another with thorough training in psychology. Methods of concentration and prayer should be studied, including the best of the Yoga and the Zen traditions. Modern man is lost unless we discover how to re-educate him for a life of concentration, contemplation, and prayer.

A group of people with an authentic and permanent vocation to the contemplative life would enrich all those who are admitted on a temporary basis. A stable contemplative vocation, however, would not exclude the possibility that some who live this life might occasionally have a sabbatical year during which they might teach mystical and ascetical theology or engage in religious formation work. Just as a contemplative vocation can develop from an active one, so a fruitful active apostolate can also develop from a more contemplative vocation, and this would be especially appropriate in the area of internal renewal.

Active communities should grant their members the right to

apply for the house of prayer whenever the special need is felt. Religious should be encouraged to spend there at least half a year to a year once or twice in their lifetimes. Shorter periods should not be excluded, even a few weeks each year, provided the religious intends to join the serious contemplative life as fully as possible for that time. Some of the members of such a house could be qualified to conduct longer retreats on an individual basis, whenever there is a need for this. Sisters themselves (and brothers, not only priests) should be trained for this work.

The financial care of the house should be assumed by the active community to which it belongs. This should not, however, prevent the members of the contemplative house from doing some work for their livelihood. The spirit of poverty and simplicity should reign but there should be no interference with concerns of a financial nature.

The house of prayer might be located advantageously in a secluded place or it might be in the midst of the city. We must study the problem of how to create an atmosphere for contemplative life in a modern environment, and this might require an establishment in the inner city. However, this should not be the only type of experiment. Some experiments should also be started with regard to the most favorable external conditions for contemplation. I would not recommend the traditional type of cloister with its austere Rules and grilles; these new houses should be models for the formation of *mature* Christians. The house of prayer must at the same time be a real community, a school of fraternal love. Genuine contemplation goes hand in hand with growth in fraternal love.

Objections to the House of Prayer

The chief objection raised against my proposal is the following: we are already overworked without this house of prayer. Some would find in it an escape from an overburdened life and the rest would be worse off than ever.

My tentative response to this is: When the program for a better professional preparation of the sisters was inaugurated, many raised the same objection. Since the leaders of the movement were convinced of the need for the program, they found ways to free the sisters. Today, all realize that efficiency is much greater when the sisters have received the best possible formation. Analogously, we are confronted with a genuine need today: we lose much energy and quite a few vocations as a result of the tensions and frustrations that come from our activism. The house of prayer, as here conceived, would be above all a source of divine energy and peace, but it would also be a source of serenity on the psychological level. If the need is genuine, and if my proposed solution seems to have some merit, men and women of faith will find the experiment a reasonable risk. It may well be that the presence of a house of prayer within the active communities would change our hectic style of life without diminishing our witness and our professional effectiveness. Is it not better to explore the possibility than simply to tolerate the evils it seeks to remedy?

II. MOTIVATION TO RESPONSIBILITY

We cannot logically regard the motivation of the religious as any different from the motivation of a good Christian. One of the greatest dangers for personnel engaged in religious formation is to allow their charges to be motivated simply by the Holy Rule and to fail to build up Christians. A religious, according to the great definition of the Second Vatican Council, is an outstanding witness to the universal vocation to sanctity and must know therefore what Christian holiness is.

One of the aspects of the New Law is that we are no longer to be subjected externally to the law but we must have insight, we must see an inner relationship to the loving will of God. For all Christians, one of the dynamics of behavior is pointed out by

St. Paul: "You are not under law but under grace" (Rom 6:14). The motive is not a written code; it is the reality of grace—God's graciousness—behind the written code, behind the Gospel: "Love one another as I have loved you."

The motivation for a Christian and especially for a religious is therefore a deep formation in faith, but a living faith. Contemplation in Christian life as well as activity in Christian life must be based on doctrine, not only as a collection of external formulas, but doctrine as a synthesis, a unified image of salvation truth, of the mystery of Christ, the Paschal Mystery, and in this light, of the mystery of the triune God. In the motivation of the Christian, one can distinguish two essential aspects: the *leitmotiv* and the single motive from the corresponding set of values.

Religious Leitmotiv

In the realm of motivation, the *leitmotiv* is most important; this is the unified view of the single motives. It can be formulated in different ways in different communities, but it must always express the Paschal Mystery, just as the Sermon on the Mount and the proclamation of the New Law in the Cenacle express the Paschal Mystery. Christ did not seek his own will, did not come to please himself, but to serve. Christ did not glorify himself but glorified the Father and so received the glory of the divinity in his human body.

The Paschal Mystery as the Lord expresses it is the *leitmotiv*. Those who seek their own lives, their own selves, lose their true selves, but those who give up their selfishness find their true selves. In one form or another, the *leitmotiv* must be the expression of the mystery of salvation, the great commandment as it is expressed in the Sermon on the Mount, "Be all goodness as your heavenly Father is all good" (Mt 5:48).

The Council pointed to the *leitmotiv* of deacons once the diaconate again becomes a state of life. For them it will be a personification of God's goodness. St. Luke expresses this *leitmotiv* as follows: "Be all compassionate as your heavenly Father is compassionate" (Lk 6:36). In the gospel of St. John (15:12), the Lord says, "Love one another as I have loved you." Christian consciousness begins when we realize how Christ has loved us; that is truly a *leitmotiv*. Everything is directed to the greater glory of God; therefore we must deeply understand the theology of the glory of God. I tried to present an integrated view of this theology in the second volume of *The Law of Christ* as the manifestation of the glory of God revealed to us in the Old and the New Testaments. God's glowing splendor falls upon us, and is then reflected back to the Lord. Just as he manifests his love in all things, so we can also mirror God's love, bringing to others and back to God that love which God has manifested to us in its fullness.

The formulation of a *leitmotiv* depends on the psychological structure of different ages and different environments, but it must always express this essential reality: God's love as it is revealed in Christ Jesus.

Individual Values

Besides the *leitmotiv*, a rich and effective motivation means insight into individual values. One of the great temptations of the past in the formation of religious men and women was to reduce everything to one formal motive: being obedient. Obedience practically became the sole value, isolated and separate from the full choir of values. So it was that the voice of obedience became rough and wrong, became louder but wrong. Obedience is of great value, no doubt, but it must be cast in the image of Christ heeding the command of the Heavenly Father. Christ knew the loving attention of his Father; his loving obedience meant deep insight into the intentions of the Heavenly Father and the needs of man.

Obedience, then, must always express what Our Lord said with respect to friends and slaves. The motivation of the slave is only external submission, external acceptance; the motivation of the friend is an intimate communion of life, an intimate communion of insight into value. Every Rule, and not only the Rules, but every commandment and every virtue, receives its value only in the light of God's love, in the light of the twofold commandment of love. Then it has an individual value and is part of the great appealing value of Christ's love.

In their religious childhood, novices have the tendency to ask: "Why do we have this Rule?" The novice master should explain the motivation of the Rule, show how the Rule is related to the great image of the Church, the great commandment of love, love of God and love of all the redeemed. We must see the purity, the pristine value of all commandments, all Rules. Pope John said over and over again that the Church must become more attractive; this attractiveness will come only when all the Rules of the Church are brought into the full light of doctrine, the light of faith through salvation, the light of the great reality of God's love and our capacity to love God and neighbor. If an individual Rule or precept cannot be explained in this light, then it must be changed. The New Law as proclaimed by Christ in the Sermon on the Mount and in the Cenacle provides motivation, because it is never separate from truth and life. If we have suffered from a lack of motivation it is because the structure of manuals of moral theology in the last two centuries created a dichotomy between morality and dogma. Commands were issued without insight into reasons behind them.

In the formation of religious, such a divorce between command and value cannot be tolerated. I made a special effort in my book, *Christian Renewal in a Changing World*, to show how Christian morality lifts all motivation into the newness of the Gospel, and so becomes open to the appeal of our new world. It is always an effort to combine the truths of salvation with the Gospel we celebrate in the liturgy and to which we witness in our lives.

Specific Motives

So far I have purposely not discussed the specific formation of religious but concentrated on that of the Christian because it is important that religious be the best Christians. As such, they must also be motivated for what is specifically their form of life. Proper motivation for the religious includes deep insight into what virginity and poverty mean, what the real meaning of obedience is under charismatic leaders: obedience in a Christian community where each one bears the burden of the others and all sustain each other by good example. There must also be depth of insight into the importance of the common life, of the sisterhood or brotherhood, of the religious family as an image of the Church, as a community of love.

Worldliness

The fear of worldliness probably accounts for most regulations that prevented full contact with the laity. Implied was the fear that involvement with lay people would diminish our "religious spirit." Some clarification is called for here.

There are four meanings of the word "world" in Sacred Scripture. One is the created universe that sings the glory of God; it is very important that we open our eyes and ears to all things that praise him. Secondly, this created universe is subjected to frustration through selfishness; so we must be careful that our witness to the created universe is not frustrated by our selfishness and our possessiveness. The created world should not be *subjected* to frustration and vanity but it should be *liberated* so that all things are considered as gifts of God, and therefore as means of service. Then there is the created universe not only subjected to sin but still remaining the created universe and being redeemed in Christ; it is good and therefore yearns for the blessed freedom of the children of God. Consequently, we must bring to the created universe a share of this freedom. The fourth meaning of "world," in St. John's Gospel, is that some of those who, having heard the message of Christ, having seen the witness of his love, refuse to accept him. These could be those religious who prefer to be buried with the dead. After having seen the example of the living community, they can be buried in the fullest sense.

A living community can contain some who are "worldly" in various ways. As a community grows in depth, in zeal, in openness, some turn out to be "worldly" in the wrong sense. We must pray to Christ the High Priest that his disciples may not be taken away from the world, from real concern for men, but that in their environment they may not be contaminated by those who are worldly in the perverted sense after having known Christ. We must have a correct understanding of what worldly means; we are not allowed to confuse the various meanings of worldliness. We should be aware that not all worldliness is holy, just as estrangement from daily life and the great events of our time has nothing to do with holiness, e.g., the concern for freedom is in itself good, but not that freedom which seeks selfish enjoyment in independence or self-worship.

Personal Responsibility

Recognition of greater personal responsibility for individual religious seems to pose a threat to the superior's authority. In the light of past training which left religious immature and not responsible enough, they doubt that self-management is possible in certain areas, especially with regard to the choice of time for prayer. It is advisable to allow people to make mistakes; otherwise they will never mature. Admittedly the transition must be gradual and calculated mistakes are not to be recommended, but if controls are abandoned gradually, the individuals will grow toward a proper use of their liberty through good motivation.

It is appropriate to give this kind of advice now: do not treat teen-agers like babies, and do not treat the adult daughter like the youngest adolescent. Sisters and brothers should be treated as adults; if some are still lacking in maturity, treat them at least as good teen-agers and help them attain adult stature. To promote growth toward maturity, we have to share our experiences and correct each other. Superiors are not expected to take on all roles themselves; they should understand their role as a community builder and community servant, a coordinator of adult persons, a sister among sisters, a brother among brothers. The superior must have the Gospel in his heart and in his manner be like inspired John, showing trust, courage, and remaining, above all, a great teacher of humility through his own example.

Humility

What a superior orders to be done is often looked upon simply and absolutely as the will of God; this is what many superiors think. I refer you to St. Paul when the people around James had urged Peter to stay away from the Christians who did not observe the law of Moses; did it look like the will of God? Paul did not break away from Peter but he spoke out, stating bluntly that it was not the will of God; Peter "was clearly in the wrong" (Gal 2:11). The superior has no direct channel to the Holy Spirit because of his office. If he is a man of prayer, docile in spirit, he will sometimes receive illumination during meditation and sometimes also from a fellow religious or a friend who may say: "Frankly, I don't think this is the will of God." In the final analysis, if the superior keeps himself within the legitimate bounds prescribed by the Rule (there are limits after all; the superior's authority is not unlimited) and if what is ordained is something that can be done in a number of ways, then let us do it in the way requested by the superior.

III. PRIMACY OF CONSCIENCE

For a fully humane and true Christian, conscience is always king. St. Paul says this clearly: "Anything that does not arise from conscience [conviction] is sin" (Rom 14:23). The Greek word *pistis* can, in the context, be translated by "faith," "conviction," or "conscience." An upright conscience has to do with the light and the earnestness of the faith. A Christian may not refer to his decision as a judgment of conscience if he has not examined it in the light of the Gospel, in the light of the Paschal Mystery. Even among religious we find people who are poorly informed or misinformed as to the real meaning of "conscience." Since formation of conscience is so fundamental to Christian life, we can benefit from a closer study of the different ways in which people understand conscience.

Historical Approaches

There are three historical approaches to conscience that bear special relevance to conscience formation. First, there is the approach of Augustine, Bonaventure, and the Scotists who conceive of conscience as that intimate power of man, namely, the power to love what is truly good. By an effective appeal to man's intimate possibility to love God and neighbor, you have penetrated the sanctuary of conscience. In this case, conscience formation consists in showing what genuine love is and attracting others by witness, example, and a loving word.

For many Thomists, conscience is defined as the power of intelligence to know the fundamental moral principles. Since, in their opinion, conscience is fundamentally knowledge, formation of conscience lies in the communication of this knowledge. Both schools have strong points in their favor; they are right as long as one school accepts the viewpoint of the other as complementary.

In my opinion, and in that of many theologians and psychologists, the correct approach to conscience involves a fuller consideration of the doctrines of St. Augustine and of St. Thomas Aquinas. The great reality that we call conscience resides in the wholeness of man, which however is always endangered on earth. It is the vital search of man's innermost being for wholeness, integrity, totality. Man's conscience is whole and healthy, strong and sensitive if the heart and mind, will and intelligence, come to a truthful harmony, if a loving will vivifies the intellect in the search for genuine love and its true objects. The conscience is whole—man in his innermost being is whole—if the light of the true good shines through the intelligence while the will is ready to embrace what the intellect presents as good and true.

Formation in Faith and Love

There are grave consequences for the formation of conscience when the latter is viewed as the totality of man. A bare, fragmented and unintegrated presentation of external laws disintegrates the conscience of man; a cold presentation of ethical knowledge risks divorcing a frozen intellect from the will. Moral teaching that cannot appeal to passions and guide them in the right direction does not bridge the intellect and will, does not serve the wholeness of man.

All the powers of man must be attracted by the good. Therefore, the good must also be presented in the form of beauty, e.g., in the liturgy, in the beauty of music, art, the beauty of witness itself. If one only sets a good example in a sullen, repulsive way without a spark of goodness, cheerfulness, and graciousness, the good example is likely to provoke resentment. If, on the other hand, we are confronted with the witness and word of a kind and joyful person, an integrated person, then we feel strongly attracted. The formation of conscience must be the formation of the integrated personality through an integrative approach and through the help of other men and women who manifest their own search for wholeness; then we see that infidelity to an appeal from God, to an impelling grace, is a breach of our totality.

Only through contrition, deep sorrow, a new encounter with the value we have spurned and a new readiness for reparation, do we return to the wholeness of our conscience, to the integrity of our personality. Therefore of very great importance in the formation of conscience is an act of sorrow after every refusal of

God's grace, after a lack of watchfulness. One of the fundamental rules in a Christian and a religious life is that immediately (as soon as God gives us the grace), in deep recollection, we ask God to forgive our lack of generosity, our turning a deaf ear to an appeal coming from him. Since God heals our weakened condition and restores us to wholeness, the act of sorrow should always be followed by an act of trust in God's compassionate love.

Formation Through Imperatives

There is a kind of "formation of conscience" which operates only through imperatives: "Do this; don't do that." It cannot be understood as the formation of a human conscience; it is more appropriately referred to as animal training. The bare imperative approach to the formation of conscience is wrong, and if the novice mistress imposes unreasonable things in order to train her charges in obedience, she is training them for infantilism, but not forming consciences. Reasonable novices refuse such irrational demands, and you should not dismiss them because of it. "You are not under law but under grace" (Rom 6:14); therefore the real motive or value must glow with the radiance and glory of God's love. Faith and goodness must have an appeal. Strong convictions arise from deep love of the Lord and penetrating insights into the mysteries of salvation.

Commercial Approach

There is another approach to conscience formation that can be labeled the commercial approach. The distortions of this approach appear in many forms. Here is one of the most curious examples I have encountered: Many sisters of one congregation serving in Germany and in France were asked why they had to pray three rosaries in Latin instead of praying them in French or in German. This large community prayed mostly in Latin in spite of the fact that not even 5 per cent had any basic knowl-

edge of Latin. Many responded with: "We are earning more indulgences. We can say only two rosaries in German, while in the
same length of time we can say three in Latin; therefore we gain
more indulgences." This is a commercial deformation of conscience. We find a similar commercial approach even in manuals
of moral theology that allow one to risk his life for another only
if he does so with direct and chief attention to his own growth
in virtue and merits. The approach is totally different from the
merciful Samaritan who paid a denarius without asking: "How
many merits will I earn in return?" He paid it because he was
merciful.

We must be very careful to pay attention to motivation when
we speak of merit. There is no doubt that there is also reference
in Scripture to merit, but the question must be understood in the
social context of those times. Merit and gain were always matters
of concern for a large family. Nobody was earning for himself individually; he was always working for the family. So merit meant
something other than what it means in our individualistic age.
Merit is a by-product of the good action of genuine love, justice,
etc. In doing good, our chief concern cannot be merit. We extend
kindness because it is good; then we know that the good in itself
brings joy and bliss and brings us nearer to God; it is rewarding.
If we always look to see how much we are earning, we are not
forming the conscience of a Christian but rather that of a good
merchant. Then we degrade good by making it a means for self-
promotion; God is not a means. The moral good relates to a genuine relationship between persons, the just and respectful relationship to our neighbor.

Dialogue Approach

A right formation of conscience can be realized through the dialogue approach. The person who appeals to us is a loving person;
it is the triune God in his love appealing to us. Therefore acting
according to the judgment of an upright conscience means giv-

ing a response to a person, to this human person through whom God speaks to me. The formation of conscience is right if you always see that it is God who solicits, God who is love. It is Christ who invites us in all things, "Follow me." Sin then is not only a "no" to a law; sin in the full sense is a refusal to a person or a refusal of greater love to Christ. This does not exclude knowledge of the law, but this too should be presented as the splendor of goodness, as a guide to a better way of loving. Behind the law is value; behind the law is the love that always motivates one to go beyond the law. Therefore we should never speak of blind obedience with regard to laws and precepts; true love is not blind.

St. Ignatius of Loyola meant something more by obedience than this unfortunate "blind" obedience. By word and example, he said great things about the right kind of obedience; why should we remember this unfortunate distortion when it never fitted into the Gospel message or teachings of the Church? We can appreciate Ignatius by recalling his formation in the united Spanish, Austrian, and Prussian army of that time. He was an officer in that army and sometimes spoke the language of the officer.

I still remember coming back after the last war and meeting my own sisters. They were very much surprised and dismayed; they asked me what kind of language I spoke! After spending five years with soldiers, I spoke their language. So it was with St. Ignatius who, not having had a novitiate before becoming an officer and soldier, was totally formed according to this language. Is it surprising that he introduced the soldier's language into asceticism? We use a happier expression; we prefer to speak more accurately of illumined, enlightened, or "seeing" obedience. A mature Christian sees the overall picture, the direction, the reasons that are behind a precept, a law, or obedience: the all-embracing motive of Christ as he heeded the command of the Heavenly Father. A mature obedience knows the various reasons and motives behind different laws and Rules.

If we see in the superior the representative of Christ, we will realize that imperfections are unavoidable in our superiors; they can never be as wise as Christ. They are messengers of Christ in their humility. We cannot speak of "enlightened obedience" unless we open our eyes wide to our own imperfections before criticizing a precept of the superior; we have to go through a serious criticism of self and be aware of our partial blindness. Some are totally blind as to their own limitations; their own way of obedience is often as blind as their disobedience, if by obedience they mean selfish conformity in the hope of avoiding trouble. We must identify our blind spots if we are to realize the extent to which we are still fooling ourselves. It is very important to be enlightened as to our own shortcomings.

One of the great contemporary problems is that the rapidly changing world is in need of a clear insight into what is abiding truth and what is rightly evolving, what can and must change, what is simply of past centuries and what is, in our time as well as in past ages, an authentic expression of the Gospel. This discernment is one of the great necessities in the formation of conscience. Conscience is king, not a slave; we have a real conscience if we can properly distinguish in all these areas. The conscience of the Christian is king when it is formed more according to the Gospel than to human rules. The chief object of the formation of religious is a deeper formation in the Gospel. In this light, the religious will then appreciate and interpret the Rule as a help to their witnessing to the Gospel.

Every Rule must be explained in the light of the Gospel. The novice master or superior makes conscience king if he humbly acknowledges that certain Rules are meaningless in this day and age. We make conscience king if we are sincere. Useless Rules are unjust to human psychology, to the Creator, and to the Gospel. We need all our strength and all our mind to understand the Gospel, the appealing love of God, and the needs of our neighbor; if we are taken up by too many unnecessary preoccupations, we are minimizing the real appeal of a loving God.

What are religious to do if the community imposes some very unnecessary, useless Rules? In themselves they do not oblige, but the final question of the Christian conscience, if conscience is king, must be: "What will the consequence of my acting in conformity with it or against it be? What will the result be for the community, for mutual love and for our witness before the world?" Sometimes it is better for the community to fail to keep all these unnecessary Rules; even temporary, wholesome scandal may be necessary.

Wholesome scandal, however, can only be given by religious who are outstanding because of zeal, kindness, goodness, and humility. If we do not observe faithfully the Rules that really are meaningful, if we are not humble, kind, and dedicated, then the scandal we give even through actions that are in themselves right will never become a wholesome scandal. We often have to observe for a time precepts and laws which in themselves are not meaningful if by so doing we promote unity and progress for the future. Patience is active and can wait!

I resort once more to the example of St. John who outran Peter and had to wait. It was very difficult for him to wait to look inside the tomb for the great news about the Master: was he risen or not? The gap between renewed thinking and unreformed structures demands great efforts at patience. We accept the situation not through legalism but through charity, not through external conformity or through renouncing our conscience, but through making a final judgment of conscience in responsible love, namely, by asking ourselves: Does it contribute to forming a community of love or does it not? Does it build up a community that is watchful for the signs of the times? The goal cannot be the "unity" of a hopeless lethargy, but unity that witnesses to the world that God lives.

IV. PRIORITIES IN THE APOSTOLATE

The virtue of vigilance comes into play here too. Founders and foundresses of communities were watchful for the signs of their times. They tried to do what was necessary in their day and if we continue to do only what they told us to do some two hundred years ago, we are not of their breed. We are then buried with their bones but not living with their spirit. In the apostolate, priority must be given to what the present opportunity, the present need demands; the decision means tremendous fortitude to resist a propensity toward laziness, a pressure to conform.

Weighty Decisions

At this point in Church history, many religious groups are making decisions as to whether or not they should be content to maintain their present apostolate only, e.g., the education of youth, or extend their apostolate to social work of some kind, continuous religious education, adult education, catechetical work, especially in the parish field. The problems are many and great; we cannot embark on experiments for which we are not prepared but we can take the first steps and plan for the future. So many communities are already overburdened. They should not overextend themselves by taking on new tasks before freeing themselves from others.

The question is one of pressures and priorities; it takes much wisdom to see what is better here and now. In some areas it is advisable to leave some personal choice to the individual religious. If a teacher can fulfill his (her) task as a teacher and devote time to a more direct apostolate, why should the community hinder or forbid it? Great decisions relative to the new directions to be taken by various religious bodies should be made by common effort that takes into account the real needs of the

Church, the world, and the possibilities open to the community.

There are certain issues of such urgency that an individual community cannot resolve them all alone. Some necessary changes call for contact with bishops and full collaboration on the level of major superiors. Far-reaching changes have to be prepared for by a common conviction on all levels, insofar as they will need the support of all. The present public discussions about our parochial school system can contribute significantly to an enlightened judgment with regard to future possibilities, especially when new methods have been tried by the fire of experimentation.

Is it not a fact that in some parochial schools, teachers are expected to take on all kinds of distracting burdens, such as fund-raising? I do not think that sisters should do this. Here, major superiors should be courageous in withdrawing sisters if the parishes are not capable of freeing them from such secondary tasks. Religious men and women need time for professional training, for leisure and for prayer. In the difficult times of today, they need more time for continual religious formation.

New Ventures

I doubt that anyone today would question the need for new structures. New forms, new structures, new concepts of policy may be demanded of us, but not everything needs to be changed. Prudence often dictates delimiting our tasks as a community, e.g., to "teaching" or to "nursing." However, teaching communities should understand their mission in a broader sense: for instance, besides teaching in the schools, religious educators could consider teaching in catechetical centers for youth and adults; they could help married people prepare their children for first communion; they could teach religion at all levels, formally and informally.

I think that the average teaching community could free some personnel for teaching in secular colleges. I am convinced that the teaching order has a definite place in the twentieth century. Modern science is so important for the life of the Church that religious should keep informed about these matters, especially the sciences related to the wholeness of man: the fine arts, and the behavioral sciences of psychology and sociology.

I feel strongly that teaching congregations should free greater numbers of brothers and sisters for catechetical training. Here we have need for a new balance; it is of prime importance to teach the Gospel on different levels and to all age groups. Not all religious are capable of this, but those who are should aspire to the possibility of continuing their formal education in theological matters.

No doubt in the future religious will be called upon more often than in the past for contributions in the area of educational television and broadcasting. Have religious congregations accepted the challenge of Vatican II with respect to the communications media? The apostolate of the press is closely related to this. More religious should go into print and make scientific contributions in areas in which they are competent.

V. FEMININE SPIRITUALITY

Is there something to be said for feminine spirituality? The principle of philosophical and theological ethics is to live what we are. Religious women have to be fully functioning persons as women; they do not have to follow all the laws and attitudes proper for religious men. Religious women of today are adults; they know better than we men the specific nature and charisms of womanhood. Comparative cultural anthropology and psychology can no longer be ignored. Womanhood today entails a role in life different from that of woman at the time of St. Paul. In our era when men and women have to collaborate so often in the apostolate, we have to develop a spirituality that is built on God's design for men and women. How then can we cooperate as consecrated men and women? A greater sense of responsibility, a better knowledge of our different roles can contribute to the development of new styles in the apostolate.

Gifts of Women

Holy Scripture reveals divine wisdom in the image of a woman, indicating thereby that woman may have a special affinity for wisdom. To be wise means to have a taste for what is good and this without the delimitations of an abstract conceptual approach. Women often have the gift of intuition that usually precedes conceptual justification; the latter is more often than not the effort of man. They seem to have a greater propensity for knowing good by connaturality, by being good and wise. Christian women should pray much for wisdom, for intuition of the good. Wise women know that the highest knowledge is a gift of God; they also realize that love is the essential condition for the most precious intuitions.

Women have their own creativity, their own way of cultivating life. It was woman who invented agriculture by introducing the most primitive forms for cultivating herbs. Woman then seems to have a special gift for protecting and for nurturing life. It would seem therefore that the greatest betrayal of a woman's spirituality lies in yielding to externalisms and lifeless activism.

Nothing is more potent than legalism for disrupting and destroying the psychological forces of a woman. Her nature clamors for life and protection, for a life that grows—not one stunted by rigid external forms. She likewise has a special tenacity toward life. She understands in an outstanding way the full meaning of tradition, namely as continuity of life—a life that is growing—not a continuity of dead formulations. Stereotyped formulas are more an invention of man than of woman; Eve is being seduced by Adam if she yields to stereotyped forms as suggested by man.

Women and Beauty

I think that women have a distinctive sense for beauty in their spirituality and beauty is certainly of great importance for spiritual life. In Holy Scripture the glory of God is the splendor, the radiance, of his goodness and truth; it is love, sanctity, and truth, manifesting themselves in beauty. Sisters should receive deep formation in all the values of beauty and be encouraged to make their contributions in artistic fields. Beauty and simplicity should characterize their houses, which, however, should be poor, i.e., not cluttered up with useless things.

I take pride in the fact that I was the first moral theologian of our time to include in his manual a long treatise about the values of beauty and art. I feel that beauty is of the essence of Christian morality. The piety expressed in our Churches, in our songs, in the liturgy, reflects an openness to beauty; this is one area where I think the religious woman has a special vocation.

The religious garb should also be pleasing but not conspicuous. The attractive simplicity of a consecrated person cannot be the beauty of a certain kind of worldliness amounting to vanity. Beauty is the splendor of goodness, harmony, and peace. A woman's good taste reveals something about her heart.

Women in Theology

We need women as leaders in theology and sister-theologians should be found in their ranks. Our theology is far too masculine. Worked out by men only, it is not surprising that it often lacks warmth, beauty, and continuity of life. We sorely need women theologians in our day. Every religious community of the post-conciliar age needs to have its own women theologians to collaborate with us men. The sisters and brothers should not totally depend on priests. Grant many sisters the opportunity for a deep theological formation but see that they keep away from legalistic moralists and negative situationists who distort theology! It is consoling to see so many sisters are involved in theology workshops. Many more could still be sent for full-time study in theology. Thank God that we no longer require, as a first condition for admission to theology, that candidates be male!

The question of feminine spirituality is a timely one because of one danger: so many religious orders of women have received their Rules from men; they were not allowed to be fully religious women. Men even prescribed their garb. I wonder what the antediluvian cardinal who recently designed a garb for sisters would say if sisters were allowed to design a simple tunic for cardinals? For too long our sisters were told to be like religious men; such dictatorial attitudes can no longer be tolerated. It is unfortunate that the feminist movement began with women claiming man's rights instead of equal human rights or specific rights as women. Women today therefore have the task of developing their own aspect of spirituality without overlooking the complementarity of men and women in the state of celibacy and in the apostolate.

Woman brings salvation—wholeness, openness, and continuity —into the world through her specific womanhood. The religious woman in the world and Church of today has to represent the best in womanhood in the warmth, kindness, motherly and sisterly attitudes she displays. She is a deaconess of salvation. In her own specific way she must express the humility of Christ as the Blessed Virgin did.

THIRTEEN | THE CHALLENGE
OF THE FUTURE

Let all who have been called to the profession of the vows take painstaking care to persevere and excel increasingly in the vocation to which God has summoned them. Let their purpose be a more vigorous flowering of the Church's holiness and the greater glory of the one and undivided Trinity (LG, 47). Such a life has a necessary role to play in the circumstances of the present age. (PC, 1)

God is love and in Christ he has manifested the full extent of his love. At the Last Supper Christ enjoins us to abide in him, to dwell in him and let his Word, that is, the message of love, dwell in us. Is it not the vital reality of Christ's love that binds us to him in a life based on the evangelical counsels? Let me express my very firm conviction that religious have a future in the Church not only because of the great merits and important role of religious in the past, but because of the great part religious are actually playing in the Church today.

There are some religious and even some communities still trailing behind the Council, behind the rest of the Church and the world, but the majority in America are joyfully, gratefully, and courageously living in this new epoch. I want to recall here the great tribute Philip Scharper paid American sisters when he told me that sisters are the most progressive and best-informed group in the American Church. If this is true, they were certainly not merely somnolent virgins before the Council. I believe the same statement can be made about congregations of brothers in America.

Church of the Future

Religious have a future in the Church, but only in the Church which is in the world, not that of yesterday or belonging to the past. There will be less clinging to customs and forms of life which do not bear testimony to present life, to divine tradition, or to authentic human tradition as continuity of life. The religious men and women of tomorrow will, in the best sense, bear witness to the Risen Lord and not merely to the three days Our Lord spent in the tomb. They will testify to the resurrection of the Lord by revealing a greater awareness of his presence in the history of salvation, in both the Church and the secular world. Therefore they will guard themselves from the backward-looking attitude of Lot's wife; they will refuse to join the ranks of grumbling and retrogressive religious who forever reminisce about the "good old days," but who like Lot's wife are petrified, lifeless, and immobile. Instead, progressive religious will be like Abraham, who left his home, culture, fatherland in pursuit of the promised land.

Religious will have a great future if they willingly agree to serve as a pioneering group in the future Church. Their chief charism of vigilance compels them to make a continuous effort at watchfulness with a view to greater spiritual depth and expansion into new areas of activity. While allowing for needed expansion, the chief effort should be directed toward increasing depth, as the condition for fruitful new ventures. There must be and there can be a new image of the Church living by faith, charity, and hope. It is therefore obvious that religious who accept the challenge of the future will show greater evidence of faithfulness and watchfulness to the Lord in coming history than they did in the past. We in no way intend of course to imply any depreciation of their past services.

Religious gain by being reminded that they have no monopoly on holiness but are witnesses and servants for the sanctification of all. We saw, during the preparations for the Council, a tendency among certain religious, even theologians, to think that if one wanted to be perfect, he had only to join our ranks and live in a "state of perfection." We do have a special role but we fail to fulfill it if we thereby cheapen the role of others. The ministerial priesthood has the specific goal of bringing all the faithful to a full awareness that they are members of the priestly People of God. Those living the witness of the evangelical counsels must be very much aware of their responsibility to encourage others to find their own way to holiness. It follows obviously that every form of jealous competition must be ruled out. Religious life must be a service and ministry for the building up of the mystical Body of Christ and therefore demands the fullest appreciation of other forms of life and service.

Religious, in their own way, should promote secular institutes and lay movements. There must be a variety of vocations; we have no doubt that God does send enough vocations if we can learn to cooperate. A kind of special solidarity could develop between certain religious orders and secular institutes. The sizable community of a religious family should sustain and inspire the smaller secular institute in its effort toward professional and spiritual formation, and the secular institute could bring "fresh air" into the religious community.

Novel Features

The future may offer new possibilities with regard to the composition of religious communities; evidently they will not be according to the old style with two social classes but may present different phases, varying degrees of nearness to the outside world, within the same community. Another form of cooperation is emerging on campuses where sisters, brothers, and laymen study catechetics in the summer. The religious have a tremendous apostolate here if they truly live in spiritual friendship with each other and with priests and laymen on the same campus. Indeed,

I know that certain sisters have played a rather important role in raising the spirit of joy, friendliness, and real community spirit of religious from other communities. All profit by this friendly cooperation. There are ways in which religious can join the laity in apostolic efforts. Undoubtedly this requires a spirit of discernment. Not everything now going on represents a genuine progress in renewal.

Cooperation of the religious with their students' parents should be explored further. The association and involvement of the parents would broaden the experience of the religious and free them from secondary tasks; it may even prove to contribute to mutual enrichment. Recently I met with a group of CFM couples. They greatly appreciated the work of the sisters but would be more appreciative if all sisters, in turn, would respect their vocation and competency as parents in preparing their children for the whole of sacramental life. Religious could certainly provide services for young couples who are not very knowledgeable in the realm of the religious and moral education of their children. Such a role should be taken up especially by sisters and brothers well trained in psychology and catechetics; they would be helping the parents realize better that they are "the first heralds of the Joyous News" (LG, 11). Such a program would be in full accord with the principle of subsidiarity and be an expression of our eagerness to respect and promote the role of others. Instead of giving religion classes only for children, religious with the help of competent laymen could offer courses for parents on how to understand the whole educational process of the child as a post-baptismal catechumenate, how to bring life and religion together in the sacramental piety of the family.

I am not in favor of a sudden discontinuance of our parochial schools. I can envision the teachers and students in the parochial school system gradually becoming integrated in the public school system. Sisters and brothers could then be salaried teachers in the poorer sections, in the slum schools of the inner city, and make a tremendous contribution toward the advancement of underprivileged minority groups besides offering reparation for our failures in the past. Moreover, we need an army of sisters and brothers for the catechetical instruction of youth in the public schools. There is also room for many religious in the Newman apostolate on secular campuses.

I frankly do not think that we should give up our Catholic colleges except in cases where the congregation or diocese can no longer afford to staff them adequately. The Catholic college can make a specific contribution through friendly cooperation with a secular college; such cooperative endeavors may well benefit the whole of our culture which is endangered by too much technological progress, where everything except the human person and his dignity receives full attention. The Catholic college should be a place where the focus of attention is on the wholeness of the person in all respects. This places strong demands on the theology department to produce a theology that specifically develops an integrative perspective of the whole of life, culture, science, and progress.

The services of religious will continue to be needed for the care of the sick, mentally retarded, and emotionally disturbed persons. However, in a welfare society like ours where appropriate institutions are available on a regional basis, parallel institutions should not be duplicated by religious orders. Instead may religious be counted among the dedicated Christians who carry on these works of mercy in state-supported institutions. I am not advocating total withdrawal of services from similar Catholic institutions, but the prospect of serious development with secular institutions deserves consideration. It is advisable that experimentation be undertaken and the results shared with other religious in this country and abroad.

Congregations which have taken the first steps toward secular institutions should not only look to the professional competency of their religious men and women assigned to such work but more to their specific apostolic preparation. Their background should reflect serious preparation in the areas of counseling, interpersonal relationships, group dynamics, and communication skills. Their social-psychological training should enable them to offer a religious perspective that will appeal to the different kinds of life they encounter while serving the People of God in this post-Vatican II era.

If religious excel in their professional competency and in religious, psychological, and pedagogical training, their presence will be most meaningful where life is being lived with great hardship but also with great opportunity for witnessing to faith. Could not religious extend their presence, influence, and witness to prisoners by visits with them and cooperation in their rehabilitation? Another area of social service well deserving of dedicated religious is that of halfway houses for ex-convicts, alcoholics, and drug addicts, all of whom are brothers and sisters in Christ.

Transitions in administrative structures have to be made gradually and with due concern for the continuity of our institutions and our effective presence. Every experiment in changing structures is a risk; some are bound to fail. We need communities ready to face this risk; some have to outrun the others. Christian solidarity can and must bind together the slow and the fast runners in this period of transition. Many new structures are already visible and are evolving rather modestly, e.g., the national conferences of major superiors of religious men and women. In some countries, such as Brazil, there is a single similar organization that brings together the major superiors of religious men and women. This gives a greater guarantee that resources will be shared for the common work: formation, the apostolate, representation, and organization.

In several countries, all orders and congregations preaching retreats and conducting parochial missions have one common institution for a continuous formation program; in full cooperation with the hierarchy, such an enterprise makes possible the transformation of the traditional system of retreats and parochial missions into new forms, in an effort to implement renewal more effectively and more quickly. Many new structures will contribute to the integration of the lay apostolate and the activity of religious orders.

Religious of the Future

I believe religious congregations have a future in the Church, and I have no doubt that the religious men and women of America particularly have a great future before them. But what about the individual religious who is to guarantee this future? He must be a mirror-image of the Church. At Vatican Council II, the church reached a deeper understanding of herself through the common efforts of the whole Church. The religious must mirror this new Church. A glance at some of her characteristics will convey the full impact of the message.

The religious of the future must be a responsible person, and better integrated into the community as such. Only those who give themselves in humble service to the community can find their true selves; they consider whatever they are and whatever they have as a gift to the community in love. They are really *persons* because they are fully responsible selves. All things find their ultimate being in God. That is why no superior can occupy the place of God or of conscience; he can only serve as a guide, giving some help in leading his fellow religious toward God.

This whole matter cannot be discussed solely on the level of local or major superiors but must also penetrate the level of the responsible self in the sight of God, of Christ who died and rose for us, in the great light of the Paschal Mystery. Much criticism and bitterness will be avoided if this line of approach is followed. How can we possibly offer bitterness and useless criticism to the Lord who died for us? The responsible self accepts the fact that in all things it is God in his mystery who appears in humble messengers. The religious of the future then must witness to how personalism and its communal realization can be combined and brought to synthesis. Then and only then will individualism no longer need to be compensated by narrow legalism and tight controls. A genuine personalism builds up community spirit and gives meaning to initiative as well as to structures.

Cooperation and Dialogue

The Council has done away with the notion that only those on the top move the whole body, leaving the others as lifeless cogs in the religious machinery. This teaching is very explicitly reflected in every chapter of every decree of the Council: everyone is to take an active part in the Church. No one is allowed to stifle charisma, the gift of the Spirit; no one can force another to bury his talent in the earth through inactivity or reduce anyone, religious or layman, to mere passivity.

There is one point that is crucial here however: there must be a common dialogue. There is need to sit down together and speak openly, frankly recognizing what is good. There must be real discussion, a weekly half hour about what has to be changed, what has to be abolished, what kind of laziness or cowardice afflicts the community, how the liturgy affects our lives, and which areas call for greater depth in our religious life. We need round-table discussions, the shouldering of common burdens, instead of the pointing out of other people's faults. Humble service must be exercised in the fraternal correction of others; at least the attempt must be made along this line. I know some communities where this has worked very well; it cannot fail if the individual is respected.

The Holy Spirit gives every individual a charisma in view of the common good; it follows that each individual gift must be appreciated. It behooves superiors, therefore, in assigning religious to tasks, to be very respectful of God's own work. They are not honoring the Holy Spirit by ignoring the gifts of the Spirit Creator. If a sister has capabilities in the fine arts, she should not be assigned to teach mathematics just because she dislikes it. Appreciate what God has given you! Collaboration is seriously called for between religious in the ranks and superiors. What type of work is one best suited for? God is the one who distributes the charisms.

It happens that young people may not know what they are best suited for. As a young man I was terribly convinced that I was called by God to preach the Gospel in Brazil. I set out to learn Portuguese and when my provincial changed his mind and asked me to specialize in moral theology, I told him: "I had a great temptation to become a Jesuit; since I wanted to be sure that I would not become a professor, I decided for the Redemptorists. As for theology, I liked everything except canon law and moral theology." My superiors told me to teach both; for some years I did public penance as a professor of canon law. Time has proved that my superiors were wiser than I and that I did the best by cooperating with them.

Conscience, Not Conformity

The religious of the future will witness to the synthesis of obedience and freedom in the true liberty of the sons and daughters of God. More is expected of a religious today than in the past. In his whole life he must manifest that he lives according to his own conscience. He is not a mere tape-recorder; he himself listens to the voice of God, recognizes his own gifts, tries to understand the values and the real needs of others, the good, while helping others. The final position must always be that of his own conscience in solidarity, humility, and fortitude, and thus he gives witness to our times. Here we come to the role of authority and genuine Christian obedience.

The world of today is filled with the dangers of external conformity, stereotyped patterns of behavior. The witness of Christians, especially of pioneers in the Church, requires a well-formed conscience. To ensure this kind of future leadership, we have to have sound vocations. If we want leaders, it is foolish to dismiss all dynamic persons. If there is so little leadership in some dioceses, in some orders of men especially, it is because all the dynamic young men were sent home. We should try to win over these promising individuals instead of dismissing them because they are headstrong and difficult. It may be that such a dynamic type is judged to be difficult because he already knows more than the superiors care to admit.

Witness to the Gospel

We must humbly accept the necessity of Rules and structures as far as they serve to warn us of the real dangers of today, but at the same time, communities must find the right balance. Rules are necessary; we must be realistic enough to know that we are not yet in the heavenly Jerusalem, but we must always remain staunch in the belief that we, here and now, can begin to do the will of God as it is done in heaven, namely, out of love, out of deep knowledge of God and the needs of men.

The religious of the future will witness to the prime importance of the Gospel, of the Sermon on the Mount. In view of this, sanctity means a continuous conversion, a continual deepening of our love for God and neighbor. Therefore religious must be formed in watchfulness in order to take advantage of the present opportunities. St. Paul keeps repeating that we must ferret out all the opportunities of the present moment (Eph 5:16; Col 4:5).

Evidently some parts of the American sisterhoods and congregations of brothers, in Christian fortitude, must serve the lower social classes. I have recommended several times that well-balanced, well-prepared religious teach in the public schools of the slums where no social prestige is involved, where family pressures prevent good lay teachers from serving. These underprivileged people who must be integrated into the mainstream of American life need dedicated people, and in my judgment, these people are American sisters and brothers. Their presence there may well be more needed than in some parochial school.

The religious of the future will be grateful to those who went before them. One of the great arts of Christian life is showing gratitude to God but also to our neighbor: gratitude to those who lived before us, who live with us, and responsibility toward those who will come after us.

Finally, the religious women of tomorrow will in an outstanding way inspire woman in her new role in the Church and in the world. Woman no doubt is a mirror of the Church in history. God has assigned a new role to women in the world and he is giving them a new role in the Church. Thus the religious woman's specific apostolate becomes: to witness to Christ, to women in the Church and in the world. The role of religious men and priests will not be diminished by this, but completed and integrated.

APPENDIX

Proposed Interim Rule *

Gal. 5.13–26   Since the Spirit is our life, let us be directed by the Spirit, who has set us free from the law of sin and death. Let us keep his law: "Love the Lord your God . . ." "Love one another as I have loved you."

The love of Christ has gathered us together, desiring the union with and in him of every human creature. Whatever will promote this fulfillment, which constitutes God's Kingdom and God's glory in the world, let us affirm; whatever will impede it, let us renounce.

We have come together in the faith that God, from his boundless goodness and love, has called all men to union with Christ and to communion with one another in the Trinity. Impelled by this faith, let us strive with gratitude and with joy to enter ever more fully into Christian community, confident that, what-

Gal. 4.6   ever our failures, we have already begun to be one with him through the Spirit given us at Baptism, so that we too may cry "Abba, Father"; and that if we are one with him, we are one with all who are in him, who are sons and daughters of the one Father by the power of the one Spirit.

We know that this faith and this hope are given us not for ourselves only but for the Kingdom: As mem-

II Cor. 5.   bers of Christ, we are a people privileged to be signs
18–20   and messengers, spreading the Good News that through Christ, lifted up in glory, the Spirit has been poured into men's hearts, reconciling the world to the

---

* This draft was prepared by members of the Interim Rule Committee of the Maryland Province of the Sisters of Notre Dame of Namur, for submission to the general chapter of their congregation.

243

Father and making it possible for men to live together in love.

Yet, only by surrendering to the power of the Spirit at work in us and in the world around us, by allowing our lives to become yet other expressions of Christ's redemptive surrender to the Father, can we enter with Christ into the glory and the joy of the Kingdom and *Jn. 17.21* be instruments for the fulfillment of his prayer: "May they all be one. Father, may they be one in us, as you are in me and I am in you." In joyous confidence, then, that whatever our weakness, his grace is sufficient for us, let us try in each set of circumstances to enter into Christ's surrender unreservedly, loving as he has loved. As he emptied himself in creative obedience even to death on a cross, transforming that death into a source of life and reconciliation for all men, let us strive to empty ourselves, surrendering ever more totally and creatively to the Spirit, that his power may be set free in us and work through us, giving life and strength to the faith, the hope and the love which unite us in Christian community and impel us to go out to the whole world as signs and messengers of the Kingdom founded by Christ.

Eph. 4.5   We know that there is one Lord, one faith, one
Eph. 4.11   baptism; yet there are a variety of gifts distributed by the one Spirit for the building up of the whole body in love. Through this diversity of gifts, the Christian community as a whole is called to embody and to show forth something of the infinite Christian reality. We believe that the gift we share as religious is a call to stable celibate community lived for the sake of the Kingdom and called into being and sustained by the Spirit of love it strives to incarnate. Through our continuing, dynamic, and joyful response to this gift, the power of the Spirit can be set free in us and work through us, revealing yet another dimension in the Christian community's witness and life, that men might understand still more clearly the meaning of Christ and the nature of his Kingdom, and that they might experience still more fully his universal love for all mankind. But if through our daily striving to live

out this permanent religious consecration we are to be instruments of the Spirit proclaiming Christ's love *Jn. 15.16* for all men and testifying that Christ is the fullness of life and that receiving of his fullness we can bear fruit which will remain, then we must support one another in love. And if we are to strengthen the witness of the whole People of God to the universality of Christ's love and contribute as effectively as we can to the Christian community's service of all mankind that the Kingdom might be extended, then we must continually seek out ways to share readily all that we are and have, striving to live in a disposition of availability and in a life of loving, joyful service.

In our lives as sisters, then, we must continually rededicate ourselves to the fundamental Christian end which we share: the union, the fulfillment, of all mankind in and through Christ. Through our witness and our varied works of education—our creative response to the mandate we have received from the Church— let us strive actively and resourcefully to proclaim God's Kingdom, and to serve it by building the human community.

Our witness and service should embody the spirit of Mary, who shows us in her life what we must strive to become in the Church and the world at large—open to the Word of God, open to change, ready to give free consent to whatever the Spirit requires for the sake of the Kingdom. In each set of circumstances, *Eph. 5.10* then, whatever the cost to ourselves, let us strive to discover and to do what the Lord wants of us.

We must try to live, too, in the spirit of our foundress, whose extraordinary insight into the goodness of God and of his creation evoked in her a single-minded response of living faith, of genuine, unreserved, dynamic love uninhibited by useless convention or by fear.

In accordance with this spirit, then, let us strive to *Col. 3.13* live in gratitude and in joy for all that we have received, giving thanks, in particular, for the Spirit who is our bond of union with God and with man, and *Phil. 1.3* giving thanks for every human person God permits us

to know, especially for one another and for all who
are our partners in the Gospel. Like our foundress, let
us continually renew our confidence in the Father's
I Jn. 2.1–2   love for us and our conviction that if any one of us
should sin, we have as our advocate Jesus Christ, who
is just. Let us avoid all unnecessary elaboration, com-
plication, or regulation in our way of life. And let us
I Jn. 3.18   seek out ways of making our love not just words or
mere talk, but something real and active.

If we are true to the spirit of our foundress, which
was permeated by the spirit of Christ and of Mary,
we will strive actively and creatively for the Kingdom's extension in time and in eternity, in accordance
with the mandate we have received from the Church,
making the fullest possible use of our gifts, as individuals and as a community. We will prove our love of
the Church by striving to be responsible members of
it, working loyally, honestly, and courageously to
strengthen, unite, and purify its life, its witness, its
Rom. 12.13   service of mankind for the Kingdom of God. We will
II Cor. 9.7   seek out effective ways to share joyfully with our
Mt. 19.21   brothers in need, and be ready even to sell what we
Rom. 12.16   have that we might give. We will try never to be con-
descending, but strive to make real friends with those
in genuine need and to become convinced of our still
greater need of them. We will seek to bring light to
those who, knowingly or through inadvertence, are
holding the poor in captivity by failing to give of their
talents and means. We will learn to rejoice in spend-
II Cor. 12.15   ing what we have, and in being expended, for the
II Cor. 1.24   deepest interests of others, not as dictators over their
faith, but as fellow workers for their happiness.

Again, if we are true to the spirit of our foundress,
we will never forget our special obligation to one an-
Eph. 6.18   other in the fellowship of our order. We will go out
Rom. 1.11–2   to one another freely, in friendship and love. We will
pray for and with one another, joyfully sharing not just
our material goods, but our spiritual gifts as well, that
we may draw encouragement from our common faith
and hope. We will speak the truth to one another in a
spirit of gentleness and humility, and be ready to

acknowledge weakness; to accept and forgive one another as freely as God has accepted and forgiven us; to bear one another's burdens, fulfilling the law of Christ; to heal and support one another in love, without thinking first of ourselves.

Eph. 4.25
Gal. 6.1–2
Eph. 4.32

Let us live together, then, in this attitude of simple love, of dynamic confidence, of gratitude, and of joy, that the Spirit may be set free in us and go out from us, bringing the Kingdom nearer its fruition. Let us never forget that because the power which must bind us to one another and go out from us to mankind is the Spirit of Christ, the Spirit of love, our lives must be rooted in love, founded on love. If we have the gift of prophecy, understanding all the mysteries there are, and knowing everything, and if we have faith in all its fullness, to move mountains, but are without love, then we are nothing at all. If we teach with all the eloquence of men or of angels, but speak without love, we are simply gongs booming and cymbals clashing. If we give away all that we possess, piece by piece, and if we even let them take our bodies to burn them, but are without love, it will do us no good whatever. Love is always patient and kind; it is never jealous; love is never boastful or conceited; it does not insist on its own way; love is never rude or selfish; it does not take offense, is not resentful. Love takes no pleasure in other people's sins but delights in the truth; it is always ready to excuse, to trust, to hope, and to endure whatever comes.

I Cor. 13.1–7

Let us love one another, then, and love all mankind, as God has loved us; and God—let us love him above all things!

Proposed Interim Constitutions

PREFACE

The Interim Rule Committee of this province suggests *interim* constitutions, based on principles derived from the Chapter. Since they can be understood only in these terms, it seems fitting to enumerate those principles which seem most relevant to the committee.

Since, by the directive of the Church, we are entering a period of experimentation, these constitutions are deliberately non-prescriptive. They assume that the details of our life will be worked out in many different ways, through experimental programs in every province and in every house. We envision substantial changes, but changes worked out through intelligent experimentation, carefully and, where possible, even scientifically evaluated.

We assume subsidiarity at every level. Responsibility not specifically reserved to the generalate belongs to the province, the local house, or the individual sister; responsibility not specifically reserved to the generalate or the province belongs to the local house or the individual sister; responsibility not specifically reserved to the generalate, the province, or the local house belongs to the individual sister.

We suppose always the supremacy of the individual conscience in the action of the individual sister. We suppose the obligation of the individual sister to educate her conscience, and of the community to provide her with opportunities to do so. We suppose the community's support of the sister in her adherence to the judgment of conscience.

We suppose the interpretation of every law with the liberty of God's children—without constraint and without selfishness. Our foundress left her congregation not an unchanging, directive formula—a constitution—but rather a living spirit of singlehearted love of God and men. Such undivided love permeates all things human and gathers all men into Christ's love which is the bond of unity.

The freedom of the Spirit should breathe in the observance of the essential guidelines which follow.

INTRODUCTION

As one means of bringing about the ultimate communion of men in the Trinity, God, through his Word, calls some Christians to a life of celibate consecration in community. Personal consecration to the person of Christ, in himself and in his members, establishes a unique relationship of the consecrated person with Christ and a unique relationship of the consecrated persons with one another and with all men. In a particular sense each of them belongs to all God's people because she does not belong exclusively to one of them. This consecration is expressed by vow. It establishes the religious community.

Our purpose is to manifest and to serve the Kingdom of God, where all men will be united with the triune God in loving community.

The congregation strives, in its limited, human way, to reflect, in the loving relationships of its members with one another, the splendor of the Kingdom.

The congregation strives to fit itself for serving the Kingdom by reverent listening to the Spirit as he speaks to its members in prayer, in one another, in the signs of the times, in the works of human wisdom, in the manifold insights of experience.

The congregation strives to serve the Kingdom by proclaiming, with all its strength, the Gospel of Christ, a Gospel of unity and peace. It is engaged in an intensive effort to learn how it may speak more clearly and with greater force, moved by the moral urgencies of our time—the failure of human societies to recognize the fundamental dignity of the human person, redeemed by Christ, and the failure of Christians and non-Christians alike to recognize the ethical imperatives of justice and charity.

The congregation strives to serve the Kingdom, the heavenly city, by serving the city of man, the secular city, in a spirit of Christian hope, recognizing with the great Christian thinkers of our era that the loving relationships of true human community must prepare men for their ultimate union in the community of the triune God. The congregation is engaged in an intensive effort to learn how it can render this service more effectively, moved by the social urgencies of our time—an age at once of unimaginable material development and of general awareness that most men live and die in the anguish of destitution.

Really to contribute to the growth of God's Kingdom by incarnating God's love, by listening to the Spirit, by proclaiming the Gospel, and by serving the city of man, ——— must gear its internal life more effectively to these corporate tasks and must prepare its members more effectively to perform them. The urgency of these alterations of our way of life is in proportion to the urgency of the ends for which they are indispensable means.

RELIGIOUS CONSECRATION IN COMMUNITY

(C1) Our consecration in community to the person of Christ, in himself and in his members, is expressed by vow. This consecration is the heart and center of our lives; it defines our unique meaning for God's people, our unique identity for ourselves, the nature of our service to the Kingdom. Through the joyous, sacrificial living out of this commitment, we find, sometimes even in a powerful experience of affective prayer, our personal fulfillment.

CELIBATE COMMUNITY

(C2) Celibate love is the gift of God which enables us to live in a community of persons in the manner which Christ chose for himself. It is our fundamental response to his love whereby each of us irrevocably consecrates her person to God and dedicates herself to the communication of Christ's love to all men in universal openness. It is rooted in the Eucharist, the source of love, and is nourished by a spirit of prayer.

(C3) We have freely come together in celibate community to incarnate in time, both individually and corporately, the love which exists in the Divine Persons. This is only possible, however, in the sharing of the Paschal Mystery of Christ's death and resurrection. Only insofar as we exist for others is our religious community an authentic sign to the world of the Word which was made flesh in selfless love.

(C4) All our human relationships, mirroring Christ's love for all, should be characterized by reverence for and unconditional acceptance of the human person; by generosity, sensitivity, and warmth.

(C5) Since to love others in a non-exclusive and non-possessive way, one normally needs to be loved, let us each consider it our personal responsibility to create an atmosphere of openness, joy, trust, understanding, and concern for all the members of our community.

(C6) A genuine community in fostering the growth of loving relationships among its members creates a climate in which friendship can develop and grow. In proportion to the strength of the love they share, friends are a vital source of love to their whole community.

(C7) As we strive to incarnate Christ's love to all men, we must realize that friction, conflict, aversion, and hostility are an inevitable condition of any pilgrim community. We must learn, therefore, to recognize and deal with these emotions; we must free one another to express them and be ever ready to serve as channels of Christ's forgiveness and healing.

COMMUNITY OF GOODS

(C8) While appreciating the value and beauty of God's creation and employing things as a means to unify all men in the love of Christ, we, as Christians, witness to evangelical poverty—an attitude of total receptivity before God. If genuine, our basic recognition of the primacy of persons over things and our poverty of spirit will find expression in simplicity of life, in joyful, but non-possessive use of material things, and freedom from unwarranted dependence upon them.

(C9) Having pledged ourselves as religious to foster community by opening ourselves in love to all persons, we shall rejoice in accepting nothing for ourselves alone and in sharing, as a community, all our resources: spiritual and material goods, time and talents. We should strive individually and corporately to use these goods as fruitfully as possible so as to spread the love of Christ, to serve his Kingdom.

(C10) We must, both individually and as a community, consider seriously how we may help to alleviate the destitution prevalent in the world today, which is inconsistent with our desire to establish a family of men joined in Christ's love. To this end we must continually re-evaluate our employment of personnel and our use of material possessions so that we may continue the selfless giving of Christ by sharing our community goods more effectively with the larger community of mankind.

COMMUNITY OF SERVICE

(C11) Mindful that our community exists in the Church with a mandate to continue Christ's work of love, let each of us listen to the Spirit as he manifests himself through the persons, assign-ments, and events of our life and our time, striving to respond creatively to all that he asks for the service of the People of God. Let us respect one another's decisions in the choice of optional apostolic activities.

(C12) Conscious that the Spirit resides within the community as a whole, which acts under designated leadership, let us strive for unity of mind, heart, and action. Where important matters are concerned, the members of the community should strive to be generous in sharing viewpoints and in mutual concession. It is the responsibility of each sister, therefore, to listen to the Spirit speaking through others and to share her insights with them in order to work toward a consensus for the good of the whole com-munity and of its individual members. The role of the sister charged with exercising leadership will normally be to articulate the community consensus. In the event that the conscientious position of a minority prevents consensus or in the case of other grave reasons, which the appointed leader should make known if possible, she should make the necessary decision. Her service is to unify the action of the community, to protect individual rights, and to strengthen the bonds of charity. Let her strive to create an environment in which all members of the community may feel at home, at ease, and at peace.

(C13) In a spirit of faith, joy, and mature obedience, let us assume our responsibility to the community and to the Church, listening to the Spirit, sharing in the process of decision-making and generously supporting decisions, whether they are arrived at by community consensus or by the action of another legitimate authority.

OTHER ASPECTS OF COMMON LIFE

(C14) In striving to make Christ's love intelligible to the world by fostering in time the loving relationships between per-sons which will exist in eternity, let us remember that "Unless a wheat grain falls on the ground and dies, it remains only a single grain." Only by the gift of ourselves to others can we bear fruit, can we foster the growth of a community of love.

(C15) Because of our dignity as persons and our social nature, we can form true community only to the extent that we are mature individuals. We must struggle constantly to promote within our communities, then, such human values as: integrity, openness, freedom, communication, mutual support, privacy, and leisure so that our members may grow toward the fullness of Christian personhood. In this reverencing of the diverse gifts of its members, the community itself will be strengthened.

(C16) In making decisions regarding correspondence, use of the phone, personal contacts, special occasions, cultural and professional opportunities, inter-house and family visits, let each sister consider her total situation—her religious consecration to the evangelical counsels and her obligation both to diffuse Christ's love to an ever wider community and to strengthen the bonds of love within her own community.

(C17) Let us strive by a responsible use of speech throughout the day to strengthen the interpersonal bonds necessary for a meaningful community life. Motivated by a habitual and loving consideration for others, let us be silent when and where charity, courtesy, or necessity require it.

(C18) In speech and in silence, in action and in contemplation, aware of the presence of God in other persons as well as within ourselves, we should strive to be attentive and responsive to God in the manner required by each circumstance.

(C19) Our health is a precious gift which enables us to serve others. Each of us is personally responsible for taking the normal measures to prevent or remedy illness. Let the local community, pledging itself to its members, provide for all, in a manner consistent with evangelical poverty, sufficient medical attention, recreation, and vacation.

(C20) Each local community should schedule its own horarium, including the Eucharistic Celebration, office, and meals.

(C21) Our dress should be simple, modest, and attractive, adapted to circumstances of time and place and the needs of the apostolate. It should include some symbol of our consecration.

(C22) We strive to serve the Kingdom by reverent listening to the Spirit in the liturgy of the Church and in communal and private prayer.

(C23) The celebration of the Eucharist is the vital center of the life of our community, as it is of the Church itself. Our life is a sharing in the death-resurrection of Christ in order that all men may be drawn into the fellowship of the Trinity. Our celebration of the Eucharist, by which we daily confirm our entrance into Christ's surrender to the Father for all mankind, presupposes our efforts to strengthen community, signifies them and makes them fruitful. It strengthens the bonds uniting the local community by helping to form one mind in it through the proclamation of the Word and by nourishing it with the one Bread of life. It strengthens the bonds of the local community with the whole community and with the Christian community. Penetrated by the Spirit of Christ, we are sent forth from the Eucharistic celebration to proclaim the reality in which we have participated and to live in conformity with its spirit.

(C24) Let us, therefore, actively participate each day in the celebration of the Eucharist in thanksgiving to the Father and in intercession for the needs of this congregation, of the whole Christian community, and of the world. As much as possible, the Eucharistic celebration should reflect the distinctive spirit and situation of the community and therefore should be open to our parishioners, students, and others associated with us in any way.

(C25) In the morning and evening let each community associate itself with the Church as she continues Christ's work of praising God and interceding for the salvation of the whole world, through recitation in common of Lauds and Vespers, or of similar prayers worked out by the local community in accordance with its special desires and needs.

(C26) As sisters of this order we have a special bond with Mary, the Virgin Mother of Our Lord Jesus Christ, who because of her unreserved faith and love is the prototype of the Church. Our communal Marian devotion should be centered on her liturgy. Let each sister honor Mary every day in a manner which is meaningful to her.

(C27) The local community must, on occasion, gather to discern the meaning of the Word of God for its unique circumstances so as to respond generously.

(C28) As Our Lady pondered the Word of God in her heart when he was made flesh in her and given to man, let us also ponder this Word in private prayer so that the glory of God may be accomplished in us. Convinced that cessation of activity and sustained effort are necessary for mental prayer, let us consecrate sufficient time to such prayer, the norm being about an hour each day. Each sister is free to divide this time and may make this prayer at whatever time and place are most beneficial to her.

(C29) Our prayer should flow from an inner stillness of heart born of awareness of God's presence in us and in all things. It needs to be nourished by the reading of Scripture and other works, about two hours being the weekly norm.

(C30) Let each of us try to set aside monthly a day of renewal, and make an annual retreat. We should seek opportunity for longer periods of renewal when we feel the need.

PENANCE

(C31) Conscious that we are one with all men in our need of continuous conversion, and realistically appraising our own weakness, let us, individually and as a community, foster a spirit of penance which will continually deepen our baptismal renunciation of sin and our conversion to Christ and will contribute to the reconciliation of all men with God and with one another.

(C32) In order to do so we should examine ourselves each day in the light of the Word of God and his great gifts to us. We should do this periodically as a community. The Sacrament of Penance must be available every week and the sisters should frequently approach it. On occasion, a communal form should be given to its celebration.

(C33) The sacramental experience of God's forgiveness should open us to one another, making possible the acknowledgment of failure and the healing of divisions through mutual forgiveness. Each community may find its own way of expressing this reconciliation.

(C34) There are no austerities of rule or custom. Our common penance consists in accepting with peace of mind and a willing, even a joyful heart, the discipline and difficulties involved in living out our religious consecration. This asceticism is especially necessary in times of change when we must be constantly vigilant in listening to the Spirit.

APOSTOLATE

(C35) Our apostolate flows from our consecration. In and through and by means of community, the love of Christ urges us to bring his light to the world.

(C36) In the tradition of our community, let us be completely dedicated to the service of the Kingdom through the work of education broadly conceived.

(C37) Our foundress believed that her sisters were destined to go all over the world. The largest branches of our congregation began as missionary enterprises. In an era when the supreme need of most non-Christian sections of the world is education, we cannot fail to help as generously as possible. Sisters destined for work in languages and cultures profoundly different from their own need careful preparation in institutions operated for this purpose. To a great extent the success of their apostolic efforts may depend on this preparation.

(C38) At this moment in time the evolutionary process is accelerating toward personalization; all nature is being transformed at an ever increasing speed for the service of man. Creative fidelity to the inspirations of the Holy Spirit demands, then, that we exert our initiative, expend our energies, and marshal our resources so that the poor and neglected, who are the special focus of our love, may share in the benefits of these developments, may realize their personal dignity and attain their final destiny.

(C39) Let us strive to promote the development of Christian community among our colleagues, our students, and all the People of God by sharing with them the love we experience in our religious community.

(C40) We must never forget that through our educational apostolate we aspire to help develop in human persons their full spiritual, intellectual, social, and physical potentialities, and especially to form consciences capable of mature Christian decisions and fully alive to social responsibility.

(C41) In our primary service of education, each sister has the right and the duty to participate as fully as she can in other communities, social, political, and professional, of which she is a member.

(C42) Because the properties we hold as a corporate body are merely a trust for the use of the People of God, they should be made available for the service of civic and professional groups serving the general welfare.

(C43) The acceleration of the process of change has given rise to a new asceticism, the radical detachment and emptying of self required by adaptations necessary to make our apostolate relevant to the people we serve. Courageous pioneering, daring experimentation, and constant re-evaluation are essential for this adaptation.

(C44) Since the apostolate of education is the work of the entire community, it is important for us to realize that all of us, whatever the nature of our service, or however deep the passiv-

ity of our suffering, actively contribute to the growth of the Kingdom.

PREPARATION FOR RELIGIOUS PROFESSION AND APOSTOLIC SERVICE; CONTINUING DEVELOPMENT

(C45) Since the congregation of the sisters of —— exists
within the Church for the sake of the Kingdom, the program of
preparation for religious profession in our community should
foster an apostolic spirituality in which the sister's love of God
finds expression in a true love of her fellow men who have been
made in God's image and redeemed by the blood of Christ.

(C46) Our life is a life of witness to Christ and service of
those who are, or who are called to become, members of his
Mystical Body. Because the strength of this witness depends
largely upon the irrevocability of the religious commitment, we
should gently lead those who aspire to membership in our congregation to an ever clearer realization that the profession of
vows is the public expression of a consecration that lasts forever.
The period of time before the perpetual profession should, therefore, be flexible. It should not, however, exceed ten years from
the time of entrance.

(C47) While maintaining our belief in the intrinsic perma-
nence of the religious vocation, let us respect the sincerity of a
sister's decision to leave our congregation, and continue to love
and cherish her, seeking to maintain a bond of mutual friendship
and support.

(C48) Sisters of —— are called to life in community. Hence
the community should be directly involved in the admission of
postulants and in the development of the young sisters. It should
share in the decision to admit them as permanent members of
the congregation.

(C49) Candidates for admission to the congregation must
possess the physical, intellectual, emotional, and moral strength

requisite for life in an apostolic religious community. Specific requirements for admission are decided at the provincial level.

(C50) Having admitted sisters to profession, we have a responsibility to love, trust, and cherish them for the rest of their lives.

(C51) We pledge ourselves to foster, to the best of our ability, the human development of each sister. A program of continuing religious development should be established in each province to encourage the growth, as a matter of primary concern, of each sister's life in Christ. Every province should also provide the professional training necessary for the realization of each one's potentialities. Let us all respond with dedicated effort to the opportunities our congregation gives.

(C52) Each province should set aside the necessary personnel to plan, execute, and evaluate this preparation and continuing development.

(C53) In the readiness to go wherever there is need and in the belief that exchange among our provinces will develop an understanding of other fields in the apostolate and so strengthen the unity of our congregation, let us generously promote such an exchange.

GOVERNMENT

(C54) The urgency of improving the governmental structures of our community at every level is in proportion to the urgency of the ends for which they are indispensable means: the building of that human community founded in justice, love, peace, and truth which is the seed of God's Kingdom.

(C55) Because this is an ecclesial community, the structures of our government will be affected by canon law now under revision. Relevant sections of this law will be incorporated in a special part of our constitutions. The juridical structures which we propose for the government of our congregation are contained in the Province's Proposals for the General Chapter. Both structures should elicit mature obedience from all members of the congregation.

(C56) The two aspects of our government: the *dynamism* of the individual members who are mature and free; and its *democratic or collegial structures,* on the general, provincial, and local levels, are interdependent and intimately united.

(C57) All human authority proceeds from the Father through the uncreated Word incarnate in Jesus Christ. In our congregation, then, no one *possesses* authority; rather, each one *participates* in the authority of our Risen Lord whose Spirit acts through us accommodating himself to our human condition.

(C58) Faithful to the inspiration of the Spirit and following Christ in humility, let us render each other the service of authority by contributing to the consensus of the community and by accepting the responsibility of office.

(C59) The first essential for effective participation in decision-making is a *free* mind: freed by love, trust, humility, and gratitude; uncluttered by fear, mistrust, fancy, and self-seeking. Striving for this interior freedom each community, meeting with its chosen leader as *primus inter pares,* through the method of deliberation and dialogue reaches an accord on significant action to be undertaken in harmony with the aim and spirit of the congregation. When the community fails to reach a consensus, or for other grave reasons, the sister in charge may make the decision herself.

(C60) Our congregation, as a community rooted in Christ, aims to be creatively present at the center of many cultures at each period in history. Realizing that only a dynamic organizational structure can achieve this presence, let us create new structures flexible enough for change and stable enough to insure continuity. In this way the unity of the congregation and the Christian freedom of each of its members will be safeguarded for the sake of the Kingdom.

CONCLUSION

God is faithful in his love. Having called us to a life of total consecration, he will not cease to call. But we can fail to respond. For this reason, let us support one another in charity, praying unceasingly that we may hold to the vows we have made to the Lord (Ps. 116.14) and prefer absolutely nothing to the love of Jesus Christ:

> Let us pray for one another and for all men, kneeling before the Father, from whom every family, whether spiritual or natural, takes its name: that out of his infinite glory, he may give us the power through his Spirit for our hidden selves to grow strong, so that Christ may live in our hearts through faith, and then, planted in love and built on love, we will with all the saints have strength to grasp the breadth and the length, the height and the depth; until, knowing the love of Christ which is beyond all knowledge, we are filled with the utter fullness of God.
>
> Glory be to him whose power, working in us, can do infinitely more than we can ask or imagine; glory be to him from generation to generation in the Church and in Christ Jesus forever and ever. Amen. (Eph 3:14-21)

INDEX

Aaron, 199
abilities, 166, 172, 236
Abraham, 61, 89, 165, 230
absolutism, 104
Academia Alfonsiana, 190–191
activism, 51, 70, 130, 190, 200, 209, 226
Adam, 107, 124, 126, 160, 191, 226
adaptation, 10, 55, 67, 119, 163, 181, 203
administration, 11, 18, 30, 100, 178, 184–185, 186, 234
agape, 11
Agar, 11
aggiornamento, 20, 105, 163
aggressiveness, 145, 147
alcoholics, 181, 234
alliances, 73
Alphonsus (St.), 18
anointed, 139, 174, 199
anthropology, 68, 225
anti-clericalism, 119
Antioch, 56, 57
apostolate, 5, 35, 50, 51, 76, 79, 99, 114, 116–117, 121, 135, 143, 145, 158, 172, 178–179, 203, 206, 223–225, 228, 231, 235, 239
appeal, 9, 50, 82, 93, 94, 96, 118, 126, 128–129, 134, 146, 169, 170, 193–212, 216, 218, 219, 221, 234
Aramaic, 63
arbitrariness, 7, 109, 117

Are You Running With Me, Jesus?, 202
Aristotle, 128
asceticism, 16, 120, 149–151, 162, 186, 198, 220
assignment, 6, 7, 34, 102, 110
atheism, 20, 38
Augustine (St.), 216
authority, 17–18, 27, 32–33, 35, 53, 87, 89, 99, 101, 105, 106, 109–117, 205, 214, 215, 237

baptism, 4, 14, 56, 126, 132, 146
Barnabas, 56, 155
beatitudes, 20, 22, 23, 29, 122, 123, 145, 162, 163, 165–166, 186, 197
beauty, 82, 90–91, 92, 187, 227
beneficia, 176, 179, 187
Bible, 28, 46, 48, 79, 123, 128, 130, 154, 163
Bonaventure, 216
Borromeo, Charles, 59, 61
Bovet, Theodor, 31
brachium mortuum, 176, 188
brotherhood, 15, 31, 33, 73, 83, 85, 142, 161, 166, 213

call, 3, 5, 15, 44, 95, 123, 127–128, 131, 133, 137, 140, 162
Calvinists, 164
casuistry, 86, 94, 164

celibacy, 5, 14, 18, 21, 24, 26, 30–32, 134, 135, 136–150, 170, 171, 228

censorship, 77

censure, 56

change, 22, 32, 33, 40, 48, 53, 55, 59, 61–65, 67, 69, 78, 98, 114, 159, 160, 179, 190, 195, 197, 201, 205, 212, 221, 224, 234

charism, 11, 35, 68, 115, 142, 171, 172, 225, 230, 236, 237

charismatic, 11, 12, 18, 100, 110, 112, 116, 148, 152, 169, 213

charity, 3, 4, 8, 12–18, 23–27, 43, 67, 71, 73–74, 78, 95–99, 101, 107, 108, 142, 154, 159, 161, 166–169, 170, 173, 183, 187, 198, 222, 230

Charlemagne, 58, 174

chastity, 4, 31, 136, 137–139, 141–145, 147, 149, 151

Christian Renewal in a Changing World, 212

Church, 3–19, 24, 25, 27–29, 33, 36, 37, 39, 30–41, 44, 45, 48, 49, 51, 54–60, 62–66, 70, 72, 74, 84, 104, 107, 111, 118, 122, 126, 136, 146–148, 156, 167, 169, 172–175, 180, 187, 192, 203, 204
    community of love, 3, 170, 213
    mystery, 3, 5, 170
    nature, 7, 9, 10
    needs, 10, 35, 114, 158, 174, 175, 180
    pilgrim, 4, 9, 10, 26, 37, 44, 148, 160

circumcision, 56, 57, 75

civil rights, 15, 102

classes, 59, 60, 73, 98, 154, 164, 173, 231

cliques, 72

collectivism, 80, 104, 180

colleges, 11, 32, 65–66, 133, 178, 224

collegiality, 12–13, 156

commitment, 21, 41, 63, 85, 134, 138, 139, 179

"common life," 171–172, 185, 213

communication, 38, 41, 63, 73, 77, 83, 179, 216, 225, 234

Communism, 73, 188

community, 15, 27, 28, 31–34, 98, 99, 104, 112, 113, 116, 119–121, 127, 143, 152, 154, 157, 160, 180, 188, 189–202, 204, 206
    building of, 26, 27, 32, 33, 35, 109, 113, 114, 142, 156, 166, 190, 215
    Christian, 14, 56, 57, 156, 171
    religious, 4, 6, 8, 9, 14, 16, 18, 31, 50–54, 59, 72, 87, 111, 117, 149, 153, 159, 175–178, 182–184, 187, 203, 207, 208, 215, 218, 223, 224, 227, 231, 232, 235, 236

compassion, 16, 59, 92, 94, 210, 218

compensation, 144, 145, 146

complacency, 10, 63

compromise, 73–75

confidence, 57, 71, 87, 90, 156, 195

confirmation, 132, 146

conformity, 7, 8, 25, 29, 32, 50, 63, 76, 80, 102, 107, 181, 184, 199, 221, 222, 223, 231

conscience, 16, 18, 45, 76, 77, 79–101, 102, 104, 110, 116–118, 129, 151, 154, 157, 173, 174, 179, 191, 199, 215–222, 237

consecration, 4, 107, 139–140, 141, 143, 203

conservatism, 52, 74

conservatives, 23, 63, 67, 71, 75, 196

consolation, 31, 144

Constantine, 58, 174

contemplation, 204–209, 210

continuity of life, 39, 53, 55–78, 105, 196, 226, 227, 230

conversion, 10, 193, 238

cooperation, 8, 82, 94, 98, 156, 181–182, 196, 231–232, 234, 236, 237

coordination, 33, 215

Cornelius, 56–57

corporate witness, 175, 178–180, 182

correspondence, 13, 116
counsels, evangelical, 4, 18, 19, 20–29, 89, 107, 136, 148, 163, 164, 167, 169, 170, 184, 185, 229, 231
covenant, 59, 136, 141, 144, 146, 147, 192
Cox, Harvey, 20, 28
creation, 64, 92, 93, 122, 123–124, 128, 161, 213
creativity, 33, 111, 202, 226
credibility, 18, 33, 46, 117, 130, 147, 171, 173, 176, 178
criticism, 71, 98, 100, 116, 119, 156, 158, 174, 184, 221, 235
cross, 21, 89, 128, 143, 146
Curia, 61, 63
customs, 7, 35, 49, 58, 63, 65, 76, 88, 110, 112–114, 153, 187, 230

deacons, 13, 136, 210
De Aeternitate Mundi, 64
Decalogue, 16
decision, 30
dedication, 4, 27, 46, 92, 107
democracy, 98, 119, 151
detachment, 6, 149, 150, 165, 186, 188
dialogue, 17, 67, 72–73, 77, 111, 113, 122–124, 129, 131, 159, 182, 219, 236
dignity, 8, 30, 38, 50, 102, 104, 107, 124, 205
discernment, 12, 15, 18, 26, 33, 53, 76, 87, 109, 199, 221, 232
discipleship, 34, 72, 168, 169, 191–194, 198, 199
disintegration, 82
dispensation, 18, 97, 183
dissension, 74
divine office, 64, 201, 202
divorce, 62
docility, 8, 26, 27, 29, 33, 34, 49, 103, 105, 108, 109, 111–113, 148, 168, 200, 215
dogma, 212

dowries, 187
dynamics (behavior), 29, 209

education, 94, 96, 149, 223, 232
ego, 124
egotism, 58, 84, 124, 138, 164, 180
Eigenkirchen, 176
employment, 183
enthusiasm, 18–19, 35, 83, 100, 115, 119–120, 141, 148
epikeia, 97
escapism, 68
eschatological, 20–21, 95, 147–148, 171, 176
ethics, 90, 96, 104, 128, 216, 220
Eucharist, 15, 106, 126, 132, 139–140, 141, 143–146, 172, 189–202, 204
Eve, 124, 160, 191, 226
exemplar, 70, 105, 110, 111
exemplary, 21, 109, 137, 172
exemptions, 6
experimentation, 66, 204, 207, 208, 223, 224

factions, 72–73, 196
faith, 4, 29, 41, 42, 45, 48, 50–52, 61–62, 76, 83–85, 93, 103, 118, 122, 134–137, 151, 162, 171, 172, 191–194, 200–202, 209–212, 216, 218, 230
fanaticism, 96, 117
farewell discourse, 46, 93, 189, 193
federation, 206
fellowship, 33, 190, 199
feudalism, 104, 179
fidelity, 38, 39, 40–41, 59, 61–63, 64, 66, 69, 77, 85, 119, 134, 137–139, 141, 142, 167, 171, 208
finances, 11, 33, 185, 186
fine arts, 225
flexibility, 17, 31, 68, 98
formalism, 37, 45, 49, 59, 184, 196
formation, 8, 79, 80, 151, 180, 185, 209, 210–211, 220, 225, 231–234
conscience, 215–222

formation (*Cont.*)
  religious, 8, 14, 16, 93, 207, 209, 212, 213, 221, 224
  theological, 8, 18, 77, 227
fortitude, 15, 19, 74, 78, 169, 223, 237, 238
founder, 10, 11, 60, 223
Franciscan, 99, 172
frankness, 12, 113, 193
fraternal correction, 142
freedom, 7–12, 18, 21, 25–28, 80, 81, 85, 89, 102–111, 138, 148–152, 158, 161–162, 165, 166, 170, 171, 176, 179, 213, 214
French Revolution, 76, 187
friendship, 4, 18, 26, 31, 141–142, 143, 149, 231
  relationship, 13, 31
  God, 4, 85, 127
  particular, 142
frustration, 14, 24, 29, 31, 51, 52, 114, 127, 146, 147, 164, 181, 209, 213
fulfillment, 18, 20, 22, 26, 96, 100–101, 104, 140, 166, 169
fund-raising, 11, 224
future, 10, 20–21, 116, 175, 200, 222–224, 229–239

garb, 49, 65, 66, 227, 228
General Chapter, 17, 60, 61, 76, 153, 169, 182, 203, 204
generosity, 11, 31, 116, 137, 140, 172, 173, 177, 183, 198, 218
Genesis, 123, 126
Gentiles, 56, 57
gentleness, 30, 34, 35, 77, 197
gift, 7, 8, 12, 14, 22–29, 34, 94, 102, 105, 106, 109–113, 132, 135–142, 147–148, 159, 162, 165, 172, 187, 193, 213, 236
"God is dead," 66
goodness, 13–16, 18, 29, 35, 85, 88, 89, 92, 103, 106, 135, 137, 144, 148, 164, 165, 193, 210, 216, 218, 220, 222, 227

Gospel, 9, 13–15, 20–25, 36, 37, 45–48, 54, 56–58, 63, 64, 88, 89, 99, 100, 103–105, 118, 124–126, 129, 130, 135, 139, 142, 145, 147, 148, 153, 154, 163–166, 169, 173, 174, 189, 192, 199, 205, 210–212, 214–216, 220, 221, 225, 237, 238
grace, 6, 8, 24, 26, 34, 35, 40, 48, 61, 70, 83, 93, 94, 96, 102, 105, 108–113, 131–134, 136–139, 147, 148, 165, 168, 182, 185, 210, 218
gradualism, 62, 92, 98–99, 182, 183
grants, 179
gratitude, 8, 23, 26, 29, 83, 84, 99, 105, 106, 131, 137–140, 147–149, 161, 186, 194, 199, 239
grave, 37, 42, 45
growth, 5–8, 24, 26, 42–45, 61, 63, 67, 73, 85, 99, 101, 103, 106, 109, 116, 194, 214–215, 219, 226
Guardini, Romano, 135
guidance, 8, 9, 12, 23, 92, 139, 148, 220

hair, 65–66, 71
happenings, 46–48, 64, 131
hatred, 73
Hebrew, 56, 63
heresy, 123, 128, 130
hierarchy, 13
holiness, 4, 16, 20, 24, 25, 39, 81, 84, 94, 96, 99, 152, 169, 172, 209, 214, 229, 230
Holy Office, 56–57
Holy Orders, 140–141, 146
hope, 21, 35, 148, 151, 195–197, 202, 230
hospitals, 178
house of prayer, 128, 200–201, 204–209
housing, 183, 187, 227
humility, 3, 6, 11–14, 18–20, 26, 28–30, 32–35, 39–41, 46, 52, 55–57, 59–61, 66, 67, 78, 83, 88–90, 98, 105, 107–111, 114, 116, 119, 132, 144, 145, 150, 151, 154, 157–158,

162, 163–188, 190–194, 198, 215, 221–228, 237

humor, 78

idolatry, 96, 103, 108
Ignatius Loyola, 110, 220
Imitation of Christ, 195
immobilism, 37, 39, 48, 52, 64, 113, 116, 162, 176, 230
imperative, 99, 142, 176, 218
impersonalism, 31, 35, 89, 110
imposition, 9, 106
Incarnation, 46, 167, 168, 173, 176
Index of Forbidden Books, 64
infallibility, 67, 68
infantilism, 27, 87, 88, 138, 218
inheritance, 182–183, 188
initiative, 6, 11, 14–15, 24, 26–27, 29, 53, 70, 99–100, 110–111, 138, 236
    spirit of, 14, 110, 168
innovation, 61, 68, 79
insight, 29, 30, 32, 34, 55, 76, 84, 90, 91, 99, 103, 118, 140, 153, 209, 211–213, 218
inspiration, 8, 32, 68, 82, 83, 111
integration, 32, 79, 85, 90, 92, 106, 115, 168, 205–206, 235, 239
    racial, 15
intuition, 226
invitation, 8, 56, 62, 124, 129, 132, 220
involvement, 20, 92, 102, 213, 232
Isaac, 89
Ismael, 61

Jacob, 89
James, 56–58, 75, 215
Jews, 58, 62, 63, 71, 75, 164
job placement, 183
John (St.), 33, 37, 42, 52, 124, 189, 197, 211, 214–215, 220
John XXIII, 20, 28, 32, 37, 50, 65, 67, 68, 118, 173, 205, 212
joy, 4, 9, 13–14, 18–19, 21, 23, 29, 32, 37, 44, 46, 83, 84, 86, 89, 92,

93, 100, 111, 129, 130, 132, 134–139, 143–145, 148, 149, 158, 159, 163–165, 170–172, 192–195, 200–203, 216, 219, 232
juniorate, 80, 94
justice, 15, 50, 74, 150, 160, 179, 183, 219
justification, 57

kairos, 47, 49, 148
kindness, 15–18, 20, 29–31, 52, 72, 73, 78, 99, 103, 117, 122, 137, 140, 142, 144, 164, 193, 197–198, 216, 219, 222, 228
kingdom of God, 4–6, 14, 18, 20–21, 23–26, 28–30, 134–137, 139–141, 143–146, 148–149, 161–164, 166, 170
knowledge, 26, 28, 35, 76, 82–84, 86–87, 90–93, 103, 109, 121–122, 147, 195, 216, 218–220, 238

labor, 163, 185
laity, 3, 11–14, 36
language, 7, 41, 63, 71, 73, 80, 92, 133, 169, 220
Last Supper, 62, 76, 93, 128, 189, 229
Latin, 50–51, 63, 91, 192, 218–219
law, 6–9, 16, 20, 25–29, 32, 39, 45, 49, 50–51, 58, 75, 84, 86–90, 92–94, 96–99, 103, 106, 109, 113, 116, 138, 147, 154, 163–165, 168–169, 175, 182, 183, 185, 189, 209, 215–218, 220–221, 225
    natural, 24, 96
    positive, 50, 96
Law of Christ, 211
Lazarus, 174
legalism, 50–51, 62, 94, 116, 162, 181, 196, 222, 226–227, 235
leisure, 21, 224
leitmotiv, 81, 210–211
letters, 77–78, 116
Levi, 199
liberals, 23, 75

liberty, 8, 38, 97, 102–103, 107, 138, 150, 214
library, 178
life
    Christian, 5, 14, 21, 54–55, 66, 81, 96, 104, 133, 145, 160, 189, 216
    religious, 5, 12–13, 20, 22, 25, 27, 30, 35, 60, 96, 104, 110, 113–116, 119, 121, 137, 142, 147, 150–153, 156, 163, 172, 175, 177–178, 190, 205, 218
    spiritual, 11, 204, 227
liturgy, 14, 37, 44, 85, 125, 129, 131, 139, 144, 148–149, 158–159, 189, 201, 212, 216, 227, 236
loneliness, 146
Lot's wife, 9, 48, 230
love, 11–16, 21–30, 32–35, 44, 52, 70–73, 79, 83–85, 89–92, 96, 98, 101–103, 105–108, 111–117, 122– 124, 130–137, 140–144, 146–147, 156, 158, 160, 162, 164–166, 168– 172, 175, 187, 190, 194, 197, 199, 204, 211, 214, 216, 218–222, 229, 235, 238
    commandment, 5, 8–10, 14–17, 80, 89, 94, 97, 114, 144, 189, 194, 210, 212
    fraternal, 14, 16, 23–24, 31, 35, 80, 108, 114–115, 121, 145, 159, 189, 200, 208
    God's, 4, 8, 9, 16–18, 23, 30, 92, 93, 106, 142–143, 211– 212
    service, 17, 35–36, 49, 95–96, 104, 115, 137, 142
Luke, 40, 69, 133, 210
luxury, 175, 177

magazines, 138
Magnificat, 40, 46
mail, 77
Malachy, 62, 91, 141
management, 11, 30, 33, 205
manipulation, 30, 102

mankind, 22, 26, 36, 37, 66, 105, 136, 144, 147, 157, 172, 205
Mark, 42, 155–156
marriage, 23, 30–31, 35, 115, 136, 137, 140–141, 144, 146–149, 171, 197
Marx, Karl, 73, 186
Mary, 39–41, 46, 69–70, 143
Mary Magdalen, 41–45
maternalism, 31
Matthew, 75, 133
maturity, 26–27, 30–34, 76–79, 82, 85, 90–91, 100–102, 104, 107, 109, 112–113, 118, 137–138, 145, 151, 184–185, 214, 215, 220
mechanism, 49, 95, 100, 114
meditation, 28, 33, 69–70, 84, 90– 91, 117, 121, 131, 207, 215
mendicants, 179
merit, 91, 219
message, 29, 37, 42, 45–47, 53–54, 62, 64, 66–68, 71, 83–84, 89, 93, 95, 118, 122, 124–127, 132–133, 163–166, 192–194, 214, 220, 229, 235
ministry, 140, 146, 231
mission, 12–13, 32, 49, 81, 104, 115, 128, 174–175, 177–178, 183, 187, 234
missionary, 129
mistakes, 99, 190, 207, 214
Möhler, Johann Adam, 140–141
morality, 38, 90–91, 128, 131, 167, 187, 212
mortification, 152, 153, 156, 158– 160, 191
motivation, 20, 30, 45, 80, 87–88, 109, 135–136, 147, 160, 186, 203, 209–215, 218–219
movies, 80, 138
mutuality, 113, 181
mystery, 3, 5, 28, 37, 44–45, 48, 115, 142, 146–147, 151, 157, 167– 168, 172–173, 176, 189, 193–195, 204, 210, 218
Mystical Body, 4–7, 25, 231

name, 127, 144, 198
Nazarene (Gospel), 165
Negroes, 15, 102
Nehemiah, 158
New Covenant, 26, 59
New Law, 93, 132, 145, 209–210, 212
Newman, Cardinal, 103
newspapers, 149–150
New Testament, 26, 95, 138, 163, 165, 211
"normal times," 55, 58
novels, 138
novitiate, 16, 32, 80, 94, 133, 142, 201, 220
nursing, 223–225

obedience, 4, 6, 9, 14, 18–19, 23, 26, 32–35, 40, 49, 52, 67–68, 80–82, 86, 93, 96, 99–101, 102–120, 136, 138, 150–151, 159–160, 167, 211–213, 218, 220, 237
    blind, 110, 114, 220
office, 75, 108, 111, 156, 185, 215
Old Testament, 164–165, 211
oneness, 82, 98, 172, 197
openness, 15, 20, 23, 30, 35, 41, 54, 68, 75, 83–84, 90, 110, 114, 116, 119, 122, 125, 127, 129, 134, 137, 146, 148–149, 151–152, 156, 162, 164–165, 194–195, 214
opinions, 117–119, 182
opportunity, 6, 10, 22, 38, 48–49, 54, 69, 76, 91, 95, 113, 132, 148, 156, 164, 194, 203, 223, 227, 234, 238
Otto the Great, 174

paradise, 124, 129, 130, 132
Parousia, 23, 47, 68
Particular Examen, 97
Paschal Mystery, 47–48, 105, 115, 193, 200, 210, 216, 235
pastoral, 100, 114, 144, 156, 173, 191
paternalism, 31

patience, 43, 52, 58, 61, 67, 70–72, 73, 75, 88, 92, 98, 117, 197, 222
Paul (St.), 21–22, 38, 48, 49, 56–58, 62, 71, 75, 86, 106, 126, 151, 155–156, 164, 169, 195, 197, 198, 210, 215, 225, 238
Paul VI, 18, 20, 32, 75, 136, 147, 150
peace, 15, 29, 32, 98, 111, 123, 132, 160, 164, 191, 209, 227
People of God, 11, 63, 64, 111, 129, 130, 147, 231, 234
perfection, 63, 81, 94, 104, 107, 128, 152, 231
permissions, 29–30, 112, 184, 185
persecution, 60, 129
personalism, 28–30, 38, 101, 126, 191, 236
personalization, 92, 193
Peter, 33, 42, 52, 56–57, 75, 193, 197, 215, 222
Philip, 193
philosophy, 180
Pilgrim Church, 4, 9, 10, 148, 160
pioneers, 30, 53–54, 58, 169, 230
Pius X, 65
Pius XII, 10, 59
Playboy, 138
pleasures, 21, 146
pluralism, 38, 76, 104, 151
politics, 75
possessions, 6, 162, 171, 177, 179, 184, 187
postulate, 94
poverty, 4, 6, 10, 11, 14, 23, 26, 29–30, 136, 143, 146, 163–188, 213
    spirit of, 6, 11, 29, 137, 144–145, 150, 162–164, 166, 169, 172, 175–177, 181, 184, 186, 208
power, 4, 6, 14, 28, 38–40, 47, 84, 103–104, 106, 108–109, 112–114, 141–142, 148, 166, 170, 176, 178, 196–197, 216
praise, 4, 92, 107, 157, 161, 171, 192, 194, 197–199, 202, 213

prayer, 17, 27–28, 30, 44, 48, 70, 74, 76, 80, 84, 117–118, 121–135, 139, 143–144, 159–160, 171, 185, 198–199, 201–204, 205–209, 214–215, 224
   life of, 4, 10, 70, 75, 118, 120, 161, 200
   spirit of, 14, 51, 67, 69, 76, 121, 135, 201–202
precepts, 3, 81, 138, 182, 184, 199, 212, 220, 222
prejudice, 29, 102, 117, 164
pressures, 29, 57, 102, 138, 223, 238
princes of the Church, 58, 61, 174
principles, 77, 85, 111, 138, 161, 175, 199, 203, 216, 228, 232
privacy, 77
privileges, 6, 173–174, 187
profession, 143, 203, 229
professional, 76, 79, 183, 205–206, 209, 224, 231, 234
progress, 9, 75, 79, 89, 106, 159, 185, 205, 222, 232
progressivism, 53, 55, 67, 75
property, 11, 163–188
Providence, 93, 122, 137, 186
provinces, 7
prudence, 15, 74, 150, 224
Psalms, 64, 91, 106, 153, 202
   Gelineau, 202
   Somerville, 202
psychology, 38, 68, 75, 77, 101, 109, 138, 145, 185, 196, 207, 209, 211, 216, 221, 225–226, 232
purification, 10

Qumran (scrolls), 86
Quoist, Michel, 202

racism, 15
radio, 149–150
rationalization, 85, 118
readiness, 55, 67–68, 73, 100, 109, 117, 161, 163, 189
Redemption, 5, 86, 122, 137, 140, 143, 164, 170, 171

Redemptorist, 31, 65
reform, 10, 35, 67, 162, 176, 181, 182, 204
regressive, 75
regulations, 9, 81, 87, 95, 98, 99, 213
relevance, 36, 42, 49, 54, 98, 120, 154, 162, 193, 216
relics, 10, 153
religion, 128
remorse, 82
renewal, 22, 37, 53–55, 58–59, 62, 67, 71, 73–75, 104, 111, 114, 117, 121–122, 127, 153, 163, 174–176, 181–182, 203–207, 232
renunciation, 29, 140–141, 143, 144, 162, 164, 167, 171–172, 182–183, 198, 200, 222
reparation, 107
repentance, 62
representative, 108
respect, 7, 9, 13–14, 18, 27, 31, 34, 73, 75, 100, 102, 104, 133, 196, 216, 232
response, 9–10, 24, 27, 41, 73, 81, 83, 93, 106–107, 122–123, 125, 128–129, 131–132, 134, 140, 151, 161, 178–179, 194, 200, 209, 220
responsibility, 11–13, 29–30, 34–35, 69, 77, 90, 100–101, 104–105, 111, 116, 119, 137, 157–160, 185, 203, 209–215, 222, 231, 239
   spirit of, 11, 29, 110–111, 116, 184, 226
resurrection, 36–37, 42–43, 45, 47–48, 54, 168, 230
revelation, 13, 39, 69, 92, 143
reverence, 100
risk, 48, 53, 209, 219, 234
Roman Empire, 58
routine, 7, 112, 154, 191, 199
rubrics, 86, 201
rule, 9, 14, 16–18, 26, 35, 40, 46, 56–57, 81, 87–88, 92–93, 95–96, 98–100, 111, 114–116, 119, 147–148, 154, 158–161, 169, 175, 181–

182, 184, 187, 199, 201, 203, 208–
209, 212, 215, 218, 220–221, 228,
238

Sacerdotalis Caelibatus, 136, 147,
150
sacrament, 4, 5, 126, 129, 131, 134,
136, 141, 144, 147, 167–168, 232
Sacred Congregation for Religious,
50
sacrifice, 16, 101, 107–108, 117, 141,
146–149, 158, 187, 191–192, 198–
199
salvation, 18, 27, 40, 44, 49, 66, 96,
105–107, 113, 122, 137, 139, 157,
162, 169–170, 172, 192, 210, 212,
218, 228–230
salvific, 107, 151, 205
sanctification, 4, 230
sanctity, 10, 15–16, 32, 100, 104,
148, 209, 238
Scharper, Philip, 220
Scheler, Max, 71
schizophrenia, 82
scholasticate, 178, 180
science, 38, 68, 79, 164, 225, 233
Scotists, 216
Scripture, 29, 39, 57, 65, 121, 123,
213
secular city, 22, 59
Secular City (The), 20
Secular City Debate, 21
self-actualization, 21, 101, 143, 196
self-denial, 16, 22, 85, 146–147, 150,
152, 156, 159, 162, 169, 191, 194
self-enhancement, 6, 129, 186
self-fulfillment, 24–25, 29, 114, 124,
126, 128–129, 135, 164–165, 172,
196
self-importance, 78
selfishness, 24, 26, 29, 85, 94, 101,
103, 109, 114, 124–125, 131, 135,
149, 151–152, 162, 164–165, 172,
180, 191, 196, 210, 213–214, 221
selflessness, 16, 37, 152
self-perfection, 128, 151–152

self-righteousness, 10, 58, 62, 64
self-sacrifice, 3
self-understanding, 5, 28
Sermon on the Mount, 16, 18, 22,
66, 93–94, 133, 145, 163, 189,
210, 212, 238
service, 4–9, 18–19, 24–26, 28, 30,
32, 41, 46, 66, 75, 95, 101, 106–
108, 109–111, 113–114, 119, 137,
140, 145–147, 149, 152, 154, 156,
158, 168–170, 172–173, 176, 180,
183, 190, 213, 231–232, 235–236
sign, 3, 5, 27–28, 49, 54, 63, 130,
137, 139, 144–145, 147, 162, 164,
166
"signs of the time," 8, 15, 35, 50,
53–54, 68, 108, 113, 134, 222–
223
silence, 18, 190
simplicity, 66, 119, 145, 146, 173,
177, 227
singing, 48, 70, 91, 129, 148, 194,
197–198, 202, 204, 227
situation ethics, 56
situationists, 227
skills, 22, 30, 234
sociology, 38, 68, 109, 185, 196,
219, 225
solidarity, 7, 13–15, 98, 109, 166,
172, 180, 182, 195–196, 231, 237
spiritualism, 181
spirituality, 5, 14, 77, 115, 121, 136,
167, 185, 203, 205
    feminine, 225–228
spontaneity, 9, 11–12, 31, 100, 110,
113, 120, 138, 152, 181, 201, 208
stereotypes, 37, 44, 45, 89, 133, 168,
226, 237
Stoics, 128
structures, 10, 22, 27, 31–32, 99,
102, 109, 113, 133, 148, 157, 161,
168, 173–174, 176, 181–182, 186,
211–212, 222, 224, 234, 236, 238
sublimation, 145, 146, 147
subsidiarity, 31, 111, 184, 232
superficiality, 80, 196

superiors, 7, 11–13, 15, 18, 26, 29–33, 35, 37, 40, 51–52, 71, 76–78, 81, 84, 87, 92, 95, 97–101, 107–109, 111–117, 119, 148, 154, 159–161, 169, 181–182, 184, 186–187, 190, 193–194, 200, 214–215, 221, 224, 234–238
symbols, 16, 66, 124, 176, 190
Synoptics, 42
synthesis, 16, 18, 80, 115, 133, 205, 210, 237

teaching, 223–225
telephone, 77
television, 17, 80, 138, 149–150, 158, 225
temperance, 149–150
temporal, 11, 175–177
tensions, 55, 57–58, 63, 73, 81, 174, 209
theologians, 65, 72, 76, 157, 173, 216, 227, 231
theology, 24, 35, 38, 50, 66, 69, 76–77, 94, 96, 119, 123, 126, 137, 141, 154, 161, 180, 200, 207, 211–212, 219, 225, 227–228, 233, 237
Thomas, 193
Thomas Aquinas, 64, 87, 93, 97
Thomists, 216
Timothy, 155
titles, 66, 173, 174
tolerance, 38
totalitarianism, 104
traditionalism, 55, 113
traditions, 10, 38–40, 44–46, 50, 52, 69, 94, 148, 152, 207, 230
tragedy, 78, 187
transportation, 177
Trent, 135, 145
trivia, 9, 66, 119
trust, 45, 90, 118, 178, 195, 215, 218

unbelief, 63
"unconditional surrender," 73–75
unction, 139
uniformity, 7, 111

union, 5, 18, 22, 137, 140
unity, 5, 7, 14, 24, 27, 31–33, 58, 63, 72–75, 82, 98, 109, 116, 140, 151, 157, 160–161, 172, 222
universities, 11, 178
unselfishness, 26, 30, 37, 84, 137, 140, 142, 159–160, 168

validity, 96
values, 38, 54, 69, 75–77, 79–81, 83–87, 90–93, 99–100, 102, 113, 124, 126, 138, 147, 152, 162, 181–182, 186, 203, 205, 210–212, 218, 220, 227, 237
vanity, 66, 213, 227
variety, 23, 27, 108, 169
Veterum sapientiae, 50
vigilance, 8, 41, 46–47, 49, 54, 81–82, 84–85, 95–96, 99–100, 133, 179, 198, 223, 230
violence, 38
virginity, 18, 24, 30, 135, 137, 140, 142–144, 147, 213
virtue, 67–92, 95, 109, 114–115, 150–151, 167, 212, 219
vision, 80
vocation, 80, 93, 94, 99, 116, 127, 134–135, 137–138, 141, 144, 159, 175, 185, 205–207, 209, 227, 231, 237
    Christian, 4, 5, 15, 159
    directors, 62
    religious, 4, 8, 51, 54, 62, 64, 159
    temporary, 85
vows, 5, 18, 85, 107, 114, 134, 137, 139–140, 142, 149, 163, 170, 171, 177, 182–183, 188, 229

Ward, Mary, 59–60
warmth, 18, 30–31, 71, 141–142, 146–147, 202, 227–228
watchfulness, 8, 46, 48–50, 54, 84–85, 95, 101, 198, 218, 222–223, 238
wealth, 22, 163–188, 230

welfare state, 171
wholeness, 32, 79, 82–83, 90, 216,
218, 233
willingness, 67, 155, 159, 182, 187–
188
wisdom, 69, 74, 78, 83, 85, 89–90,
92, 121–122, 124, 190, 226
womanhood, 38–39, 225, 228
work, 185–187, 208
world, 10, 22, 28–30, 36, 38, 45–47,
49, 53, 59, 64, 69, 82, 84, 104–
105, 107, 127, 142–144, 149, 154,
161–162, 168, 171, 178, 181, 186,
192, 196, 205, 212–215, 221–224,
228, 230, 239
    Johannine, 67
worldliness, 213–214, 227
worship, 107, 123, 127, 201
Wust, Peter, 121

Yoga, 207

Zen, 207

Conciliar Documents

LUMEN GENTIUM: Dogmatic Constitution on the Church
Chapter 1: (1–8) Mystery of the Church
            (5) Coming of God's kingdom, 3, 6, 94
            (8) Christ as Mediator, 11
Chapter 2: (9–17) The People of God, 8, 9
            (11) Sacraments and priestly community, 232
Chapter 3: (18–29) The Hierarchical Structure, 12
            (25) The teaching authority, 13
            (28) Ministerial priesthood, 13
            (29) Deacons, 13
Chapter 4: (30–38) The Laity, 3, 12–13
            (30) Laity's mission, 12
            (37) Laity-hierarchy relationships, 14
            (38) Witness of laity, 36, 54
Chapter 5: (39–42) Universal Call to Holiness
            (39) Holy Church, 24, 25
            (42) Way to holiness, 107, 169, 170
Chapter 6: (43–47) Religious
            (43) Evangelical counsels, 81
            (44) Vows, 3, 4, 28, 107, 170
            (45) Jurisdiction of religious, 143
            (46) Personality development, 35, 36, 114
            (47) Perseverance in vocation, 229
Chapter 7: (48–51) Pilgrim Church, 4, 9, 10, 26, 37, 44, 148, 160
Chapter 8: (52–69) Blessed Virgin Mary, 46

GAUDIUM ET SPES: Pastoral Constitution on the Church in the Modern World

Art. 16: Conscience, 79
    34: Value of human activity, 185
    35: Regulation of human activity, 185
    52: The family, 76
    67: Labor and leisure, 185
    69: Purpose of created things, 186

PERFECTAE CARITATIS: Decree on the Appropriate Renewal of Religious Life

Art. 1: Religious life in the Church, 23, 167, 203, 229
    2: Renewal of religious life, 20, 22, 55
    5: Contemplation and apostolate combined, 151, 167
    6: Spirit of prayer, 27, 121, 189
    12: Chastity, 31, 136
    13: Poverty, 163, 167, 174, 177, 181, 183, 184, 185
    14: Obedience, 9, 34, 102, 105, 107, 108, 109, 110, 111, 114, 159

ECCLESIAE SANCTAE: Norms for the Implementation of the Decree *Perfectae Caritatis*

Art. 18: Subsidiarity, 112
    21: Mental prayer, 204
    22: Mortification, 152

Constitution on Divine Revelation, p. 39
Constitution on the Sacred Liturgy, 37, 42

Cum permissu superiorum
P. Gerhard Mittermeier, C.Ss.R.
Provinzial
Munich, 9 January 1968

NIHIL OBSTAT
Rt. Rev. Msgr. John A. Goodwine, S.T.L., J.C.D., Censor Librorum

IMPRIMATUR
Most Rev. Terence J. Cooke, D.D.
Archbishop of New York
New York, May 17, 1968